How Shall They Be Saved?

*The Destiny
of Those
Who Do Not
Hear of Jesus*

Millard J. Erickson

Baker Books

A Division of Baker Book House Co
Grand Rapids, Michigan 49516

Published by Baker Books
a division of Baker Book House Company
PO Box 6287, Grand Rapids, Michigan 49516-6287

Printed in the United States of America

Library of Congress Cataloging–in–Publication Data

Erickson, Millard J.
    How shall they be saved? : the destiny of those who do not hear of Jesus / Millard J. Erickson.
       p.   cm.
    Includes bibliographical references and indexes.
    ISBN 0-8010-2065-4 (pbk.)
    1. Salvation outside the church. I. Title.
  I. Title.
  BT759.E75   1996
  234—dc20
                                                    95-39123

To
Marvin E. Beckman
Senior Vice President of Operations and Corporate Counsel
Moody Bible Institute

Man of God
Learned in the law
Wise counselor
Good friend

Contents

Preface

Some theological matters come to the forefront of discussion because of intellectual issues; others gain attention because of practical matters that involve doctrinal questions. This book attempts to survey theological developments that have drawn inspiration from both theoretical and practical sources. Consequently, the question of the eternal destiny of those who do not hear of Jesus Christ during their lifetime is one that in various ways currently engages theologians, philosophers, anthropologists, and missiologists. The literature on the subject has mushroomed in the past decade or two.

Yet much of the material sent forth on this subject carries rather strong ideological flavoring. Firm positions are taken, sometimes without real appreciation for the type of considerations that motivate those of opposite persuasions. In many cases, more is read into the Scripture than is exegetically supported there. Thus, another work on the subject seems justified. In this book we first attempt to survey the several different positions or "schools of thought," before going back over the issues that are at stake and sifting the evidence with an attempt to come to a balanced and responsible viewpoint.

This volume is the second produced under my current appointment as research professor of theology at Southwestern Baptist Theological Seminary. The terms of my appointment permit me to offer an elective each year on a subject that I wish to research and write on. I appreciate this opportunity afforded me by Dr. Russell Dilday, former president of Southwestern, and Dr. Bruce Corley, former dean of the school of theology at Southwestern. I also wish to thank all those who have interacted with me on these matters. This especially includes the students in my elective course during the fall 1993 and fall 1994 semesters and a Doctor of Ministry course in October 1994 at Southwestern. Chapters 7, 9, and 12 were also presented in a Doctor of Ministry course at Grace Theological Seminary, Winona Lake, Indiana, June 19–20, 1995. Portions of chapters 1, 2, 6, 9, and 12 were given as the W. H. Griffith Thomas lectures at Dallas Theological Seminary, Dallas, Texas, February 8–11, 1994. Cross-cultural exposure of these concepts was obtained in two settings: a Master of Theology course taught at the Faculdade

Teológico Batista de São Paulo in São Paulo, Brazil, November 8–11, 1994, and lectures at the International Theological Conference at the Seminãrio Teológico Batista do Sul do Brasil, Rio de Janeiro, November 1–4, 1994. Several chapters were also given as messages at the pastors' continuing education seminar of the Middle East Baptist Conference, Burton, Ohio, February 21 and 22, 1994. Rev. Herbert Skoglund, since retired as Director of World Missions of the Baptist General Conference, and a former missionary to Japan, who has done graduate studies in world religions at Garrett-Evangelical Theological Seminary and the University of Chicago, read the entire manuscript and offered helpful suggestions, especially on chapters 8 and 14. My graduate assistant, Mr. Darrell W. Brown, a Ph.D. student at Southwestern, assisted with research and checking references. Numerous other conversations on these matters have also helped sharpen and stimulate my thinking. Maria denBoer's editorial work did much to improve the style and clarity of the manuscript.

Thinking and discussion on these matters will go on within the church, for these are issues it can ill afford to ignore. It is my hope and prayer that this contribution will help lead some readers to conclusions that are pleasing to our Lord.

Part 1

Introduction

1

Introduction

From its very inception Christianity has been an evangelistic religion. Its adherents have believed they have a responsibility to spread to all persons the Good News of Jesus Christ and salvation through faith in him. This belief, in turn, entailed several conceptions. One was the actual need of all persons to receive salvation, or, in other words, the belief that all persons are sinners, guilty and condemned. It also included a certain understanding of the nature of salvation, namely, that faith in Jesus Christ was required, and that this involved believing certain information. While there never was exact agreement on the number or the relative percentage of the human race that would be saved, there was general consensus that not all who have lived will receive eternal life.

In recent years controversy has arisen about this conception, however. The uniqueness, exclusiveness, and necessity of Jesus Christ and belief in him for salvation are being questioned by some Christians. In light of this and other considerations, it is important that we investigate carefully the questions of who and how many will be saved, and on what basis. The study of these questions is especially important at this time for a number of reasons.

Current Confusion about the Subject

The first reason is that there has been confusion regarding these matters recently, even in those circles where this has traditionally been given the highest value. The Barna organization has for a number of years polled the American population regarding their religious beliefs and related issues. Their polling data published in 1992 indicated a rather high degree of correct understanding of the basis of salvation. When asked to describe their belief about life after death, 62 percent of the general sample responded, "When you die, you will go to heaven because you have confessed your sins and have accepted Jesus Christ as your Savior." Only 6 percent said, "When you die you will go to heaven because you have tried to obey the Ten Commandments"; 9 percent said, "Because you are basically a good person"; and 6 percent said, "Because God loves all people and will not let them perish."[1] When asked to respond to the statement, "All good people, whether they consider Jesus Christ to be their Savior or not, will live in heaven after they die on earth," somewhat different responses emerged. Of those who said they had made a personal commitment to Jesus Christ (which in turn constituted 65 percent of the total adult sample), 25 percent agreed strongly and 15 percent agreed moderately; 16 percent disagreed moderately and 33 percent disagreed strongly; 11 percent did not know. Thus, of the persons who would hazard an opinion, those who disagreed outnumbered those who agreed by less than a 5 to 4 ratio! Even 29 percent of the born again and 26 percent of the Baptists agreed, either strongly or somewhat. Those most opposed were the charismatics and pentecostalists, with 18 percent agreeing and 78 percent disagreeing.[2] It appears that while a strong majority agree in theory on what qualifies a person for entrance into heaven, when the question shifts to who will actually get there, a very different view is taken by a significant portion of the sample.[3]

It is interesting to note the apparent conflict between the personal testimonies of many people regarding the basis of their own salvation and their belief regarding the salvation of other persons. Probably the emotional factor has overwhelmed the rational. It may be that many people feel sympathy for others, desiring to see all persons receive the same benefits of salvation that they themselves have received, rather than relating this belief to rational or doctrinal considerations.

Effect on Doctrinal Tenets

A second major reason why this study is important is because of the effect doctrinal considerations in this area have on other doctrines. Doctrine is organic. Rather than comprising a loose collection of scattered

1. George Barna, *The Barna Report 1992–93: America Renews Its Search for God* (Ventura, Calif.: Regal, 1992), pp. 76–78, 294–95.
2. Ibid., pp. 50–52, 262.
3. Independent confirmation of these results was obtained by a recent Doctor of Ministry class.One student was an institutional chaplain, seven were senior pastors of Southern Baptist churches in Texas, and one was a senior pastor of a Southern Baptist church in Oklahoma.When they polled their predominantly very conservative constituents, the pastors were quite surprised to find the degree of openness toward more inclusive views of salvation, particularly in a denomination known for its strongly evangelistic emphasis.

ideas, theology properly done is a whole, so that the position a person takes on one doctrine affects conclusions in other areas as well. Even when this is not done consciously, and there is internal inconsistency within a doctrinal scheme, sooner or later the logic of the matter prevails. Whether the person holding that view perceives the connection himself or herself, or whether someone else does, the logical implications of the idea held will bear upon the other doctrines, bringing about modifications in them.

The Person of Christ

One very obvious connection is between one's view of the extent of salvation and the doctrine of the person of Christ, specifically, the incarnation. If, as Christianity has traditionally claimed, Jesus was God's unique entry into the human race in personal incarnation, then the relationship to him is potentially also unique and indispensable to the proper relationship with God. John Hick has edited or co-edited two books whose titles bear an interesting similarity: *The Myth of God Incarnate* and (with Paul Knitter) *The Myth of Christian Uniqueness*. If God has become incarnate in Jesus, then the Christian faith is unique. Hick puts it this way: "If Jesus was literally God incarnate, the second Person of the holy Trinity living a human life, so that the Christian religion was founded by God-on-earth in person, it is then very hard to escape from the traditional view that all mankind must be converted to the Christian faith."[4] The logical flow may of course move in either direction. If Jesus was not the unique incarnation of God, then there is no necessity of believing in him and in him alone, or at least the usual reason for requiring that belief is not valid. Conversely, by the logic of denying the consequent, if for some reason we are convinced that all of humanity need not necessarily be converted to belief in Jesus, then it must not be the case that he was the literal and unique incarnation of God.

The Trinity

A second doctrine closely and logically connected with this issue is the Trinity. This conception of God causes Christianity to stand out as unique among the world's religions. On the one hand, it brings Christianity into conflict with strictly and rigidly monotheistic religions, such as Judaism and Islam. On the other hand, it places it in irreconcilable contradiction to pantheistic Eastern religions, such as Hinduism. Thus, any attempt to say that people may be saved by any one of several religions because they are basically all the same would appear to founder on the unique doctrine that cannot simply be assimilated into the doctrinal

---

4. John Hick, *God Has Many Names* (Philadelphia: Westminster, 1982), p. 19.

views of these other religions. The effect on the doctrine of the Trinity is in one of two directions. In the one case, the doctrine's legitimacy is challenged by the claim that the Bible does not really teach such a doctrine. The other approach accepts the doctrine but calls into question its uniqueness, maintaining that parallels can be found in other religions.[5]

Divine Sovereignty

Other aspects of the doctrine of God similarly bear upon and are borne upon by this matter. In part, the question may be posed in terms of whether God really is God. What are his rights? Does he have the right to do whatever he chooses, or must he follow, and be judged by, some antecedent standard of right and wrong? Does he have a right to condemn those who have because of the circumstances of life been at a disadvantage regarding the possibility of meeting the conditions requisite for salvation?

The form of Christian theology that comes in for the most severe criticism in the discussion of these matters of salvation is Calvinism. According to this theology, God has from all eternity sovereignly destined some persons to be saved and others to be lost. He has done this without any consideration of works on their part, or even of any foreseen faith on their part. The question is now being raised, however, whether this is just, whether God *may* rightfully do this, even if he *can* do this. Note that the issue is therefore somewhat different from one form in which it is sometimes put—as a question of whether God can do this, that is, whether he has the ability to do so. The objection is that such action would be in conflict with human freedom, which is considered indubitable. Here it is that whether he has the ability to do so or not, he does not have the right to do so. Thus, rather than calling into question his omnipotence, it is his omniscience (i.e., the knowledge of what is good and right), and even more, his justice, which need to be rethought.

Scripture

The doctrine of Scripture is also affected by the doctrine of salvation. The first point of apparent tension or need of revision comes when one examines certain scriptural passages that appear to teach that relatively few will be saved, such as Jesus' statement about the small gate and narrow road, which few find (Matt. 7:13–14). If on other grounds one is convinced that many, perhaps a majority, of those humans who will live upon this earth during the duration of human history are to be saved, then one must find some other way of interpreting the biblical passages

---

5. Raimundo Panikkar, *The Trinity and the Religious Experience of Man* (New York: Orbis, 1973), p. viii.

or of regarding the status of what is taught in the Bible. One ploy may be to assert that the Bible indeed teaches such a matter, but is wrong. Another may be to say that the Bible contains varying, even conflicting statements. Either of these positions will call for some revision of the usual understanding.

A second point at which the doctrine of Scripture will be affected is in terms of the uniqueness of biblical revelation. A traditional understanding of the Bible is that it alone contains the truth one must know and believe in order to be savingly related to God. One concern of the current discussion, however, pertains to those who have never heard the gospel or have never been evangelized. These people have no access to the content of the specially revealed truth preserved for us in the Bible. Some believe that salvation may be possible through "implicit faith," or by responding to what can be known about God and the human predicament from general or natural revelation. If this is the case, however, then what is the unique status of special revelation? Is it really necessary, or could it have been foregone?

Authority

An extension of this issue is the complex of factors known as religious (or in this case, specifically, Christian) authority. Some varieties of Protestantism, such as the Scholastic orthodoxy of the seventeenth century and some streams of twentieth-century fundamentalism, have emphasized the Bible exclusively. Classical Reformation thought had spoken of a twofold authority: the external or objective authority (the Bible) and the internal or subjective authority (the internal witness of the Holy Spirit). Roman Catholicism, and to a lesser extent, Anglicanism and Eastern Orthodoxy, emphasized tradition as a channel of divine authority. There have always been movements, usually on the fringe of Christianity, which have emphasized a direct, present speaking by the Holy Spirit. In the twentieth century, Pentecostalism, followed by the charismatic movement and the "Third Wave," represented this approach. Methodism, following John Wesley's lead, spoke of the fourfold basis of authority: Bible, reason, tradition, and experience. In recent times, the emphasis on personal experience has grown, both in extent and in intensity. With respect to the issues that we will be discussing, personal experience frequently plays a major, indeed even the major, role. If this is the case, however, then logically the Bible's authority must be downgraded to some extent. Thus, the controversy over the saved potentially at least creates controversy over the authority of the Bible.

The Nature of Salvation

Another and more obvious point of effect of the discussion is in terms of the nature of salvation. What does it mean to be saved? This raises a whole raft of issues in contemporary thought. Whereas salvation was traditionally thought of as restoration to fellowship with God, canceling guilt and condemnation and bringing about positive favor with the Lord, this has been challenged in our time. The various nuances of liberation theology see salvation as at least partly the deliverance of a person or group from oppression, with this oppression being seen as racial (black theology), sexual (feminist theology), or economic (third world liberation theologies).

There has also been a strong emphasis in recent years on salvation as holistic. Rather than being simply a spiritual matter, or affecting the person's spiritual standing with God, salvation involves the whole person. Thus, for example, Clark Pinnock, in discussing the famous passage in Acts 4:12 ("Salvation is found in no one else, for there is no other name given to men by which we must be saved"), includes physical healing in the concept of salvation. Assuming that Peter is saying that the healing of the cripple is an instance of the salvation found in Christ, rather than an evidence of Christ's uniqueness as the giver of salvation, he says, "Peter tells us that physical healing is part of biblical salvation. There is more than a touch of irony here, I think, when one considers that those who quote the text to support the exclusivist paradigm seldom in my experience acknowledge physical healing as part of salvation. They appear to be using the text to prove something it does not really say, while at the same time ignoring what it plainly does say."[6]

Including physical healing or freedom from oppression either as supplements to or substitutes for the older idea of salvation as primarily justification, regeneration, and the like, however, encounters broader problems. For if God's failure to provide salvation in the older sense to all persons is a difficulty, then the failure to provide these other dimensions must be an even more severe problem, since many who are devoutly religious and even devoutly Christian suffer ill health or injustice. How can such things be? The nature of salvation seems to bear on the whole issue of divine justice, and thus the matter is in need of further discussion.

The Nature of Truth and Logic

The doctrine of salvation also bears on the nature of truth and logic. In an earlier way of thinking, the truth of a proposition entailed the false-

---

6. Clark Pinnock, "Acts 4:12—No Other Name under Heaven," in *Through No Fault of Their Own?The Fate of Those Who Have Never Heard*, ed. William V. Crockett and James G. Sigountos (Grand Rapids: Baker, 1991), p. 109.

hood of its contradictory. Two contradictory statements could not both be true at the same time and in the same respect. Thus, one way to refute a statement was to verify its contradictory. Conversely, arguing for the truth of a position or proposition might require refuting its contradictory. This was because logic was believed to apply.

There is some difficulty for this position in the current discussions of salvation. Traditionally Christianity and its competitors, the other major world religions, were thought to contradict one another. These contradictions were sufficiently significant so that both religions could not be true simultaneously and in the same respect. If, however, contemporary pluralism is correct, then these apparently contradictory views are actually the same thing at root. To say this, however, requires one of two tactics. One would require a criticism of one or both of the religions, showing that it does not teach what it has been thought to teach, or if it does teach that, we are not bound to accept that teaching. The other tactic would be to revise logic, so that two statements can actually contradict one another and yet both be true. On this basis, the locus of truth would not be objectively within the propositions of the view, but subjectively within the effect produced within the person exposed to them.[7]

Hermeneutics

This teaching or this set of issues also has an effect on hermeneutics. One solution to the problem of the apparent conflict of biblical teachings, either with the teachings of other religions or with the contentions of a theory such as pluralism or inclusivism, is to interpret those exclusivist passages, such as Jesus' words, "I am the way and the truth and the life. No one comes to the Father except through me" (John 14:6), as metaphorical rather than literal. When one uses this device, however, other potential complications follow. Does one interpret all biblical teachings in this metaphorical fashion? If not, on what basis does one distinguish among them? Is there a consistent basis for this, or is it simply ad hoc or random in nature? One's hermeneutical theory and practice are put to the test by these issues.

Religion

Finally, this discussion raises and sharpens the question of the very nature of religion. For much of its history, Christianity was considered largely a matter of doctrine or ideas, so that what separated it from various religions was different teachings. Faith was then also thought of in

7. See, for example, Søren Kierkegaard, *Concluding Unscientific Postscript* (Princeton, N.J.: Princeton University Press, 1941), pp. 169–224.

corresponding fashion. Being a Christian, or being Christianly religious, was a matter of what one believed, of believing the doctrines of Christianity rather than those of some competitor religion.

The nineteenth century opened this issue to debate, however. Immanuel Kant had written three massive analyses (critiques) of human experience. In the first of these, the *Critique of Pure Reason*, Kant argued that we cannot have theoretical knowledge of what lies beyond sense experience. That excluded many of traditional Christian theology's objects of belief. It is not possible to prove, by theoretical reason, the existence, or for that matter, the nonexistence, of God. In the second critique, however, the *Critique of Practical Reason*, Kant reintroduced these doctrinal concepts as necessary postulates. God is needed as the source and guarantor of ethical values. The third critique, the *Critique of Judgment*, dealt with esthetic matters. The conclusion of Kant's reasoning was to make God and other theological matters not so much objects of belief, but a practical necessity, and religion not a matter of believing certain claims or thinking in a certain way, but of ethics, or acting in a certain way. While Albrecht Ritschl chose to follow Kant, making religion a matter of value judgments, Friedrich Schleiermacher relegated religion to Kant's third realm, and made it a matter of feelings, specifically, the feeling of absolute dependence. Much contemporary religious discussion and practice have followed a similar track.

This same debate regarding the nature of religion, and specifically, of the Christian religion, is also present as a major component of the discussion of salvation. On their surface, the ideological contents of the various world religions seem to differ considerably from one to another. If, however, religion is a matter of a certain feeling experience, rather than its ideological conceptions, then the various religions may be more generic than has been thought. Indeed, this seems to underlie John Hick's pluralism, as he describes at some length worship experiences of different religions, and documents this with excerpts from the literature of various religious sources.[8] It is also found in the writing of Raimundo Panikkar, who claims that the Trinity is not distinctively Christian, and interprets each of the persons of the Trinity in terms of experience, showing that each of these three types of experience is found in several different religions.[9] Thus, the whole question of the nature of religion, whether it is an autonomous sphere of human experience, or can be assimilated to some other type of experience, is and will need to be part of the agenda generated by this type of discussion.

8. Hick, *God Has Many Names*, pp. 62–66.
9. Panikkar, *Trinity and the Religious Experience of Man*.

Cultural Changes

Globalization

Another major reason for the importance of the subject of salvation is the changed situation in our world today. One major phenomenon of our time is globalization—the fact that persons living in one part of the world are in contact with and influenced by events transpiring elsewhere in the world. This means that our understanding of reality must be formulated in a much broader context than formerly. For much of the history of the world, the majority of persons lived their lifetimes without coming in contact with persons of very different persuasions or cultures. People might never move more than twenty or thirty miles from their place of birth. Some Roman Catholics, for example, never encountered any non-Catholic Christian, let alone anyone of another religion. Some persons never met anyone who did not speak their language. In such a setting, it is very easy to be ethnocentric, to think of one's own way as the right way, and indeed, as the only way. When something different was encountered, it was immediately thought wrong by virtue of being different, for one's way had been experienced for so long that it simply was not possible to identify with anything different or to enter into another way empathetically.

This has changed in our day, however. A large percentage of the earth's population now has had contact with persons from other religions. This may take place through international travel, where one can observe firsthand the worship by those of a different religion. Even for those who cannot afford the luxury of such travel, however, the contact with different cultures and religions is virtually unavoidable. Refugees from other countries are coming to the United States, bringing their customs, languages, and religions with them. Persons from other countries are traveling, so that tourism is not a unidirectional phenomenon. And, in fact, missions activity is not restricted to Christianity. Islam has become aggressively evangelistic and missions-oriented on a worldwide scale.[10] One can no longer assume that by staying at home one will have no contact with followers of other religions. Other religions are now coming to our own homes.

10. Russell Chandler, *Racing Toward 2001: The Forces Shaping America's Religious Future* (Grand Rapids: Zondervan; and San Francisco: Harper San Francisco, 1992), pp. 183–85.The religion section of a Minneapolis newspaper carried a note about a National Basketball Association player, Al-Hahjj Mahmoud Abdul-Rauf of the Denver Nuggets, who "will conduct a free basketball clinic and talk about the Islamic faith . . . at the Islamic Center of Minnesota."The use of this evangelistic technique took place not far from a Christian megachurch that conducts an annual baseball clinic involving evangelical Christian players on the Minnesota Twins team."Point guard to make a point," *Star-Tribune, Newspaper of the Twin Cities*, Saturday, April 16, 1994, p. 12E.

Even those who do not come in direct personal contact with adherents of other religions are seldom unexposed to those religions. Several series on public television have introduced world religions to Americans, often in a powerful way. The general impact of television has made Americans aware of various cultures, although not always accurately.

In light of these developments, we must ask ourselves what our attitude toward these persons is. Christians have traditionally tended to be condescending toward other religions. They were either regarded as idolatry, or at least as clouded or mistaken constructions of the revelation given to all persons. We must now, however, as a result of a closer contact, ask ourselves about the status of these persons and their religions. What should be our attitude toward them? Should they be evangelized, or regarded as fellow travelers, who although they express themselves differently, are really bound for the same place we are?

Missions Crisis

This question has become more urgent because of the missions crisis. Especially in mainline denominations, there has been a retrenchment in missions. The number of missionaries under appointment by the mission boards of those denominations has steadily declined over the years. At the same time, evangelical missions have grown rapidly, compensating for the decline of these other organizations' missions programs.[11]

This prosperity of evangelical missions may soon come to an end, however, for changes are taking place within evangelicalism. One is the strong orientation of ministry toward the consumer. In some cases this is bringing large numbers of persons to church and even into the membership, but the nature of their commitment is somewhat different from that of the preceding generation of evangelicals. In particular, their support of missions is on a rather different basis. A generation ago it was popular to ask people simply to support a program. Thus, people would give to underwrite the budget of a mission organization. A shift took place toward personalized giving, in which churches and individuals would subscribe part of a given missionary's support. More recently, however, evangelical Christians of the baby-boomer generation have shown reluctance to make long-term commitments to programs of which they have only secondhand information. They want personal, direct acquaintance with the work they are asked to support, and they are

11. James Leo Garrett, Jr., "'Evangelicals' and Baptists—Is There a Difference?"in James Leo Garrett, Jr., E. Glenn Hinson, and James E. Tull, eds., *Are Southern Baptists "Evangelicals"?*(Macon, Ga.: Mercer University Press, 1983), p. 81.

more inclined to give to limited, concrete projects, rather than to ongoing programs.[12]

The upshot of this is that missions giving is now declining in such churches. Actually, giving of all kinds is declining. In part this is due to the nature of the appeal. Rather than emphasizing responsibility or stewardship, many of these churches have been built on the idea of the church meeting the needs of those to whom it ministers. In this setting, taking has not always moved on to giving. One large contemporary ministry numbers only about 15 percent of those who attend as givers of any kind. Some churches are attracting large numbers of "seekers" but are not succeeding in transforming them into "finders" in sufficient numbers to sustain a growing ministry. Consequently, the per capita giving of such ministries, especially when adjusted for inflation, is not growing. Even established churches are finding that such a decline is taking place. While it has been popular to attribute this to a reaction against organized religion as a result of the televangelist scandals of the late 1980s, or the economic recession and stagnation of the United States and the entire world economy, the problems seem to go beyond this. With a shortage of financial support, ministries outside the local church are the first to be cut. Thus, missions, even in conservative circles, are falling on hard times. Much of the missions giving is being done by persons fifty-five years of age and older. As these people come to retirement age and then die, a financial crisis will be upon the churches, hitting missions first. In denominations affiliated with the National Association of Evangelicals per-member church contributions declined from 6.72 percent of personal income in 1968 to 4.62 percent in 1992. Much of this is attributed to consumerism among churchgoers, who expect more gratification from their churches, rather than giving to missions projects.[13] James Engel and Jerry Jones find that only 10 percent to 15 percent of Christian baby boomers have a high interest level in spreading the gospel overseas through conventional missions.[14]

All of this will force us to rethink our stance toward missions. Some in mainline circles have attempted to be optimistic by concluding that perhaps inability to send missionaries to evangelize those who have not heard is not such a great tragedy after all. Perhaps these persons really possess the truth, so that they do not need to be told. The inability to do

---

12. James F. Engel, *Averting the Financial Crisis in Christian Organizations: Insights from a Decade of Donor Research* (Wheaton, Ill.: Management Development Associates, 1983), pp. 51–52.

13. Helen Lee, "Churches Struggle with New Factors in the Giving Equation," *Christianity Today* 30.5 (April 24, 1995): 48–49.

14. James F. Engel and Jerry D. Jones, *Baby Boomers and the Future of World Missions* (Orange, Calif.: Management Development Associates, 1989), p. 27.

so may raise questions on a subjective level that may be answered differently than in the past.

Some even suggest that evangelism is not only unnecessary, but may even be improper. Possibly it is simply exporting our own cultural quirks to others. It has not been uncommon to attach to the Christian message typically Western or Northern culture, customs, and tastes. So, for example, we have sometimes taught indigenous persons to dress like Westerners, or to build houses of worship that are typically Western. I once remarked to an Argentine pastor that a seminary building in Buenos Aires looked quite North American. He said, "That's not surprising. The plans were drawn in Nashville." Beyond that, we have been equally provincial or ethnocentric in calling upon Buddhists, Hindus, Muslims, and Jews to abandon their religious beliefs and practices to become Christians.

Perhaps those who find in the various religions simply variations on a theme are right. Some developments within American evangelical popular religion seem to indicate that the uniqueness of Christian religion is more apparent than real. For example, some see in certain varieties of contemporary evangelical worship, and especially its music, much that resembles the practices of other religions. One new faculty member at a certain seminary attended the all-school retreat that preceded the beginning of the school year, and remarked to the dean after the first period of singing, "We haven't sung anything that a Hindu could not have sung!" Some have seen in the countless repetitions of the words of a song parallels to the mantras repeated in some Eastern religious practices. The changing culture of Christian churches and their changing worship practices make this inquiry and discussion all the more pertinent.

Criticisms of Exclusivism

Divine Justice

A study of the doctrine of salvation is important because of the increasing crescendo of criticisms being leveled at the traditional exclusivist approach. One of these, alluded to earlier, criticizes the concept of God's justice. If God chooses to save some persons by providing them with an opportunity to fulfill his conditions by enabling them to hear, and condemns others who have not fulfilled those conditions or obeyed his command to believe on his Son, largely because they have not really heard of him, how can he be termed just? And if this is to be referred to as just, what has happened to the meaningfulness of language? Does God prescribe different standards for us than what he practices himself? If this does not count against justice, then what could possibly do so? Has not the term become so elastic as to be virtually meaningless? How can we appeal to other humans to be just in their dealings with persons, when we apparently do not know what that means ourselves?

The problem takes a slightly different form when we consider the future state of the unevangelized. The traditional doctrine has been that such persons spend eternity in an endless punishment in hell. How can this be reconciled with God's love? Did not Jesus teach that we are to forgive those who wrong us, to love not only our friends but also our enemies? How then are we to understand a God who apparently does not love his enemies, who takes vengeance on them, and eternally so, who is never satisfied with the punishment of these people?

Human Injustice

A second major criticism of the traditional view is that it has actually led to injustice within the human race, in the treatment of human by human. The mission enterprise and colonialization have proceeded together, or at least in parallel. The brown and black populations of the colonized countries were regarded by the Europeans as inferior and therefore in need of a higher guardianship. This characterization embraced their culture and religions. Thus, one moral justification of the imperial enterprise was that it served the end of raising the unfortunate people of the colonized countries. The political subjugation of a people was justified by the benefit that resulted from or accompanied this, namely, their conversion to a superior religion, Christianity. John Hick says, "But without going into further detail it is, I think, clear that in the eighteenth and nineteenth centuries the conviction of the decisive superiority of Christianity infused the imperial expansion of the West with a powerful moral impetus and an effective religious validation without which the enterprise might well not have been psychologically viable."[15]

Disregard for Other Humans

A further criticism of the traditional exclusivist position is that it represents a disregard for other humans. It fails to respect other peoples' culture and religion, accepting them for what they are, and accepting in return their respect and acceptance of one's own position. To elevate one's own culture and religion above that of others is to elevate oneself above the other. As such, Christianity's exclusivism is just another version of the Western imperialism that considers the Western way the right way, all

---

15. John Hick, "The Non-Absoluteness of Christianity," in *The Myth of Christian Uniqueness: Toward a Pluralistic Theology of Religions*, ed. John Hick and Paul F. Knitter (Maryknoll, N.Y.: Orbis, 1987), p. 20.

others being in need of correction. Exclusiveness is actually an expression of hostility toward others.

Political Impossibility of Exclusivism

Not only is the approach improper; it is literally impossible in our present-day world. We live in a world community in which culture and religion are often seen as more closely fused than what persons in the United States are accustomed to. Forced recognition of the official status of certain religions is mandatory. For example, U.S. troops stationed in Saudi Arabia during Desert Storm had to abide, at least outwardly and officially, by the strictures imposed by the Muslim state religion. There could be no open practice of Christianity, and attire and other practices had to conform to Islamic standards.

Exclusivist Doctrinal Idolatry

Finally, the whole exclusivist approach is accused of setting up doctrines or ideas as idols. The conceptions are limitations on what God can do, or stipulations of what he must do. This mistakes a human conception of God for God himself. As such, it is an illicit substitution, usurping commitment to God with commitment to particular doctrines.

Insufficient Past Treatment

The discussion of the topics considered in this book is also important because they have never received definitive treatment by the church. No official council has given them the concerted attention and authoritative ruling that were given to such doctrines as the person of Christ and the Trinity, for example. Elements of the doctrine of salvation were certainly treated, especially by councils such as Trent, but the question of how many will be saved and the ultimate destiny of the lost, or the duration of punishment for unbelievers, did not receive such attention. It is unlikely that an ecumenical council with such a broad representation of Christianity will ever again be assembled, and even if such were the case, its pronouncements could not carry effective authority in today's atmosphere of individualism and autonomy. This means that there is a backload of unresolved issues, for not only has there not been a council, but there also has not been the extensive type of discussion that has been devoted to some issues in the past.

Recent Attention

This discussion also is needed because of the large amount of attention given to the topic in recent years. Controversy has erupted in print, revealing that long-accepted positions are no longer going unchallenged. The literature produced by pluralists such as John Hick and Paul Knitter is being responded to by persons like Carl Braaten.[16] The Roman Catholic Church's Second Vatican Council modified considerably the earlier exclusivist position of the church, as have individual Catholic theologians, most notably Karl Rahner. Even groups as conservative as the Evangelical Theological Society are stirred by debate regarding these matters, with Clark Pinnock, John Sanders, and others taking more inclusivist positions. Literature has sprung up in response to this.[17] The question of annihilation has proven especially troublesome in evangelicalism in recent years, with such staunch conservatives as John R. Stott, Philip Edgecumbe Hughes, John Wenham, and Michael Green declaring themselves to be believers in this view. Indeed, debate over the doctrine of annihilation broke out at a Consultation on Evangelical Affirmations, so that no statement could be adopted by the assembled theologians.[18]

One measure of the level of interest in the subject on the scholarly level is the amount of material being published in journals. An index of this is *Religious Index One: Periodicals*. An examination of this index of articles by subject shows that there has been an especially strong increase in articles dealing with religious pluralism. For example, in the 5-year period 1970–74, 48 articles on religious pluralism were indexed, while the 5-year period 1987–91 totaled 246 articles. The number of articles on universalism increased from only 25 to 43.[19] This has come in a number of different kinds of journals. Because this is not only a matter of theology but also deeply affects such fields as missions, the literature has come from a variety of sources.

---

16. Carl E. Braaten, *No Other Gospel!Christianity among the World's Religions* (Minneapolis: Fortress, 1992).

17. E.g., *Through No Fault of Their Own?* and Larry Dixon, *The Other Side of the Good News* (Wheaton, Ill.: Victor Books, 1992).

18. *Christianity Today* 33.9 (June 16, 1989): 62–63.

19. *Religious Index One: Periodicals*, ed. R. Dean Hudgens (Evanston, Ill.: American Theological Library Association, 1993), vols. 10–11 (1970–74), pp. 534–35, 708–9; ed. G. Fay Dickerson, vol. 19 (1987), pp. 260, 341; vol. 20 (1988), pp. 317, 417; vol. 21 (1989), pp. 280–81, 370; ed. Don Haymes, vol. 22 (1990), pp. 290, 386; vol. 23 (1991), pp. 318–19, 420.It should be noted that the number of periodicals indexed increased during this period from 295 to 506, which is partly due to an increase in journals in existence and partly to a wider coverage of existing journals.

Practical Implications for Ministry

There also is real need for discussion of these topics because of their practical implications for ministry. This is especially true of evangelism, whether domestic or foreign. Traditionally, evangelism was motivated at least in part by the conviction that all must be reached with the good news of the gospel, because apart from faith in Jesus Christ all are lost and under divine condemnation for their sins. Now, however, there is a potentially changed understanding of the status of the unevangelized. Perhaps they are not lost. They may be savingly related to God on the basis of the knowledge all humans can obtain from the study of nature and of themselves. Perhaps those who have not heard during this life will have an opportunity to hear after death, and such a presentation might well be more convincing than that which an ordinary human evangelist could make. Thus, if not already "saved," they may well be in the future, even without human instrumentality. Rather than bringing about their salvation, our efforts at evangelism and missions may aggravate their predicament. Further, those, if any, who are lost may not experience eternal suffering, but rather simply cease to be.

These discussions are spurring new debates regarding the necessity of evangelism. While the more inclusivist views do not eliminate evangelism, they do suggest a need for rethinking its grounds. As we noted at the beginning of this chapter, the church has throughout its history believed it must reach out to bring the good news to others. Some major attention to this set of issues is in order, for this is no merely ivory tower theoretical endeavor. It is of the utmost importance in terms of the church's very understanding of its own basis for being.

Reflections of Wider Cultural Issues

Finally, the debate is important because of much wider issues. To some extent, this interaction is part of a larger collision between traditional beliefs and values and those arising in our day. As such, the struggle between two different cultures is affected by this. One issue we have already noted is the status of God and his authority and justice. Is he bound to follow any external standard of what is right and wrong? Does he have any inherent obligations to humans, other than to fulfill the promises and covenants he has made with them?

Another of these issues is the nature of responsibility. To what extent are people properly responsible for their decisions and actions? This question does not apply so much to the matters of implicit faith and postmortem evangelism, for there the question involves the justice of condemning persons who have not really heard and thus have not really rejected the offer of salvation. Further, some of these discussions include the idea of degrees of punishment in proportion to the knowledge involved. Rather, this issue becomes especially operative with respect to annihilation. Traditionally, the sense of freedom and responsibility required the idea that one is held responsible for the consequences of one's actions, and should make such choices enlightened by awareness of those results. More recently, however, the culture has tended to blunt the unfortunate results of poor choices. This is probably one factor behind the fact that in many schools it is no longer possible to fail; the "F" grade has disappeared, being replaced by the "no credit." It can also be seen in the type of rhetoric being expressed in connection with the "pro-choice" position on abortion. What one often hears is that "a woman should have the right over her own body." Many in the "pro-life" camp agree formally with that contention, and consequently are strongly opposed to rape. They would contend, however, that except in the case of rape, by the time a woman has become pregnant she has already to some extent surrendered that right. What she wishes to do is to exercise the right to reverse an earlier decision, whether made consciously or by default, not to practice birth control in the sense of pregnancy prevention. She is choosing to substitute another form of birth control, pregnancy interruption. Insisting on the right to make this choice is really a case of "pro-second choice."

I have sometimes used an illustration drawn from golf. It is the eighteenth hole of the final round of an important professional tournament and one golfer is lining up a short putt. If he makes the putt, he will tie one other golfer for the lowest score, and they will enter a sudden-death playoff. He carefully lines up the putt and strokes the club through the ball. The ball rolls straight toward the hole, then curves slightly, rims the cup, and rolls away. The gallery groans. The golfer, however, walks over, picks up the ball, turns to the crowd with a sheepish grin, and says, "Sorry. I didn't mean to hit it." He then places the ball in its original location and prepares to putt again. In many areas of life, we get only one chance. Annihilation does not give one a second chance. However, if the traditional position on this doctrine is correct—that the Bible teaches eternal suffering as the consequence of rejection—it is an attempt to nullify the full extent of the effects of one's choices.

Part **2**

The Varied
Perspectives on
the Question

2

Traditional
Roman Catholic Exclusivism

We wish now to examine the traditional Roman Catholic view on the salvation of those who have not heard the gospel of salvation. It is important to note that the Catholic Church has not always been monolithic in its view on this issue, or for that matter, on many of its doctrinal tenets. Through a long process of interaction and dialogue, the church came to declare certain views "orthodox," as the official position that all members of the church must hold. In this process, the church was also formulating a theory of its own authority, the culmination of which was promulgated at the First Vatican Council, which began in 1871, to the effect that when the pope, the bishop of Rome, speaks *ex cathedra* in matters of faith and practice, he is infallible. That virtually guaranteed a universal acceptance of certain views, at least in a formal fashion. We now turn to that consensus.

There is a certain difficulty in interpreting the Catholic position. The official view, which we will be discussing here, was the doctrine of *extra ecclesiam nulla salus*: Outside the church there is no salvation. We have to ask ourselves, however, whether this formula actually addresses the question under discussion here. For it may mean that those who have not consciously included themselves in the Roman Catholic Church are lost. On the other hand, it may mean simply that those who consciously exclude themselves from the church are lost. These are two quite different statements. In other words, the issue may be what it means to be inside the church, or even the meaning of the church.

In light of this latter observation, we must consider the possibility that different persons subscribing to the same formula may understand it in

33

different ways. In order to make a complete assessment of the traditional Catholic position, therefore, it is necessary to see the elements from which it was drawn, and its various forms at different times. In some cases, the view is only present implicitly; at other times it is quite well thought out and consciously held.

Another issue is involved in this interpretation of beliefs: at what point we consider "Protestantism" to have begun. Is it an innovation, first occurring in the sixteenth century? To put the point differently, was the Reformation a departure from the basic consensus or a return to that tradition? May it be that the later Roman Catholicism actually represented the departure or deviation?

Representative Statements

Early Theologians

Even before the development of the "high" view of the church and its authority, there were theologians who held out little hope for the heathen. Tertullian, for example, describes how great his joy will be in seeing the pagan philosophers, kings, playwrights, and poets suffering the torments of hell.[1] Origen said, "Let no man deceive himself. Outside this house, i.e. the Church, none is saved."[2] Cyprian made a similar point: "He cannot have God for his Father, who has not the Church for his mother."[3] Ambrose states categorically that those who die unbaptized go to hell.[4] It should be noted that of these, including Augustine, all except Origen are Latin or Western theologians, and of those, all except Ambrose are Africans.

Augustine

We turn then to Augustine, the great churchman and theologian, who was undoubtedly the most influential theologian of the first millennium of the Christian church and one of its five or six greatest theologians of all time. Augustine's thought may seem to us somewhat ambiguous. To someone reading him in the twentieth century, his ideas sound at times quite Protestant, even quite Reformation, in nature. In other places, however, he resembles much more closely what we know as Catholicism. The reason is that the seeds of both these movements were present in his thought. We ought not to think of this as a confusion

1. Tertullian, *The Shows* 30.
2. *Homilies on Joshua* 3.5, in *Patrologia cursus completus, series graeca*, 12:841.
3. *On the Unity of the Church* 100.6.
4. Ambrose, *On Abraham* 2.11.

of these two streams of theology. To do that would be an anachronism. Rather, they simply had not yet been separated at this point. Some of Augustine's themes address the question of what has come to be called predestination, or what he labeled that. Other motifs are concerned with the necessary conditions for salvation.

Augustine addresses the question of those who have never heard the message of salvation through faith in Jesus Christ, in a letter to Deogratias, in which he seeks to respond to some of Porphyry's weightier arguments against the Christians. If, says Porphyry, Christ is the only Way of Salvation, the Grace and Truth, and in him alone and only to persons believing in him is the way of return to God, what then are we to think of those who have lived before Christ? What is to be done with those innumerable souls who were in no way blameworthy, since Christ had not yet made his appearance in human flesh? Both in Rome and throughout the whole world were those who were very zealous in the worship practiced in heathen temples in that time. In light of this great zeal, why did Christ withhold himself for such an extended period, merely enlarging the time of inability? Porphyry will not allow the answer that provision for those who lived before Christ had been made through the old Jewish law. It was only after a long time in the history of the race that the law came, and then it only flourished within the narrow limits of Syria, progressing only gradually toward Italy and arriving there no earlier than the reign of Caius. "What then," asks Porphyry, "became of the souls of men in Rome and Latium who lived before the time of the Caesars, and were destitute of the grace of Christ, because He had not then come?"[5] This would seem to provide Augustine an excellent opportunity to clarify his view in such a way as to articulate either an exclusivist or what we would today term an inclusivist view.

Augustine replies by affirming that Christ is the Word of God, by whom all things were made, and is the Son, because he does not merely belong to the past but abides unchangeably with the unchangeable Father. He is the one predicted by the prophets and has fulfilled all their prophecies. In all these ages he is the same Son of God, co-eternal with the Father. He is the unchangeable Wisdom by whom universal nature was called into existence, by participation in whom every rational soul is made blessed. "Therefore," Augustine says, "from the beginning of the human race, whosoever believed in Him and in any way knew Him, and lived in a pious and just manner according to His precepts, was undoubtedly saved by Him, in whatever time and place he may have lived."[6] Those of us living since Christ's earthly ministry believe in him

5. Augustine, *Letter to Deogratius* 8.
6. Ibid., 12.

as both dwelling with the Father and having come in the flesh, whereas those in earlier ages believed in him as dwelling with the Father and coming in the flesh. The nature of faith is not changed by what was foretold having now come to pass.

In light of this, then, Augustine affirms that although the true religion was formerly set forth and practiced under other names and different symbolic rites than it now has, and was less clearly revealed and to fewer people than it now is, it is one and the same under both periods.[7] Thus, he appears to allow for some, not merely in the Hebrew religion, but in other religions as well, to be saved by Christ, even though their knowledge of him was partial and imperfect. This move, however, is not primarily based on belief in the efficacy of general revelation. Although he holds that all humans have access to general revelation, through which God makes known his nature and his ethical demands, sin obscures and perverts the natural human's understanding of the truth. Salvation requires explicit knowledge of the Messiah.[8] Augustine believes that many, both within and outside of Israel, were saved before the coming of the Messiah, but it appears that he holds that this was through God's special revelation of himself to them, so that their status was much like that of Job in the Old Testament era.

Why, however, was this gift of faith and consequent salvation given to some and not all? Make no mistake about it, says Augustine: It was given to some and not to others, rather than indiscriminately to all. The believer really should feel no distress over this fact, however. From one (Adam) all have gone into a condemnation that is righteous. Even if no one were saved, that would be just, for all deserve condemnation. It is a matter of great grace for many to be delivered, so that their salvation is not on the basis of any merit whatsoever. Their merits are no greater than those condemned. Why, then, does God deliver one rather than another? This is a great, inscrutable mystery. God's ways are past finding out. We simply cannot begin to criticize God for these matters. Augustine cites Romans 11:33: "O man, who art thou that repliest against God?" It would be better to hear or to say that, than to dare to speak as if we could know the things he has chosen to keep secret. Beyond that, however, we know God's deeds must be just, because he cannot will anything unrighteous.[9]

This still, however, leaves us with the question of why Christ appeared as late in the history of the human race as he did. Augustine affirms that Christ willed to appear to humans and have his doctrine

7. Ibid.
8. *The City of God* 8.6, 10–12.
9. *On the Predestination of the Saints* 16.

preached to them at a time and place in which he foreknew that some would believe on him. He foreknew that at the times when the gospel was not preached, all people would react as many did in the time of his bodily presence, when people refused to believe even if he raised persons from the dead.[10]

There are, then, according to Augustine, three categories of persons with respect to salvation. There are those to whom the gospel was not preached, because God foreknew that they would not believe. Second, there were those to whom the gospel was preached, even though God foreknew that they would not believe, so that they might serve as examples for condemnation. Third, there were those to whom the gospel was revealed and who believed. Only those in this third category were saved, but this was not unjust.[11]

Who, then, will be saved? Only those who hear and believe the gospel of Christ. All others, the unevangelized, are condemned to hell. This, Augustine maintains, involves large numbers of persons: "Many more are left under punishment than are delivered from it, in order that it may be thus shown what was due to all."[12] While some might recoil from such a seemingly harsh statement, Augustine maintains that it should instead motivate believers to gratitude, seeing what might have been their fate but for the grace of God.

What about Catholicism's later development? Here we should observe that there is both a broader and a narrower version of the exclusivist position. The broader form argues from the necessity of believing the gospel and the essential facts about Jesus Christ. In light of this, those who have not heard cannot be saved, for they are incapable, even if through no fault of their own, of meeting the necessary conditions for obtaining that salvation. The second version is an argument from the necessity of the church for salvation. This is tied to the sacramental system, and consequently developed later, as that system gradually evolved. The former variety has much in common with Protestant exclusivism. The latter, on the other hand, is unique to Catholicism.

The Athanasian Creed

It is helpful to examine some representative statements of the Roman Catholic Church. The first is found in the Creed *quicumque* (the Athanasian Creed). It appears that this creed definitely is not from Athanasius, although it certainly is of ancient derivation, having been variously assigned to St. Ambrose of Milan and Fulgentius Ruspensis.

---

10. Ibid., 17; *Letter to Deogratius* 14.
11. *The City of God* 18.47.
12. Ibid., 21.12.

It is, however, one of the earliest such statements, and afterwards was accorded such great authority in both the Western and Eastern churches that it was accepted in liturgical use. It therefore can be considered a rather definitive articulation of the faith. It reads, "Whoever wishes to be saved, needs above all to hold the Catholic faith; unless each one preserves this whole and inviolate he will without a doubt perish in eternity." Then follows an enumeration of the tenets of trinitarian belief and of incarnation. Without these, says the creed, one cannot be saved. "This is the Catholic faith; unless every one believes this faithfully and firmly, he cannot be saved."[13] Note that belief, or holding the Catholic faith, is emphasized, rather than ecclesiastical connection or remaining in communion with the church. We should note further that the belief required is quite extensive. Not merely the basic tenets must be believed, but one is required to preserve this "whole and inviolate." The items enumerated as necessary for belief are considerable and detailed. They include the Trinity and several qualities of God: eternality, uncreatedness, immensity, omnipotence, and coequality of the three persons. With respect to Christ, the prescribed beliefs include the full incarnation, his suffering, descent into hell, resurrection, ascension, session at the right hand of God the Father, second coming, and judgment. A faithful and firm belief in these matters is essential to salvation.

Innocent III

A papal pronouncement expressing this perspective comes from Innocent III, who wrote in a letter "Eius exemplo," to the archbishop of Terraco, on December 18, 1208: "By the heart we believe and by the mouth confess the one Church, not of heretics but the Holy Roman, Catholic, and Apostolic (Church) outside which we believe that no one is saved."[14] This pronouncement definitely limits salvation to members of the church. As far as the unsaved, Innocent seems to have in mind heretics and schismatics, rather than the unevangelized. It is at least conceivable that the latter might be regarded somewhat differently, because they are outside the church passively or by omission, while the former are apparently deliberately so.

The Lateran Council IV

The Lateran Council IV (1215) put the matter more emphatically, and emphasized the role of the church's sacramental ministry, in its Ecumenical XII, against the Albigensians:

13. Henry Denzinger, *The Sources of Catholic Dogma*, trans. Roy Deferrari (St. Louis: B. Herder, 1957), pp. 39, 40.
14. Ibid., p. 423.

One indeed is the universal Church of the faithful, outside which no one at all is saved, in which the priest himself is the sacrifice, Jesus Christ, whose body and blood are truly contained in the sacrament of the altar under the species of bread and wine; the bread (changed) into His body by divine power of transubstantiation and the wine into the blood, so that to accomplish the mystery of unity we ourselves receive from His (nature) what He Himself received from ours. And surely no one can accomplish this sacrament, except a priest who has been rightly ordained according to the keys of the Church which Jesus Christ Himself conceded to the Apostles and to their successors.[15]

This is a reflection of St. Cyprian's statement, "There is no salvation outside the Church," in Epistle 73, to Jubaianus.[16]

The Council of Florence

One of the clearest statements comes from the Council of Florence (1438–45):

It firmly believes, professes, and proclaims that those not living within the Catholic Church, not only pagans, but also Jews and heretics and schismatics cannot become participants in eternal life, but will depart "into everlasting fire which was prepared for the devil and his angels" [Matt. 25:41] unless before the end of life the same have been added to the flock; and that the unity of the ecclesiastical body is so strong that only to those remaining in it are the sacraments of the Church of benefit for salvation, and do fastings, almsgiving, and other functions of piety and exercises of Christian service produce eternal reward, and that no one, whatever almsgiving he has practiced, even if he has shed blood for the name of Christ, can be saved, unless he has remained in the bosom and unity of the Catholic Church.[17]

This statement is remarkably clear and explicit on several points. First, it is clear to whom it is referring. Pagans, as well as Jews and schismatics, are enumerated. Second, the basis of salvation is clear. The connection with the sacraments is crucial in terms of the benefit for salvation. Those not so connected cannot be saved, no matter how pious their lives may have been. Thus, it is one of the most definitive statements of the "outside the church, no salvation" position. Coming from a council, it carries the sort of ecumenical authority only such a group can confer. It cannot be said that the Roman Catholic Church is not on record regarding this crucial matter.

15. Ibid., p. 430.
16. Cyprian, *Epistle* 73, n. 21.
17. Denzinger, *Sources*, p. 714.

The Council of Trent

The Council of Trent has been considered especially significant and authoritative for prescribing the positions of the church in the more modern period. The Profession of Faith of the Council as found in the Bull of Pius IV, "Iniunctum nobis," November 13, 1565, says: "This true Catholic faith, outside of which no one can be saved . . ."[18] The statement itself is quite detailed and explicit, including everything in the Apostles' Creed, as well as all traditions and other observances and constitutions of the church. Similarly, Benedict XIV (1740–58), in the profession of faith prescribed for Orientals (Maronites), said, "And that this faith of the Catholic Church, without which no one can be saved, etc. . . ," referring to the statement of the Council of Trent.[19]

Gregory XVI

More recent popes have also spoken on this matter in much the same tone. Gregory XVI (1831–46), writing about indifferentism, or the opinion "that the eternal salvation of the soul can be acquired by any profession of faith whatsoever, if morals are conformed to the standard of the just and the honest,"[20] comments: "For, since all restraint has been removed by which men are kept on the paths of truth, since their nature inclined to evil is now plunging headlong, we say that the 'bottom of the pit' has truly been opened, from which John [Apoc. 9:3] saw 'smoke arising by which the sun was darkened with locusts' coming out of it to devastate the earth."[21] We need to be careful not to generalize too much from this statement. It simply rejects indifferentism's idea that any profession of faith whatsoever is acceptable, if only the moral behavior is of a certain type. It does not exclude the possibility of some professions of faith which, including the substance of the gospel without its particulars, might make the person acceptable to God. In logical form, indifferentism held that all A is B. This edict says that some A is not B. That does not exclude, however, the possibility of some A being B.

Pius IX

Pius IX (1846–48) also addressed the issues posed by indifferentism. A syllabus or collection of modern errors has been made from his various allocutions, encyclicals, and epistles. Among the false ideas condemned are the following: "16. In the worship of any religion whatever, men can find the way to eternal salvation, and can attain eternal salva-

18. Ibid., p. 1000.
19. Ibid., p. 1473.
20. Ibid., p. 1613.
21. Ibid., p. 1614.

tion. . . . 17. We must have at least good hope concerning the eternal salvation of all those who in no wise are in the true Church of Christ."[22] But he also said,

> For, it must be held by faith that outside the Apostolic Roman Church no one can be saved; that this is the only ark of salvation; that he who shall not have entered therein will perish in the flood; but, on the other hand, it is necessary to hold for certain that they who labor in ignorance of the true religion, if this ignorance is invincible, are not stained by any guilt in this matter in the eyes of God. Now, in truth, who would arrogate so much to himself as to mark the limits of such an ignorance, because of the nature and variety of peoples, regions, innate dispositions, and of so many other things?[23]

Evidently Pius is distinguishing between those who consciously and knowingly depart from the faith, or reject it, and those who do so ignorantly. As such, he seems to pose something of a paradox. It may be understood, and the paradox removed at least partly, through the observation that he is reluctant to set limits on the possible mercy of God. In other words, those who are outside the church are lost, but he is at least agnostic about the status of those who are "invincibly ignorant."

What shall we now make of these pronouncements of the church? We can summarize them as follows. We must interpret these statements in light of the situations they were intended to address, namely, the polemical discussions. In large part, they were discussing the status of heretics and schismatics, those who consciously and willingly rejected the Catholic tradition. They are less clear and categorical about those who are invincibly ignorant of that tradition, and therefore have not actively rejected it. There seems to be some possibility of hope for those in this group who display marks of morality fitting what God requires of persons. There is not necessarily the same tolerance for those of other religions, which are mentioned explicitly in some of the statements. It is not always clear whether they are in mind in the document under consideration. It may well be that what we have here is a rather clear exclusivist position, but with respect for God's sovereignty, so that there is reluctance to state the limits of his mercy and grace. Thus, in these areas of virtual agnosticism, there are enough openings so that later interpreters would be able to fit such concepts as "baptism by desire" into them.

22. Ibid., p. 1716, 1717.
23. Ibid., p. 1647.

Roman Catholic Theological Matrix

All that we have said in the foregoing must be understood within the theological matrix of Roman Catholic theology as a whole. In the introductory chapter we referred to the organic character of theology. To the extent that a given theology is logically coherent, its various doctrines are interrelated, so that the position taken on one of them influences the others. Consequently, the correct understanding of any given theology, such as the extent of salvation in this case, must be developed within the context of the theology as a whole.

The Nature of Salvation

A first and obviously most crucial doctrine concerns the nature of salvation itself. In particular, the Catholic understanding of justification is not forensic. That is to say, it does not consist primarily of God somehow declaring a person just, or imputing to him or her a righteousness not actually possessed by that person. Rather, justification tends to be more a matter of impartation, the actual coming to be of goodness within the person. The central concept is that of sanctifying grace, which from a Protestant or at least a Lutheran perspective, seems to fuse together the doctrines of justification and sanctification. A person is as righteous in the sight of God as he or she is actually holy or good in condition. This should not necessarily be thought of in terms of salvation by works, as if one accomplished this by one's own effort. Rather, it is something that must be given by God, and that through the sacraments.

Justification

In particular, Roman Catholic theology objects to the Protestant concept of justification. To the Catholic, the Lutheran doctrine of justification by grace means that the person remains sinful but God ignores the sin: "Our souls remain indeed hideous in themselves, but God covers them over with the merits of Christ so that these are looked upon by him as being ours; our sins are not 'imputed' to us, but the merits of Christ are."[24] In contrast, the Catholic view is that "we become just before God not through a non-imputation of sin but by an interior renovation which blots out sin. This is effected by sanctifying grace, which is explained as a reality poured forth upon us and inhering in us."[25] Such biblical expressions as "born again," and "new creature" speak

24. *The Teaching of the Catholic Church: A Summary of Catholic Doctrine*, ed. George D. Smith (New York: Macmillan, 1958), 1:550.
25. Ibid., p. 551.

powerfully of this character of sanctifying grace. To the Catholic the Protestant alternative is abhorrent:

> All this is directly contrary to the awful teaching of Protestantism which would make the soul even of the just man a sinful thing, essentially corrupt and loathsome. There can, then, be no doubt about what is the correct view of the matter: sanctifying grace is a real quality, of surpassing beauty, infused by God into the soul and making that soul worthy of the Creator who fashioned it and the Redeemer who won it from the thraldom of sin.[26]

The Divine Method of Working

This further leads us to an understanding of God's working, or more generally, of his method of providence, with respect to the spiritual needs of humans. Since Christ's ascension, God carries on his work through the church. Jesus' conferral of the power of the keys on Peter (Matt. 16:19) was a commissioning of the church to act on God's behalf on earth. This is his chosen means of working, and grace comes to humans through this channel.

The Church

Key to this Catholic doctrine is the nature and status of this exclusive church. The church is supernatural in origin, having been established by Christ himself. Because sacramentalism is a large part of Catholic theology, the church is indispensable. God gives his grace to persons through certain rites of the church, such as baptism, the Eucharist, extreme unction, and the like. Because the church holds the power of these sacraments and controls who may receive them, it has the power to transmit or withhold God's sanctifying grace. A corollary to sacramentalism is sacerdotalism, the doctrine that only a properly ordained priest has the authority to administer these sacraments. Without a priest present to pronounce the proper formula, the Eucharist, for example, would not be the Eucharist. It would simply be a meal of bread and wine. Because such authority is conferred from above and ultimately derives from Christ, one cannot simply choose to establish a Catholic Church. The church must descend by apostolic succession from Peter, who in turn received his authority from Christ himself. Within this context, the idea of no salvation outside the church makes good sense, for grace must be given for salvation to be received, and that grace is limited to the church.

26. Ibid., pp. 551–52.

What, then, are we to make of the paradoxical combination of the *extra ecclesiam nulla salus* principle and some who are apparently saved even though they have never heard of Christ and thus cannot possibly have consciously believed? The church maintains that this doctrine does not mean that the church condemns and must condemn all non-Catholics. Rather, it is not the church's task to inflict eternal damnation. That role belongs to God alone, who can scrutinize the conscience as the church cannot. Rather, the church maintains that it has always taught that "nothing else is needed to obtain justification than an act of perfect charity and of contrition. Whoever, under the impulse of actual grace, elicits these acts receives immediately the gift of sanctifying grace, and is numbered among the children of God."[27] Such would not, however, include anyone who, knowing that God has commanded everyone to join the church, willfully remains outside her fold, because the love of God necessarily involves obedience to him.[28]

Strictly speaking, those who receive grace without having formally united with the visible church are not entirely outside the church. The desire to fulfill all of God's commandments implicitly includes a desire to be united with the church, because although these individuals do not know it, this has been commanded by God. Hence, they would certainly unite fully if they were aware of the command, and therefore can be said to belong to the church by desire. Even in those cases where God saves persons apart from the church, he does so through the church's graces. Such persons can be said to be joined with the church in spiritual communion, although not in visible, external communion.[29]

Toleration

Some Catholic theologians, perhaps because the Catholic Church has been criticized for intolerance, emphasize the toleration implicit within these qualifications of the traditional formula. So Pohle, for example, maintains that the church is tolerant and kindly considerate of non-Catholics, and even non-Christians. He says, "In her tolerance toward the erring the Church indeed goes farther than the large catechism of Martin Luther, which on 'pagans or Turks or Jews or false Christians' passes the general and stern sentence of condemnation: 'wherefore they remain under eternal wrath and in everlasting damnation.'"[30]

27. George Heyward Joyce, "Church," in *The Catholic Encyclopedia* (New York: Encyclopedia Press, 1913), 3:752.

28. Ibid.

29. Ibid., pp. 752–53.

30. Joseph Pohle, "Toleration," in *The Catholic Encyclopedia* (New York: Encyclopedia Press, 1913), 14:767.

It is probable that this conception has developed over the years, so that even the pronouncements of the Second Vatican Council only expanded and elaborated what was already present in less complete form. This is seen particularly in the letter of the Holy Office to Archbishop Cushing of Boston in 1949, intervening decisively in the heresy trial of Leonard Feeney. Feeney, a priest, had insisted on a strict interpretation of the *extra ecclesiam nulla salus* principle. He subsequently was excommunicated. The pope's letter spoke definitely to two extremes on the issue: Feeney's position and the view that other religions besides Catholic Christianity could serve as means of salvation. He reaffirmed the Catholic Church's traditional position that Christ himself established the church, and that consequently it is the means appointed by God for salvation, "without which no one is able to enter the kingdom of heavenly glory."[31] The statement then goes on to say that "for someone to obtain eternal salvation it is not always demanded that he is in fact (*reapse*) incorporated as a member of the Church, but what is absolutely required is that he should adhere to it by wish and desire." Nor is it necessary that this wish always be explicit and conscious, for "where a man labours under invincible ignorance God also accepts an *implicit wish*, as it [is] called, for it is contained in that good disposition of the soul whereby a man wishes to conform his will to the will of God."[32] The statement indicates that Pius "reproves those who exclude from eternal salvation those who adhere to the Church by implicit wish alone, and also those who falsely assert that men can equally well be saved in any religion." This implicit wish is defined, however: "But it is not to be thought that any sort of wish to enter the Church is sufficient for a man to be saved. It is required that the wish whereby someone is directed to the Church should be informed by *perfect charity*." And, lest someone think that this type of faith or wish is a human accomplishment, the pope says, "nor can an implicit *votum* have effect unless the man has supernatural faith."[33]

It is not clear just how many persons Catholic theology expects to be saved, whether relatively few or relatively many. Pohle seems to indicate that there will be many: "Otherwise the gentle breathing of grace is not confined within the walls of the Catholic Church, but reaches the hearts of many who stand afar, working in them the marvel of justification and thus ensuring the eternal salvation of numberless men who . . .

---

31. *The Teaching of the Catholic Church as Contained in Her Documents*, prepared by Josef Neuner and Heinrich Roos, ed. Karl Rahner, trans. Geoffrey Stevens (Staten Island, N.Y.: Alba, 1967), p. 244.
32. Ibid.
33. Ibid., pp. 244–45.

cannot appreciate her true nature."[34] This is not quite so clear from the other statements we have examined, however. Pius XII's letter to Archbishop Cushing places great emphasis on the charity being perfect. There is no official definition of this, but it sounds so extreme as to be quite rare. It is a quality only seldom found even among those who are formally and externally united to the visible church. Pius made quite clear that not just any wish would suffice for salvation under such circumstances.

The other factor introducing qualification into this alternative means of obtaining sanctifying grace is the specification that such an implicit wish is not simply a human accomplishment, but itself the result of actual grace. While this is not elaborated further, it seems apparent that this supernatural impartation of actual grace requires special divine intervention. In this respect, it may be more like the Protestant exclusivist view that God gives special revelation to some outside the reach of the gospel, than it is like the view that persons come to implicit faith through general revelation.

Evaluation

Positive

This position, which has exerted such a strong influence during the years of Catholic dominance in the Christian world, must now be evaluated. A number of positive features of this approach deserve special notice.

1. This approach understands and takes seriously the importance of the question of the essence of Christianity or of religion. It realizes that the question, "What makes Christianity different from other religions?" or "What distinguishes a person as a bona fide Christian?" is an important one. While this may be disregarded or underemphasized in some other varieties of treatment of the problem of inclusivism or exclusivism, these theologians have wrestled with this question and have offered a rather clearcut answer. Whereas much debate about the extent of salvation's reach has really failed to come to grips with the opposed position because of a failure to deal with the basic question, this group has potentially assisted all who debate the overall issue by identifying the crucial problem.

34. Pohle, "Toleration," p. 767.

2. Having asked this question and having concluded that the intellectual content of religion, or the doctrinal basis, is important, these theologians have not underestimated the differences between Christianity's doctrinal structure and that of other religions. They have rather carefully delineated the respective systems. There is no facile treatment of different religions as simply different expressions of the same thing.

3. Catholic exclusivism has also taken seriously humans' need for salvation. Whereas some other forms might tacitly assume that failure to arrive at the correct position does not have serious consequences, these persons have seen, on the basis of Scripture, tradition, and experience, that there is clearly something wrong with the human, and that serious intervention is necessary to rectify that.

4. At least in its earliest forms, Catholic exclusivism takes very seriously the question of the nature and content of faith. Unlike some more recent schools of thought, which reduce or even virtually eliminate the question of the precise details of the object of belief, these theologians have asked, "What and how much must one believe to be saved?"

5. The approach to the relationship with Christ has been consistent with the rest of the theological system. To be more specific, the understanding of salvation and of grace is related in a consistent way to the understanding of the church and the means of grace.

Negative

Countering these positive points are a number of problems with this theology, some of which are inherent in Catholic theology of any variety.

1. The whole question of exclusiveness, insofar as it is related to connection with the Catholic Church as a historical institution, rests logically on the historical data establishing a connection between the present church and Christ's founding act. That historical data, however, is, to say the least, ambiguous or disputed. Much of the presentation of the position seems to assume, rather than argue, this historical connection.

2. In the later forms of this theology, the effort to maintain the original terms of the position seems somewhat strained. This appears in such areas as "baptism by desire," where the language becomes quite extended and even stretched to the point where meaningfulness itself is in question. There is insufficient clarification of just how much can be covered by the concept.

3. The definition of the doctrine of salvation is also ambiguous. What are the relative places of faith and works, and the exact definitions of these concepts?

4. This theology emphasizes the necessity of adherence to the infallible body of teaching given by the church; yet there is some difficulty in identifying precisely that infallible body of teaching. This problem shows itself, for example, in the question of infallible *ex cathedra* papal statements. There is little agreement regarding just which or how many such pronouncements have been made throughout the church's history.

5. There is difficulty in determining, for purposes of our discussion, the extent of rejection of any deviation from the Catholic faith. This is because most of the statements are directed to specific varieties of belief deemed heretical. Thus, for example, the rejection of indifferentism is a rejection of the idea that any view whatsoever is acceptable. Does it follow from this, however, that no views other than the official Catholic orthodoxy are acceptable? Similarly, statements about Christian heretics cannot simply be used by later theology as indications of the attitude toward those who have not really been exposed to Christian teaching at all.

3

Protestant Exclusivism

Corresponding to Catholic exclusivism is a Protestant parallel. It would not be correct to speak of this as a Protestant version of the Catholic view, for they are in some ways very different species of the same genus. In certain respects, the Protestant view even represents a reaction against the Catholic emphasis on the exclusiveness of the church as a channel of grace. The conceptions we are looking at here began considerably later than the Catholic form. In many cases, Protestant exclusivism built upon Protestantism's unique theological principles. In general, exclusivist views are found more commonly among Calvinists than Arminians. More correctly, we should refer to Augustinianism rather than Calvinism. In this connection, because Martin Luther was an Augustinian monk, his view is in many ways similar to that of Calvin, making the continental Reformation virtually unanimous in its exclusivism.

We need to review briefly those basic theological doctrines. While not found in all their detail in each instance of Protestant exclusivism, they are representative of the theological stance of those who do maintain that there is no salvation outside the Christian faith and belief in the gospel.

1. All persons have sinned. There is no such thing as a person who obeys God completely. All humans not only sin, but they are sinners by nature as well as by choice.
2. God is completely holy, and as such expects his human creatures to be holy as he is holy.
3. As a violation of God's law and person, sin must be atoned for by payment of the penalty attached to it.

4. This provision of atonement for human sin has been made through Jesus Christ's sacrificial death.
5. The salvation accomplished through Christ's atoning death must be accepted by sinful humans. Its efficacy is not automatic.

Representative Statements

John Calvin

As in so many other areas, John Calvin gave the view its definitive form. The starting point is his view of general revelation, because those who argue for inclusivism often do so on the grounds that general revelation serves to bring persons to enough knowledge to constitute saving faith. For Calvin, however, general revelation is ineffective. Indeed, since the fall, persons apart from Christ are unable to make anything of the knowledge of God the Creator from observation of the creation. The "natural course" of things was "that the fabric of the world should be a school in which we might learn piety, and from it pass to eternal life and perfect felicity."[1] This does not happen, however, for several reasons, including sloth and ingratitude. Sloth means that our minds are so blinded that they cannot perceive the truth. And ingratitude means that our senses are so corrupted that we wickedly rob God of his glory. Thus, Calvin says, "It is certain that after the fall of our first parent, no knowledge of God without a Mediator was effectual to salvation."[2] He recognizes but rejects the efforts of those who hold that salvation extends to some who have not heard and believed. He says, "The more shameful, therefore, is the presumption of those who throw heaven open to the unbelieving and profane, in the absence of that grace which Scripture uniformly prescribes as the only door by which we enter into life."[3]

What, then, are we to make of other religions and their teachings? These are worshiped by large numbers of persons, representing unbelievers' distortions of God's truth. Calvin says, "The Scripture, in order to direct us to the true God, distinctly excludes and rejects all the gods of the heathen, because religion was universally adulterated in almost every age."[4] What value did this general revelation serve for the pagans, then? Calvin replies that its only effect was to make them guilty or without excuse. So he says, "But as all, without exception, have in the vanity of their minds rushed or been dragged into lying fictions, these impres-

---

1. John Calvin, *Institutes of the Christian Religion*, trans. Henry Beveridge (Grand Rapids: Eerdmans, 1953), 2.6.1.
2. Ibid.
3. Ibid.
4. Ibid., 1.10.3.

sions, as to the unity of God, whatever they may have naturally been, have had no further effect than to render men inexcusable."[5]

Even the chosen people were saved only because of the Mediator. The prophecies pointed toward him. The Hosannas given at Jesus' triumphant Palm Sunday entry into Jerusalem indicate a general preparation and knowledge of the things concerning him. Salvation is only through him. First John 2:23 says, "No one who denies the Son has the Father."

Charles Hodge

This tradition was carried through later Protestant theology as well. It can be found in the Old Princeton School, the Princeton Seminary of the second half of the nineteenth century. One prime spokesman for this movement—and, in view of his major textbook, one of the persons most influential in terms of number of people influenced—was Charles Hodge. He discusses the divine calling of those who have been elected to eternal life and the means by which this calling is accomplished, because predestination of the end (eternal life) also involves predestination of the means (faith on the part of the person), and in turn the means that enable such faith. He is quite clear about special revelation's crucial place in this process: "The call in question is made only through the Word of God, as heard or read. That is, the revelation of the plan of salvation is not made by the works or the providence of God; nor by the moral constitution of our nature; nor by the intuitions or deductions of reason; nor by direct revelation to all men everywhere and at all times; but only in the written Word of God."[6]

Are there not instances, however, when persons who did not seem to have the written Word of God at their disposal nonetheless had saving knowledge of God? Here would be included the various "God-fearers" mentioned in both the Old and the New Testaments, such persons presumably as Job and Melchizedek. There may, Hodge acknowledges, have been cases in the past where God revealed himself directly to persons, but these were of the nature of a miracle, rather than to be attributed to a universal general or natural revelation. He says of these, "For such supernatural revelations of truth after its being made known in the Scriptures and committed to the Church with the command to teach all nations, we have no promise in the Scriptures and no evidence from experience."[7] In other words, we have no grounds for expecting such, and certainly should not presume that such will occur.

5. Ibid.
6. Charles Hodge, *Systematic Theology* (Grand Rapids: Eerdmans, 1952), 2:646.
7. Ibid.

Hodge argues for this position on the basis of several considerations. One is the argument of consensus. He says, "It has ever been, and still is, the doctrine of the Church universal in almost all its parts, that it is only in and through the Scriptures that the knowledge necessary to salvation is revealed to men."[8] Whether this is a correct statement will have to be evaluated in light of all the data considered in this book, but the claim here is that Hodge's position is not to be thought unusual or innovative. He also offers several inferential arguments from various doctrines and other teachings of Scripture. One of these is the Old and New Testament teachings regarding the status of the heathen. The constant biblical witness is that they are in a "state of fatal ignorance." It can also be inferred from the biblical teaching regarding the nature of the gospel. This is based essentially on the saving work of Christ. For adults, it is necessary, for this to become effective, that they consciously accept Christ and his work. Further, this conclusion can be drawn from the fact of the Great Commission. Why would this have been given, if the preaching of the gospel had not been necessary? If persons could somehow be saved without believing the content of that message, it would surely be superfluous.

Most of all, however, Hodge contends that this requirement of persons hearing explicitly and believing is true because the Bible expressly teaches it. Many references could be cited. Among them are especially texts such as Romans 10:14, 17. Surely, Paul would not have written what he did there, if hearing the supernatural gospel had not been indispensable.

Hodge admits that this is an awful doctrine, one in which he takes no joy.[9] This should be borne in mind when we come to some later comments of theologians who suggest that those who hold the exclusivist position are somehow indifferent or cold-hearted. The exclusivist view is that the message of the Bible, specifically our Lord's teaching, is that the way is small and narrow, and few find and enter in. This could produce a reaction on our part: abhorrence or blaming of God, or repulsion that causes us to turn away or immobilizes us. Rather, it should prompt us to increased exertion in taking the gospel to those who have never heard.

It should be noted, however, that for Hodge and the other members of the Old Princeton School, this view did not necessarily lead to the conclusion that the number saved would be relatively few. Rather, they concluded that a large number would be saved, perhaps the vast majority of those who have lived. This suggests that although the relative fewness concept has usually accompanied the exclusivist view, it need not

8. Ibid.
9. Ibid., p. 648.

necessarily be so. This, however, is because of a special feature of this theology. These men were postmillennialists, who believed that the kingdom of God would be established prior to Christ's coming to earth visibly and bodily in his second coming. This would be accomplished through the successful preaching of the gospel, so that large numbers of persons would respond favorably and turn to faith in Christ in the endtimes. Because presumably a higher percentage of the earth's population would be alive in the last times than at earlier periods, this means that those converted from among them would in turn constitute a large percentage of the whole of all who have ever lived. Such a view also has other implications. If there is a theoretical limit to the number of persons who can live on the earth at any given time, once that limit is approached or reached, the Lord's return would need to occur quite soon or majority conversion must be true of each generation. As soon as a few generations at that level of population have lived and died, the persons alive at any given time would constitute a diminishing minority of the total number.

John Sanders considers this optimism uncharacteristic of the exclusivist position, which he terms "restrictivism."[10] If by "characteristic" he means simply that historically it is a fact that more exclusivists have held that there would be few saved than have held that many would be saved, this is certainly correct. If, however, he means by "characteristic" more than merely what is customary, he would be saying that this is somehow virtually contrary to the principles of this school of thought. That, it would seem, is a confusion of two distinguishable although interrelated issues: the number who are saved and the means by which they are saved. This may indicate that by "restrictivist" he means something somewhat different than what we mean by "exclusivist," as we are using it here. He may mean that the restrictivists not only restrict the means of salvation to explicit faith, based on hearing the Word of God, but that they also restrict the extent of salvation, the number who are saved. It should be noted that in the sense in which we are using the term here, these men are clearly exclusivists. Salvation is exclusively through Christianity, and through a conscious faith in the realities expressed in the gospel, but it is believed that many will be successfully evangelized.

Louis Berkhof

Twentieth-century Reformed theologians have held a similarly exclusivistic position. In his formerly widely used systematic theology

10. John Sanders, *No Other Name: An Investigation into the Destiny of the Unevangelized* (Grand Rapids: Eerdmans, 1992), p. 76.

textbook, Berkhof notes that some hold that there are other ways for the unevangelized Gentiles to be saved than through a faith response to the preaching of the gospel. He believes that this view rests on the assumption that the only sin that really condemns a person is explicit rejection of Jesus Christ. Scripture, however, never says this. Thus, the position is based on a hypothetical conjecture. We do not know what things there may be that we do not know.

Rather, the Bible does explicitly point out that the Gentiles are lost. Representative texts that teach this are Romans 1:32 and 2:12, as well as Revelation 21:8. Berkhof's comment is that "there is no Scripture evidence on which we can base the hope that adult Gentiles, or even Gentile children that have not yet come to years of discretion, will be saved."[11] In other words, he would not exclude the possibility of such a hope for salvation independent of special revelation, but the Bible should itself give some indication of this alternative approach.

Loraine Boettner

Another twentieth-century Calvinist who has addressed this issue is Loraine Boettner. He affirms that those who have not heard the specially revealed gospel know nothing about Christ. He willingly accepts the charge brought against some forms of Christianity, that the majority of persons who have lived to this point were lost, because they really did not have an opportunity to hear or, in other words, have the means of grace available to them. Boettner sees this as providential, and as virtually involving the principle set forth in the Calvinistic doctrine of predestination. For a long period of time the Jews, really a small group of people, were the only ones to whom God made a special revelation of himself, and Jesus confined his public ministry and that of his disciples to the Jews. "Multitudes were left with no chance to hear the Gospel, and consequently died in their sins," says Boettner. They do not hear, and consequently do not believe, because God has not elected them to eternal life. "If God had intended to save them undoubtedly he would have sent them the means of salvation." If God had chosen to Christianize India and China a thousand years ago, he certainly could have done so. Rather, "they were left in gross darkness and unbelief."[12]

Boettner cites a large number of Scriptures in support of this view, among them Ezekiel 33:8; Acts 4:12; Romans 2:12; 10:13, 14; 1 Corinthians 3:11; John 15:5; 14:6; 3:36; 17:3; 1 John 5:12; Hebrews 11:6. Most of these, of course, speak of the exclusiveness of the basis of

11. Louis Berkhof, *Systematic Theology* (Grand Rapids: Eerdmans, 1941), p. 693.
12. Loraine Boettner, *The Reformed Doctrine of Predestination*, 8th ed. (Grand Rapids: Eerdmans, 1954), p. 117.

salvation, namely, that there is salvation in no one other than Christ, but do not address the question of the exclusiveness of the means of salvation, that is, whether one can be saved only by consciously knowing of Christ and believing in or committing oneself to him. One clear exception is Romans 10:13–14, but there Boettner does not consider whether those *and only those* who call upon the name of the Lord will be saved. In connection with the other statements about the necessity of having Christ, he does not consider in any real depth what this means or how it may be obtained. He appears to assume that having equals hearing. Thus, although his position is clearly exclusivist, the basis advanced does not help us greatly in the conflict between exclusivists and inclusivists.

Somewhat unique and interesting is Boettner's apparent argument from analogy. He observes that the heathen do not really receive many of the temporal blessings of God either: "We readily see that so far as the pleasures and joys and opportunities in this world are concerned the heathens are largely passed by; and on the same principle we would expect them to be passed by in the next world also."[13] It should be clear, however, that if people are in situations in which they will never hear, it is because God does not intend for them to be saved:

> Those who are providentially placed in the pagan darkness of western China can no more accept Christ as Savior than they can accept the radio, the airplane, or the Copernican system of astronomy, things concerning which they are totally ignorant. When God places people in such conditions we may be sure that He has no more intention that they shall be saved than He has that the soil of northern Siberia, which is frozen all the year round, shall produce crops of wheat. Had he intended otherwise, he would have supplied the means leading to the designed end.[14]

There are also, within nominally Christian lands, multitudes to whom the gospel has never been presented in any adequate way. Their condition is the same as those in unevangelized countries and for the same reason.

Boettner also advances what is actually a pragmatic argument, whether he realizes it or not. He states that the belief that the heathens are lost has been one of the strongest arguments in favor of foreign missions. If there were enough light within the other religions to save the persons who adhere to them, there would be much less need for preaching the gospel to them. He says, "Our attitude toward foreign missions is determined pretty largely by the answer which we give to this ques-

13. Ibid., p. 120.
14. Ibid.

tion."[15] Being a strong Calvinist, Boettner of course believes fervently in divine sovereignty. Thus, one cannot limit what God could and might do. He can save some adult heathen people if he chooses to, for the Spirit works as he chooses and where he chooses, with or without the use of means. However, if this happens, it is not through general revelation. It would rather be a miracle of pure grace, some special manifestation by God of himself to such persons, a case of special revelation outside the Bible. It is a case of extraordinary hearing of the gospel, presumably similar to cases of special revelation not preserved in the Bible (cf. John 21:25). It therefore is not an instance of inclusivism.

There is one significant point of difference among these unsaved, however. The fact that they all are lost does not mean that they all suffer the same degree of punishment. There will be varying degrees of punishment, based, at least in part, on opportunity. Boettner bases this conclusion on two passages from Jesus' teachings. One is Luke 10:12–14, where Jesus indicated that in the day of judgment it would be more tolerable for Sodom than for those cities that had heard his message.[16] The other is found in the parable of the faithful and unfaithful servants (Luke 12:47–48), where the punishment is more severe for the servant who, knowing the master's will, failed to do it, than for the one who was ignorant of the master's will and failed to do it. Thus, Boettner concludes, "So while the heathens are lost, they shall suffer relatively less than those who have heard and rejected the Gospel."[17]

R. C. Sproul

A contemporary Calvinist who has defended the exclusivist position is R. C. Sproul. He notes that the form in which the question is put is something like, "What happens to the poor innocent native in Africa who has never heard of Christ?" He recognizes the commendable motivation behind this question in the compassion of one human for the fate of others. Yet he also observes that the way in which the question is framed tends to prejudice the issue.[18] If the question is really asked in this form, the answer is easy and obvious: "The innocent native who never hears of Christ is in excellent shape, and we need not be anxious about his redemption. The *innocent* person doesn't need to hear of Christ. He has no need of redemption. God never punishes innocent people. The innocent person needs no Saviour; he can save himself by his innocence."[19]

---

15. Ibid., p. 119.
16. Ibid., p. 120.
17. Ibid., p. 121.
18. R. C. Sproul, *Reason to Believe* (Grand Rapids: Zondervan, 1978), p. 48.
19. Ibid., p. 49.

The framing of the question this way, however, "betrays the assumption that there are innocent persons in the world." If there are, which Christianity definitely denies, then we do not need to be concerned about them. The real question is, "What happens to the *guilty* person who has never heard?" What often underlies the former question is the idea of relative innocence, the idea that some persons are more wicked than others. This is often specifically because those who live wickedly, knowing the details of God's commandments, appear guilty of more heinous wickedness than persons who do not know them.[20]

If the remote native is in some sense guilty, however, in what does his guilt consist? Is he being punished for not believing in Christ, of whom he has never heard? This point is pertinent, in light of the statements of some who claim that the only sin for which one is condemned is the sin of rejecting Christ. Sproul acknowledges that "if God were to punish a person for not responding to a message that he could not possibly hear, that would be a great injustice."[21] Because God is just, we can be sure that no one is ever punished for rejecting Christ if he has never heard of him.[22] If indeed the only damnable offense against God were rejection of Christ, then we ought to leave the native alone. This would be the most helpful thing we could do for him, because by informing him about Christ, we are placing his soul in eternal jeopardy. Now he knows about Christ, and if he does not respond to him affirmatively, he can no longer claim ignorance as an excuse.

What about this assumption that the only damnable offense is rejection of Christ? What if the person who has never heard of Christ *has* heard of God the Father and rejected *him*? Is this as serious as rejecting God the Son? Sproul's answer is that it would seem to be at least as serious, if indeed not more serious.[23] The question, then, is whether those who have not had the gospel preached to them may nevertheless have heard about God, and if so, how this is accomplished.

Sproul maintains that the New Testament says humans are universally guilty, and relates the guilt to this very point. He believes the New Testament announces Christ's coming to a world that had already rejected God the Father. That is why Christ could say, "I came not to call the righteous, but the sinner to repentance. Those who are well have no need of a physician" (Matt. 9:12–13).[24] The biblical assessment of the status of those who have never heard of Christ is given in Romans 1:18 and

20. Ibid.
· 21. Ibid.
22. Ibid., pp. 49–50.
23. Ibid., p. 50.
24. Ibid.

following. Verse 18 says, "For the wrath of God is revealed from heaven against all ungodliness and wickedness of those who by their wickedness suppress the truth." It is suppression of the truth that is the occasion of God's wrath being revealed. What, however, is this truth that is being suppressed? Paul makes that clear in the remainder of the passage (vv. 19–21).[25] He says that what can be known about God is plain to them, because he has shown it to them: his invisible nature, namely, his eternal power and deity. Since the creation of the world this has been shown them so that it is clearly perceived in the things that are made. Although they knew God, however, they did not honor him as God or give thanks to him, so they are without excuse. Consequently, they became futile in their thinking and their senseless minds were darkened. This, Sproul observes, is what is usually referred to as the "general revelation."[26] He makes five observations about this revelation:

1. It is clear and unambiguous.
2. It "gets through." They *knew* God.
3. It has been going on since the foundation of the world.
4. It comes by way of creation.
5. It is sufficient to render man inexcusable.[27]

What is the excuse that is eliminated by this revelation? Sproul says it is ignorance. Because God has clearly revealed himself to all humans, no one can plead ignorance as an excuse. He acknowledges that there are circumstances under which ignorance may function as an excuse for certain things. The Roman Catholic Church has distinguished between vincible and invincible ignorance. The former is ignorance for which one is responsible, in the sense that he could have known the information, if he had chosen to take the necessary steps. Invincible ignorance is that ignorance that cannot possibly be overcome. In the Catholic scheme, it does excuse.[28]

In Sproul's understanding of the human condition, persons who have never heard of Christ can plead ignorance at that point, but not ignorance with respect to God the Father. Those who live in remote areas of the world are religious, of course. Some would say that those who worship totem poles, cows, or bee trees cannot be expected to do better than this, for they do not know better. They do, however, insists Sproul, based on what Paul has written. They have known the truth, but have ex-

25. Ibid., p. 51.
26. Ibid., p. 52.
27. Ibid., pp. 50–52.
28. Ibid., pp. 52–53.

changed it for a lie. They have turned to worshiping things made with human hands instead of worshiping the true God. This does not excuse them; it aggravates their situation, for the supreme insult to God is reducing him to the level of the creature. This strips God of his deity.[29]

What, then, will be the basis of the judgment of the heathen? Sproul says that "the New Testament makes it very clear that people will be judged according to the light they have."[30] While not all of the Old Testament law is known to them, they do have a law "written on their hearts," according to Romans 2:15. The pagan has an ethic, but does not live up to that, and consequently will be judged for it. He may not know of Christ, and therefore is not judged and punished for not accepting him. He has, however, a revelation of God the Father, and is punished for rejecting the Father.[31]

Christians need to take the message of the gospel to these people. In so doing, their opportunity for believing is increased. Of course, at the same time, their responsibility is increased, because their knowledge is increased. It is a two-edged sword. The Christian, however, must also realize that there is a second responsibility, this one devolving upon himself or herself. The Christian must ask, "What happens to me if I never do anything to promote the world mission of the church?" The concern for the remote native must begin with compassion, and be responded to with compassion, as well. Thus, the question of the fate of those who have never heard must be answered not only with words but also with actions.

It is apparent that Sproul's view places him squarely within the exclusivist camp, and is one of the more completely articulated views. He definitely feels that all have had a chance to hear of God through general revelation, and all have rejected. They are therefore guilty, not of the sin of rejecting Christ, but of rejecting God the Father. For them to be saved, they must hear the gospel that has been specially revealed, and respond in an affirmative fashion. It should be noted that while Sproul deals with the question of the suppression of the truth, and thus the rejection of the Father, in Romans 1, that merely establishes the universal sinfulness of humans. He does not equally grapple with the possibility that Romans 2:14 ("do by nature things required by the law") is teaching that perhaps some of these sinners come to repentance and abandonment to the mercy of God.

Carl F. H. Henry

A final representative of the exclusivist position is Carl F. H. Henry. Because of his stature as perhaps the premier theologian within evan-

---

29. Ibid., pp. 54–55.
30. Ibid., p. 55.
31. Ibid., pp. 55–56.

gelicalism, his convictions on this topic are of special significance. They are especially clear in connection with his discussion of the view propounded by J. N. D. Anderson. Henry grants that Anderson protests against the idea that nonbiblical religion may be a means of salvation for Christian grace, but accuses him of believing that these other religions contain elements of truth.[32] Anderson holds out the possibility of salvation even apart from explicit faith in Jesus Christ on the basis of the analogy of those who lived before the time of Christ. Their salvation was based on the work Christ was to do in the future. Yet Abraham, Moses, David, and others did not know Jesus except as a "vague hope of the future which they proclaimed but only dimly understood."[33] May it be that those who live after the time of Christ but never hear of him during their lifetime may be saved in a similar fashion to Old Testament believers? Anderson poses the question this way: "What if the Spirit of God convicts them, as he alone can, of something of their sin and need; and what if he enables them, in the darkness of twilight, somehow to cast themselves on the mercy of God and cry out, as it were, for his forgiveness and salvation? Will they not then be accepted as forgiven in the one and only Saviour?"[34]

Henry's reaction to this idea is quite negative and critical. He notes three features of Anderson's "projection": "(1) its exceedingly hypothetical character; (2) its lack of clear and unequivocal support in the New Testament which, as Anderson concedes, stresses the Christian duty to proclaim the gospel universally; (3) its theological weakness." He also feels that a further weakness in Anderson's view is that "it detaches the Holy Spirit's ministry ever since New Testament times from an explicit witness to the historical Jesus as the mediating Messiah."[35] It is this express witness to Jesus Christ that enables persons today to distinguish the Holy Spirit from false spirits. In the nonbiblical religions, there is of course no need for an absolute mediator, because their system of theology calls for no salvific substitute. He also finds fault with Anderson's suggestions that those who may turn to God in the twilight, in repentance and faith, still need to be told the gospel, because they lack the assurance, conscious companionship, and confident message that can come only from a full knowledge of Christ and what he has done. He says, "these very deficiencies suggest that Anderson separates from a

32. Carl F. H. Henry, *God, Revelation and Authority*, vol. 6, *God Who Stands and Stays*, pt. 2 (Waco, Tex.: Word, 1983), p. 367.

33. Norman Anderson, "A Christian Approach to Comparative Religion," in *The World's Religions*, ed. Norman Anderson (Grand Rapids: Eerdmans, 1976), p. 234.

34. Ibid.

35. Henry, *God, Revelation and Authority*, p. 368.

cohesive and unitary plan of salvation the possibility of a personal rescue that in fact cannot be thus isolated."[36]

Finally, Henry objects to Anderson's use of Abraham as a model for adherents of nonbiblical religions who realize their own wickedness and seek divine forgiveness, even though they do not know the name of Jesus any more than did Abraham. He responds by saying that

> We may properly challenge this claim, however, for God's covenant with Abraham, bringing blessing to the nations, has for its context revealed religion that already focuses on the Mediator-Messiah, involving as it does a divinely approved sacrifice, if only in an elementary and preparatory sense. If God's covenant-relationship is attenuated merely to man's repentance and divine forgiveness, we imply that God is tolerant of sin in a manner that Old Testament faith precludes; moreover, we anticipate Judaism's later error of essentially identifying the covenant with a works-religion.[37]

To some extent, it appears that Henry is preoccupied with the features of nonbiblical religions, and not enough with the biblical statements about general revelation or any description of its recipients. Thus, other than brief discussions of Cornelius and Abraham, he does not really enter into a thorough consideration of the persons in Scripture who seemed to have become part of the covenant without previous extensive exposure to the content of the message. It is clear, however, that he identifies himself as an exclusivist, one who believes not only that the work of Christ is essential for salvation, but that there must also be conscious awareness and acceptance of it. In one of his earliest books, he considered the possibility of persons, on the basis of the natural light they have, trusting in God to provide the indispensable sacrifice for their sin. His comment is, "That men will find their way to it, apart from the preaching of the Gospel, is most unlikely."[38]

Summary

It is now time to summarize the Protestant exclusivist position, as we have seen it stated in the thought of these several theologians.

1. All humans are sinners who live apart from God. This combination of disbelief and disobedience means that they are under God's condemnation.
2. Even those who have never heard of Jesus Christ are responsible for their sin and guilt. There is a genuine general revelation of

---

36. Ibid.
37. Ibid., p. 369.
38. Carl F. H. Henry, *Giving a Reason for Our Hope* (Boston: W. A. Wilde, 1949), p. 41.

God in nature and in the human personality, and from this all persons know God sufficiently so that they should have been able to respond positively to him, but have in fact suppressed this truth.

3. Salvation cannot be by works. It is only available through God's merciful, gracious provision in offering Jesus Christ as a sacrifice for the sins of all humankind.

4. In order to be forgiven and saved, it is necessary to understand the basis of this salvation, in other words, to have the special revelation that gives knowledge of the gospel.

5. No one is innocent. Because all have sinned, the question of the condition of the unevangelized is not a question of the innocent. All deserve divine judgment. If God were to give each person what he or she deserves, none would be saved; all would be lost.

6. Adherents of other religions, no matter how sincere or committed, are spiritually lost unless they come to belief in Jesus Christ.

7. Death brings to an end the opportunity for accepting Jesus Christ, and thus for eternal salvation. The decisions made in this life have eternal consequences.

8. Jesus Christ's return will be followed by a great judgment, at which point persons will be consigned to eternal fellowship with God if they have accepted Christ, or to eternal separation from God and to eternal punishment if they have not.

9. In light of the foregoing, Christians have an obligation to take the good news to unbelievers by telling them of Jesus Christ.

Evaluation

How shall we assess this view, which has had such wide popularity in Protestantism over the years, and is probably the view held rather unreflectively by many lay persons today?

Positive

There are a number of positive strengths of this position, as it is usually formulated.

1. Exclusivism takes seriously the didactic passages of both the Old and New Testaments that, at least on the surface, sound strongly exclusivist. The condemnation of the other nations and the warning to Israel to avoid their religious beliefs and practices, Jesus' statements about his unique status as a channel of salvation, and

the preaching of Paul and other apostles to a non-Christian world can well be accounted for by this theory.

2. This view takes seriously the biblical teaching about the universality of sin and guilt. It recognizes that the issue is not the destiny of the innocent, but whether persons really are innocent or guilty.

3. This approach emphasizes the role of doctrine as a determinant of the object to which one is related in faith, in a day in which faith is becoming rather generalized by the feeling orientation of much popular religion.

4. In at least some forms of this view, there is a realization of the necessary connection between the end (salvation of persons) and the means (their knowing what must be believed). This is particularly spelled out in Boettner's position.

5. The advocates of this view also generally see that evangelization is a two-edged sword. If the severity of punishment of the lost is proportionate to their knowledge, then those who hear the gospel but do not believe are worse off than if they had never been told the message about Christ. The good news, in other words, becomes for them bad news, and worse news than would otherwise have been the case.

Negative

Despite these strengths, there are a number of problems with the usual form of this view, and a number of points at which unresolved issues must be dealt with.

1. There tends to be too much deduction from other tenets, without careful evaluation of the suppressed premises in the argument. For example, passages like Romans 10:9–12 and Acts 16:31 indicate that believing in Jesus Christ or calling upon his name leads to salvation. The passages do not necessarily say, however, that only those who do so will be saved, although no other alternative is considered in those contexts. To say that those *and only those* who believe in Jesus will be saved is an illicit deduction.

2. Too much is also inferred from the Great Commission. To be sure, Christ's giving this confers an importance and urgency on the task of missions and evangelism. It is not stated, however, that this is because those to be evangelized cannot possibly be saved otherwise.

3. Perhaps the most serious problem with this view is that it has not really grappled adequately with the problem of human responsibility. That is to say, how can people who have not heard the gos-

pel be without excuse if they could not possibly have believed and if such belief is indispensable to salvation? As the statement of the position usually stands, people are condemned for failing to do what they could not possibly have done.

4. In Boettner's version of the position, there is inadequate consideration of the relationship between what is and what should be. That people are placed in situations where they cannot hear the gospel may make it certain that they will not be saved. Does it follow from this, however, that God does not will for them to be saved? In other words, can we be sure that they ought to remain in such conditions, or may it be the case that God intended for them to live where they are, but also that Christians were to take the message to them? The underlying issue of passivity in light of foreordination rears itself in Boettner's variety of Calvinism, perhaps by unintention.

4

Classical Universalism

Periodically in the course of the church's history, a view has arisen that is sharply opposed to the exclusivist views we have been examining. Rather than dividing the human race into two camps, the saved and the lost, this view in various ways has asserted that eventually all persons will actually be saved. Salvation, in other words, is to be universal, not merely in the sense of being available to all persons, but in the sense that all will actually be saved. While this position has had a long and checkered history, we wish to examine the form that it took in the first half to two-thirds of the twentieth century. In many cases this was before knowledge of world cultures had become as widespread as it is today.

In classical universalism, certain elements of the Christian view are presupposed, and in some cases, a fairly orthodox understanding of Christianity is present. For example, the conception of the deity or of ultimate reality is basically that of theism. Jesus Christ, however understood, is regarded as a significant object of faith. The end or destiny of human beings is believed to be fellowship with God, including in the future. Thus, when the universalists we are here examining speak of salvation, that salvation may rather strongly resemble the usual Christian understanding of salvation.

Even within the twentieth-century manifestations, there are a variety of forms of this view. In some there is relatively little discussion of how God would save all persons, whether through implicit faith, postmortem evangelism, or just what. Rather the emphasis is on why God will save all persons. The reason, rather than the means, is the primary object of interest here. Others, however, discuss the circumstances or the means by which humans come to this proper relationship. For some, it may require an opportunity for faith after death. It may even require, in some views, something like hell as a remedial experience to bring people to the conditions under which God can accept them. All are agreed, however, that certain conditions are required for this universal salvation. None holds that God will simply admit persons, regardless of their lives or beliefs, into his presence unchanged. There truly is a need for saving these persons from what they are, not simply from what might befall them.

This school of thought could be examined in many ways. We will begin by noting the reasons advanced in favor of the position, followed by a response to some of the usual objections raised against this type of view. Then we will look at some specifics of the understanding of the means to the changes in a person required for salvation.

Arguments for Universalism

The arguments usually adduced in support of universalism are of basically three types: biblical, doctrinal, and emotional. Universalism is in some senses a rather orthodox Christian variety of belief. This is particularly true of those theologies that emphasize biblical testimony as the basis for their universalism.

Biblical Arguments for Universalism

C. H. Dodd has especially argued that the Bible witnesses to universalism. His is no simplistic or naive approach to Scripture, and the hermeneutic involved is crucial to understanding the Scriptures appealed to. Dodd observes that there were two conflicting tendencies or attitudes within the early church. One party insisted on and wished to preserve the value of the national distinctions of Judaism. The other maintained that such distinctions had been superseded in the church; they were part of Israel as the object of the old covenant, but had no place in the new covenant. Paul was on the side of the latter group, and in Galatians we see his polemic on this point, whereas in Romans the battle is substantially won and letters such as Ephesians simply assume the issue as now settled.[1]

Beyond that, however, there was another more subtle movement in Paul's thought. He had certainly held that the church was not simply restricted nationally, but, Dodd concedes, in the earlier writings it is still exclusive in another sense. The church is made up only of those who are saved, who constitute only a part of the human race. In the later writings,

1. C. H. Dodd, *The Authority of the Bible* (London: Nisbet, 1928), pp. 207-8.

however, the church "is truly universal, for by an inward necessity it must ultimately include all mankind, and form the centre of a reconciled universe."[2]

One specific passage Dodd cites in this connection is Romans 11:11–32. In particular, the key verse in the passage is verse 32, which reads, "God has consigned all men to disobedience, that He may have mercy upon all." In the early chapters Paul has discussed the universal sinfulness of humanity and God's accompanying judgment on all humans. In this passage, he reiterates that theme but now links it with another important dimension of truth. The universal sinfulness of the human race is pictured as within God's purpose, although not necessarily in the sense of a causation that would conflict with human freedom. "But," says Dodd, "the final aim of that purpose is a state in which God's **mercy** is as universally effective as sin has been. In other words, it is the will of God that all mankind shall ultimately be saved."[3] In Dodd's judgment, Paul is here teaching a clear universalism.

It might seem strange and even incredible to some, however, Dodd observes, to claim that Paul held such an absolute universalism. On that line of interpretation, the Greek word for all is not to be thought of in numerical terms. It means primarily "mankind as a whole" rather than "all individual men." Moreover, it is contended that the very form and trend of Paul's argument do not justify such a completely universal conclusion. Paul has been arguing in terms of large groups, namely, Jews, Gentiles, and the Christian church, rather than in terms of individuals.[4]

Despite these reservations, Dodd finds universalistic conclusions here. For one thing, the arguments by which Paul claims that all Israel will be saved apply equally well to the whole of the human race. This is seen within this epistle, in which we see God reaching out to all men. There is the universal revelation to all men, found in nature (1:20) and in the law written on their hearts and attested to by conscience (2:14–15). It is true that they have sinned against the light, but so has Israel, and they are to be saved because God never goes back upon his gifts and call (11:29). If, then, this guarantees the salvation of Israel, it must do so as well for all men, because there is one God who is God of the Jews and the Gentiles alike (3:29–30) and there are no distinctions (3:22). So, says Dodd, "Whether or not, therefore, Paul himself drew the 'universalist' conclusion, it seems that we must draw it from his premises."[5] In

2. Ibid., p. 208.
3. C. H. Dodd, *The Epistle of Paul to the Romans* (New York: Harper and Brothers, 1932), p. 183.
4. Ibid., pp. 183–84.
5. Ibid., p. 184.

other words, Dodd seems to be saying that Paul may not have explicitly held and taught universalism here, but that he did so implicitly.

Dodd appeals to a still broader principle of interpretation in dealing with Romans 11. He notes that in the epistles there is evidence that Paul believed in and expected an ultimate reconciliation to God of the spiritual powers that were at that time hostile both to him and to human salvation. In Colossians 1:16–20 this is made inclusive of both the earthly and the heavenly, or physical and spiritual forces. Ephesians 1:10 is similarly cosmic in scope. Indeed, the subjugation of all the spiritual forces appears to be part of what is involved in the ultimate redemption of even the physical universe (Rom. 8:21).[6] From this principle, Dodd then draws a conclusion for the interpretation of this passage: "But if Paul believed that such a thoroughgoing redintegration of the universe was the end of the divine purpose, then he cannot but have thought that a complete redintegration of the human race was included in it; and he may be allowed to have meant what he said in its full sense: that God would **have mercy upon all.**"[7]

We need to understand what Paul meant by this final triumph. It might be construed as involving simply the destruction or the suppression of the hostile elements, whether human, subhuman, or superhuman, to which the whole creation was subject. In Paul's later writing, however, it is apparent that this is not meant. Rather, this ultimate unity of all things to God is secured "by bringing them all into harmony with the will of God as expressed in Christ."[8] Dodd adds, "We may further observe that if the whole created universe is salvable, then there can be no finality in the distinction between 'the things of the Lord', and 'the things of the world.'"[9]

It is not just the later Pauline epistles that show this universalistic purpose of God, however, according to Dodd. In the Synoptic Gospels, we see the unfolding of God's plan for all persons. They contain a conflict between the local or provincial and the universal. Even in Matthew, the most nationalistic of the three, we find reports of Jesus' more universalistic preaching, as we do in Mark. It is especially in the writings of the third evangelist that we see a deliberate design to make clear the progression and extension of God's redemptive plan. The very selection and expression of events and messages indicate the movement from any sort of exclusive society of the true God to a truly universal one.[10]

   6. Ibid., pp. 184–85.
   7. Ibid., pp. 185–86.
   8. C. H. Dodd, *New Testament Studies* (New York: Scribner's, n. d.), p. 125.
   9. Ibid.
   10. Dodd, *Authority of the Bible*, pp. 209–11.

John A. T. Robinson, in somewhat more direct fashion, indicates that the New Testament teaches universalism, and uses the term that Origen, the real founder of universalism, used. He says, "The New Testament asserts the final *apokatastasis*, the restoration of all things, not as a daring speculation, nor as a possibility, but as reality—a reality that shall be and must be, because it already is."[11] He cites a number of texts supporting this contention. In 1 Corinthians 15:22 Paul draws a parallel between the universal condemnation resulting from Adam's sin and the universal enlivening through Christ's death: "In Christ shall all be made alive." Similarly, in Romans 5:18 Paul says that "through one act of righteousness the free gift came unto all men to justification of life." Robinson affirms that Paul is saying that the end is simply the realization of something already accomplished at the resurrection. This is seen quite clearly in Ephesians 1:20–22, where Paul speaks of God, through the resurrection, putting Christ in a position of rule or dominion over everything, not only in this world but also in the world to come. This picture of the future is a myth, but a myth that represents the translation of an accomplished fact into the future: "The promise of universal restoration is assured by the past: there cannot be any other outcome."[12] A similar expression is found in the midst of Paul's great discourse on the resurrection in 1 Corinthians 15:24–28. There is, as we shall shortly see, another type of myth in the New Testament as well, but this one cannot be disregarded.

Nels Ferré also sees more than one tradition within the Bible. One tradition in the New Testament is "the sovereign victory of God in Christ over all, in terms of His own love."[13] There are, to be sure, a number of specific texts that teach this, such as Philippians 2:10–11. On the basis of texts like this, biblical scholars such as C. H. Dodd find strong universalism in the Bible. Yet Ferré believes that all such verses, however many they may be, are as nothing in comparison to the total message of the New Testament. He says: "The total logic of the Bible, however, is forthright and fine. *God would have all to be saved and with God all things are possible.* Either God would not or could not effect such a sovereign victory of His love, but He can and will!"[14]

Doctrinal Arguments for Universalism

The case for universalism, even when made on the basis of biblical texts, is not exclusively or necessarily even primarily made on those

11. John A. T. Robinson, *In the End, God* (New York: Harper and Row, 1968), p. 110.
12. Ibid.
13. Nels F. S. Ferré, *The Christian Understanding of God* (New York: Harper and Brothers, 1951), p. 246.
14. Ibid.

grounds. Most prominent among these considerations is the Christian doctrine of God.

Robinson believes that the connection of the doctrine of God with the issue of the salvation of all is what makes universalism such a crucial, rather than a peripheral, matter. Where we come out on the question of who and how many will be saved both determines and is determined by our understanding of God's nature and his way of working. Some maintain that "God *will* be all in all *despite* the damnation or destruction of many of his creatures."[15] This view is in irreconcilable conflict with the universalist's understanding of God. From the universalist's perspective, "The God I believe in, the God I see in Christ, *could not* be all in all *in these conditions*: such victory *could not* be the victory of a God of love."[16] God's method of vindicating himself as God and the nature of his final lordship is the answer to what he essentially is.[17]

One issue distinguishing different views of God's nature is the relationship among the attributes, especially the central and basic attributes of God's love and justice. Robinson examines Thomas Aquinas's treatment of the problem of affirming that God's will is always accomplished and yet that God wills for everyone to be saved. How can this be? Aquinas's solution is to distinguish between God's antecedent or absolute will and his consequent or conditioned will. God wills in general that everyone should be saved, but is like a benevolent judge who would not want to see anyone sentenced to death but must nonetheless will this if a person is convicted of homicide. God's consequent will is that some should be damned, because his justice demands it. What seems to be a change in God's mind is actually an expression of the internal constancy of his nature.[18]

In Robinson's judgment, however, this interpretation is based on separating that which cannot and should not be separated. He speaks, indeed, of "the absolute identity of the divine love and the divine justice."[19] Rather than these being two parallel attributes, each representing a different requirement of God's nature, justice is a quality of his love, a designation of his way of working. Justice is not a substitute for love, which comes into play when love has failed. It is an expression of love's working. Thus, divine love cannot be mere sentimentality, and justice cannot be arbitrary or vindictive.[20]

15. Robinson, *In the End, God,* p. 113.
16. Ibid.
17. Ibid., p. 114.
18. Ibid., pp. 114–15.
19. Ibid., p. 115.
20. Ibid.

This means that a justice that is satisfied with condemning the sinner as an assertion of its rights is unacceptable to the Christian. A purely retributive justice would be a contradiction of love. If judgment were God's last word, it would indicate love's failure. As important as judgment is, its purpose and function is to lead people to receive the mercy that cancels it.[21] Because God is omnipotent and his love is what it is, there must be another end: "God is the eternal 'Yea,' and if his last word is any other than his first—a creative, affirming 'Let there be!'—then his love is defeated and he is not omnipotent. But that word of affirmation can only be pronounced upon a creation which is in every respect 'very good.' Only if and when all men respond with that 'Yes' which they are called into being to give, can God utter the final *'consummatum.'"*[22]

An even more pervasive emphasis on the doctrine of God's love is found in the writings of Nels F. S. Ferré. To understand fully the depth of Ferré's emphasis, it is necessary to know a bit about his biography. He grew up in the home of a very strict fundamentalist Baptist pastor in Sweden. His father preached the old doctrine of hellfire and brimstone. The younger Ferré underwent an emotional conversion experience, which resulted in great joy in his life. This was the first conversion, to orthodox Christianity. Soon questions began to bother him greatly, however, with the most severe being how a loving God could send persons to hell who had never heard of Jesus Christ during their lifetimes. During college, he resolved to be completely honest, and found that he could be both honest and Christian. This was his second conversion, to honesty. His third conversion was to love, as he came to a faith that viewed God as both love as kindness and love as severity.[23]

Ferré's starting point for our thinking in this area, as, indeed, in all areas, is therefore God's complete sovereign love. This sovereign love will produce God's total victory. It can accept nothing less. "Love will win unconditional surrender from all that is not love, and God will rule everywhere and forever, apart only from new pedagogical processes where God works to share yet more His boundless grace."[24] While this might sound as if it conflicts with human freedom, Ferré insists that God is freedom and that he has given freedom to humans as well. The nature of the universe and our selves is such that the more freely we are allowed to choose, the more we learn that God's way is best for all concerned.[25]

21. Ibid., pp. 116–17.
22. Ibid., p. 117.
23. Ibid., p. 135.
24. Ibid., pp. 219–20.
25. Ibid., p. 220.

Ferré is abundantly clear about his belief in the reality of life after death. Without this there is no solution to the problem of evil, a problem to which every religion that would hope to be accepted must offer some solution. Ironically, the better life here becomes, the more evil it is that it should come to an end. Duration may indeed be unimportant to the quality of an experience, but it is not unimportant to fellowship. The Christian view, however, is clear that God is not the God of the dead but of the living, that even Abraham, Isaac, and Jacob live unto him now. This is crucial, for if God is only the creator of this life, there is question of how good he really is. Whether this future life is thought of in terms of resurrection or immortality, whether it be called Greek or Hebrew, is immaterial to Ferré. It is sufficient to know that this is part and parcel of the Christian faith. We know and understand relatively little about the exact conditions of this future state, but believe that it will display both continuity with and discontinuity from our present state.[26] We do know that no one will ever be saved apart from God's gracious purpose in Christ Jesus. We must bear in mind, however, "that 'God's gracious purpose in Christ Jesus' is the totality of God's activity, and though conclusively expressed in the historic Jesus, must not be limited to him. We are saved by accepting the Christ, not by idolizing a historic, human personality."[27]

When we come to consider the Christian doctrine of the last things in a systematic fashion, it is immediately apparent that the doctrine is squarely based on the eternal and faithful love of the sovereign Lord. In this picture, however, "eternal hell is naturally out of the question, both as subjustice and as sublove." It is subjustice, because it inflicts infinite punishment for finite transgressions, which no human judge has a right to do. Only the infinite could sin infinitely, and because pure negativity is a logical contradiction, infinite sin is impossible. To be sure, we sin against an absolute God and an absolute law, but we do so not as God but as weak creatures confused within ourselves and an ambiguous outside world. Ferré is very emphatic in the terms in which he rejects the concept of an eternal hell:

> The very conception of an eternal hell is monstrous and an insult to the conception of last things in other religions, not to mention the Christian doctrine of God's sovereign love. Such a doctrine would either make God a tyrant, where any human Hitler would be a third degree saint, and the concentration camps of human torture, the king's picnic grounds. That such a doctrine could be conceived, not to mention believed, shows how

26. Ibid., pp. 222–23.
27. Ibid., p. 224.

far from any understanding of the love of God many people once were and, alas, still are!

No worse insult could be offered to Christ and no blasphemy of God could go deeper than this. God's name has been libeled beyond belief even by those who sincerely think they know Him, love Him, and serve Him. Yet an idol they serve, not the God of the Christian faith.[28]

What, then, is the correct understanding of hell? It must be seen, not as eternal punishment, but as reclamatory, as an instrument of love, for the sake of the sinner. It is not enough to say that hell is not recriminatory, although that is surely true. There are no incorrigible sinners; God has no permanent problem children. To those who truly love all, heaven can only be heaven when it has emptied hell. Everyone, including each one in hell, is completely important to God. Just like the Good Shepherd who insists on finding the hundredth sheep, God cannot be sovereign love without salvation "unto the last."[29]

Hell is not heaven unattained, but heaven rejected. Just as heaven begins in this life for those who accept the new life in Christ, so hell begins in this life for those who reject him, but it is intensified beyond this life. This is part of the purpose of hell: "What the intensification of that suffering and sorrow will be like we cannot tell, but we can be sure that it will be adequate to cause the sinner to know that the strange country is not good for him and to come to himself enough to want to go back to his father and home. God will put the screws on hard enough to make men want to change their ways, precisely because he loves them enough to do so."[30] There will be no mere forgetting of sins. They have to be faced, repented of, and forgiven. The consequences of sin will have to be paid, by both the individual sinner and society as a whole.

The other aspect of the doctrine of God that bears strongly on this issue is his omnipotence. It is one thing for God to desire strongly and sincerely to save everyone. What, however, if he is unable to accomplish this end? Thus, the omnipotence of God, his ability to accomplish his ends fully, is a vital part of the salvation of all persons.

Robinson is quite emphatic about this point. He says, as part of his response to Thomas, "In the last resort there is no way of avoiding the conclusion that any modification of the antecedent will of God to save all implies a concession to a power outside himself."[31] The will of God extends beyond this life. His power is his ability to fulfill his love, and if this should not completely come to pass, the reason must be found out-

28. Ibid., p. 228.
29. Ibid., p. 229.
30. Ibid., pp. 229–30.
31. Robinson, *In the End, God*, p. 117.

side him. Nothing within God could lead to his willing anything other than life for anyone. If, therefore, he does not save everyone, this must indicate that something external to God is stronger than he is, preventing him from accomplishing what he has willed. This, however, is impossible:

> Whether he had to condemn to extinction one or millions, God would have failed and failed infinitely. For love could not will such a thing, nor contemplate the prospect of it with anything but abhorrence. Whether this failure is represented simply as the bounding of his omnipotence of love, or as a resort to a power of compulsion other than that of love, it makes no difference. In either case a contradiction would be set up within the divine being: God would simply cease to be God.[32]

A similar emphasis is found in Ferré's theology. Among the traditions in the New Testament he finds that of "the sovereign victory of God in Christ over all, in terms of His own love."[33] There are, to be sure, a number of specific texts that teach this, such as Philippians 2:10–11. On the basis of such texts, biblical scholars like C. H. Dodd find strong universalism in the Bible. Yet all such verses, however many they may be, are as nothing in comparison to the total message of the New Testament. He says: "The total logic of the Bible, however, is forthright and fine. *God would have all to be saved and with God all things are possible.* Either God would not or could not effect such a sovereign victory of His love, but He can and will!"[34] The Christian position is that God is sovereign love. God knows what actions and operations should be produced or prevented, and knows he directs everything to its end, so that nothing upsets or frustrates his plans. Ferré clearly opts for this third motif as the primary or highest. He says: "Those who worship the sovereign Lord dare proclaim nothing less than the total victory of His love. No other position can be consistently Christian."[35] While Robinson does not give us explicit indications of how God's omnipotence accomplishes this final reconciliation of all to himself, Ferré holds that there is such a place as hell, which is part of God's overall working to accomplish his goal.

Ferré, then, if we have correctly understood him, holds and teaches that even when persons rebel against and resist God, he continues to love them with a perfect and sovereign love and endeavors to overcome that opposition. Although with some persons that may take a long time,

32. Ibid., p. 118.
33. Ibid., p. 246.
34. Ibid.
35. Ibid., p. 247.

ultimately that love will triumph, bringing persons to respond in love to him. While some traditions suggest the idea of an endless hell and of annihilation of the wicked, the one that most fully embodies Christian truth is the idea of sovereign love being triumphant in the end.

Emotional Arguments for Universalism

Intermixed with these arguments, particularly the doctrinal ones, is an overtone of emotional abhorrence that sometimes becomes quite overt. This may stem from a sense of the injustice of an ostensibly good God condemning some and saving others. Thus, Ferré speaks of the idea of an eternal hell as subjustice. Beyond that, it is sublove. Ferré's description of eternal hell uses terms like "tyrant," "insult," "blasphemy," and "libel," and compares such a God unfavorably with Hitler, who by comparison would be a "third-degree saint." These are expressions of moral outrage that go beyond mere intellectual objection.

Responses to Objections

A number of objections have been raised to such universalistic views. In the responses universalists give to those criticisms, we gain further insight into their views, including the doctrinal framework of the specific conception of the last things. We will consider two major objections, one specifically biblical, the other logical in nature.

The Biblical Objection

The biblical objection is frequently raised and is rather obvious. It calls attention to the fact that while there are texts that definitely sound universalistic in tone, others speak quite clearly of two groups of persons in the future, one of which seems destined by God for eternal separation from him. How can universalism be reconciled with this biblical data? Basically, three different responses are made by the three different universalists whose thought we have been examining.

Dodd, as we have observed, recognizes in Paul's writings the presence of this element of judgment and eternal lostness. His major strategy for dealing with this, however, is to appeal to what he terms development within Paul's thought and writings. He grants, for example, that in the two letters to the Thessalonians, Paul anticipates, perhaps even with some satisfaction, God's destruction of his enemies. It is perhaps clearest in 2 Thessalonians 1:6–10, where the revelation of Jesus will involve taking vengeance on those who do not know God and do not obey Jesus Christ. They will be penalized with eternal separation from the presence of God.[36] In 1 Corinthians, there is a notable change in emphasis. As Dodd sees it, Paul may at this time have still believed that Christ would destroy pagans and unconverted Jews, but does not say so. He comments: "In any case the change of emphasis is unmistakable. The main interest at least is no longer in the destruction of the human enemies of the Church, but in the overcoming of spiritual powers of evil, to make way for a grand unification of the universe in Christ."[37]

In the later epistles after 1 Corinthians, this tendency is carried much further. For example, whereas the final rejection of the Jews is explicitly taught in 1 Thessalonians and seems to be implied in Galatians, in Romans 11 Paul presents an extensive argument to the effect that their rejection cannot be final. Temporarily God has turned away from them to take the gospel to the Gentiles, but when the "full strength" of the Gentiles has been brought into the church, then all Israel will be saved. While this expression "full strength" might simply be taken to mean completing the number of the elect to salvation, Dodd believes it actually means all Gentiles. Paul does, after all, say, "in order that he might have mercy upon *all*" (v. 32). The shift here in Paul's thinking is now complete.[38]

This change can be seen in another respect: the attitude toward the law. In Galatians, Paul depicts it as an instrument used by the angelic powers to enslave God's people. In Romans he presents it as something good, just, and holy, but because of the weakness of the flesh, it cannot achieve its true purpose of giving life. By 2 Corinthians, however, Paul discusses it as containing in veiled form the truth that is plainly revealed in Christ. Accordingly, we find a softening in Paul's controversy with the legalists, as shown, for example, in his plea for unity between the Jewish and Gentile wings of the church. This also fits well with his emphasis in Ephesians on the unity of Jew and Greek in the church. While not claiming that there is any logical connection between belief in the ultimate salvation of the Jews and this greater tolerance of Jews, both within and outside the church who continue to emphasize the law, Dodd definitely believes that there is a psychological connection.[39]

We have noted earlier Paul's broadening of the scope of inclusion of what redemption is to affect. In 1 Corinthians 15 Paul speaks of Christ triumphing over "principalities and powers"; he goes on to speak of Christ redeeming "all things" in Colossians 1:16 and Ephesians 1:10,

36. Dodd, *New Testament Studies,* p. 121.
37. Ibid., p. 122.
38. Ibid., pp. 122–23.
39. Ibid., pp. 123–24.

and even speaks explicitly of the redemption of the whole creation in Romans 8. This is further evidence of the evolution of Paul's thought.

What is the explanation for such a phenomenon in Paul's thinking? Dodd sees Paul's pre-Christian position as being that of the Jewish writing extant at that time, especially well represented in the Apocalypse of Ezra or 2 Esdras. This outlook was markedly dualistic. Paul, however, from the very beginning of his Christian life, was called to be a missionary to the Gentiles. This created something of a tension in his life and thinking, which he gradually overcame. As Dodd puts it, "This dualism is very deeply rooted in the apocalyptic eschatology which moulded the *Weltanschauung* with which Paul began; but he outgrew it."[40]

What, then, are the implications of this understanding of Paul's development for the interpretation of the passages that present difficulty for a universalist view? The conclusion of Dodd appears clear: The later views supersede the earlier ones and are therefore to be taken as more authoritative. The decisive change seems to be associated with the period of 2 Corinthians, although this is somewhat complicated by uncertainty about the dating of Galatians. Dodd says:

> But though we may have to confess that we cannot have any certainty on these points [of the relative dating of 2 Cor. 10–12, Galatians, 2 Cor. 1–9 and 2 Cor. 6:14–7:1], it does at least seem clear that after the period represented by Galatians and by II Corinthians as a whole, there is a growing emphasis on the idea of reconciliation, and a growingly clear expression of a belief in the ultimate universality of salvation in Christ.[41]

A rather different approach to this problem is taken by Robinson. He readily acknowledges the presence in Scripture of the myth of the last judgment, of the sheep and the goats, along with the myth that speaks of the ultimate salvation of all. The difficulty for interpretation comes if we treat them as parallel objective statements of the final outcome of the universe. If so regarded, then one must surely be false and the other true, for they are clearly mutually contradictory.[42] Rather, we must see that they represent two different standpoints, two sides of the truth that is in Jesus. The one says "Christ is all in all, and always will be," while the other says "Christ has to be chosen, and always must be." The former is the truth as it is for God; the latter is the truth as it is for the subject facing decision.[43]

40. Ibid., p. 126.
41. Ibid., pp. 125–26.
42. Robinson, *In the End, God*, p. 129.
43. Ibid., pp. 129–30.

Robinson claims that the intention of this myth that depicts both heaven and hell is not to give an objective description of the final outcome that will occur. It is to describe the infinite seriousness of choosing death and hell, to make clear that no one who rejects Christ can claim a finite hell. The person who sins, presuming that grace will abound, cannot be forgiven. To objectivize it, however, to make it a picture of the final outcome of persons, is to transpose matters from the key of *kairos* into the key of *chronos*: "Infinite seriousness is translated as endless time: what is of eternal movement becomes what is of everlasting duration."[44] While Robinson does not here invoke the name of Rudolf Bultmann and demythologization, his admiration for that methodology expressed elsewhere[45] suggests that the proper designation for this interpretation of the myth of eternal heaven and hell as two separate everlasting states is to take it existentially.

Ferré's handling of the biblical problem can be seen in connection with his treatment of heaven and hell. He acknowledges that the idea of hell as eternal suffering is found in the Bible, but it is only one of three such views there, the other two being annihilation and the final salvation of all. He says that it is uncertain whether Jesus actually taught the eternal suffering view. He was much misunderstood, and his teaching, coming from a distance, has been much diluted. These concepts are given in parables, and cannot be taken in terms of predictive or descriptive truth, except for the one point the parable makes. For example, Jesus' teaching in Matthew 25 was intended to teach the point that faithfulness, rather than merely profession, is what makes the difference. In other words, Jesus may have preached existential hell, where true and needed, and not hell as an explanatory category. Ferré fears that "wooden and leaden thinking on our part on this subject has caused much harm among the spiritually sensitive and the intellectually seeking."[46]

His own selection of the third view, the final salvation of all, is not based simply on the existence of certain texts that teach this, although they certainly are there. Rather, it is to be chosen because of the total logic of the New Testament: God is sovereign love, who would have all persons to be saved and with whom all things are possible.[47] In other words, individual passages are to be understood in light of the overall theme of Scripture, even if at some points they appear to contradict that broad sweep.

44. Ibid., p. 132.
45. See, e.g., *Honest to God* (Philadelphia: Westminster, 1963), pp. 23–24, 32–35, 44.
46. Ibid., pp. 245–46.
47. Ibid., p. 246.

Why, then, was this logic not clearer than it is? The reason, Ferré says, may very well be that the New Testament is very existential and does little with the explanatory perspective. In addition, however, its implications come slowly. Perhaps Jesus knew that the disciples could not bear these implications. Perhaps he never saw them himself, misunderstood, or left the question to the Holy Spirit to lead believers into all truth. Perhaps Paul saw them, but whether he or Jesus did makes very little difference. When a great new truth comes bursting into history, it so startles and shakes the first persons to see it and its implications are so revolutionary and far-ranging that those first discoverers cannot fully see them.[48]

The Logical Objection

The other charge frequently brought against universalism is that it contradicts human freedom—a charge that is usually lodged against Calvinism by its opponents. Indeed, it could be argued that this is a Calvinistic view of human destiny, in which God in effect elects everyone, not merely part of the human race, to eternal salvation. If this is so, however, does it not contradict human freedom, in terms of persons' ability to resist or reject God's will and working for their salvation?

Robinson has been particularly aware of and sensitive to this charge. He takes this issue very seriously, for any view that in any way compromises human freedom is self-condemned. Without freedom, love cannot be love. This concern is not only from the human standpoint, but from that of God as well, for in order for omnipotence to be acknowledged, there must be the freedom to respond or to reject.[49]

If we would deal with the problem properly, however, says Robinson, we must understand it correctly. This is sometimes put as if it were a matter of two irresistible forces pulling in opposite directions, so that if God gains an inch it is at the expense of the other's loss. This, however, is the wrong way of conceiving of the matter. Rather, we should think of it on the analogy of human experience. Here, we are sometimes approached by another person in an act of great love, shown in self-sacrifice, forgiveness, or something of the sort. It is in such situations that we feel most strongly moved to respond. Yet there is no external compulsion, nothing forcing us to act in such a way. None of us, in such a case, feels that we do not act freely when we respond. In fact, there is a sense of most fully being ourselves, of attaining that for which we are intended, and that such fulfillment is intimately bound up with this decision.[50] This sense of fulfillment reaches its ultimate when the ap-

48. Ibid., pp. 246–47.
49. *In the End, God*, pp. 120–21.
50. Ibid., pp. 121–22.

proach and the response involve God. Robinson says: "Under the constraint of the love of God in Christ this sense of self-fulfillment is at its maximum. The testimony of generations is that here, as nowhere else, service is perfect freedom."[51]

One more thing needs to be said in general about the issue. Robinson has deliberately chosen to discuss it by appealing to personal experience because that is the context in which such a discussion should proceed. It is only from the perspective of the person, in relationship to other persons, that this makes sense. Robinson endorses Kierkegaard's, Brunner's, and Buber's conceptions here, that truth is both subjective and subjectively known. Part of the problem comes from trying to deal with the question of freedom and divine sovereignty as if this were an objective matter of logic. "Freedom is essentially something that belongs to, and is only real in, the world of the *Thou*. Attempt to net it within the categories of logic and scientific thought, and it slips through the mesh. It eludes the schema of cause and effect and cannot be contained within the simple disjunction of the law of non-contradiction."[52]

This involves the whole idea of theology. Objective logic always insists upon either grace or free will, or perhaps first the one and then the other. If the one is true, the other cannot be. A theology based on such an objective approach, or what some would call a scientific theology, will thus encounter such difficulties. A theology that is trying to remain true to the personal realities it is trying to systematize, however, must refuse to try to resolve this contradiction in an objective fashion. It must accept the fact of the paradox. In the world of *I-Thou*, the person who responds to God's love feels no tension. Even though the person knows that the divine victory of love is necessary, there is no sense of being compelled, but rather this knowledge brings great joy, peace, and a sense of freedom.[53]

Evaluation

Positive

What are the relative strengths and weaknesses of the position we have been considering? Let us note first the considerable commendable qualities of this school of thought as presented by the authors whose work we have examined.

51. Ibid., p. 122.
52. Ibid., p. 125.
53. Ibid., pp. 125–26.

1. These men are clear about their commitment as *Christian* theologians. They are not advocates of a pluralism that offers several alternative approaches to salvation as found in different religions. Nor do they adhere to the tepid type of Christianity in which Christ is the *preferred* religious teacher. These men clearly hold that faith is to be placed in Christ alone, that there is no other way of salvation. If all are to be saved, they are to be saved within the context of Christianity's distinctive beliefs.

2. A genuine biblical basis is offered for the views espoused. While this may seem to be a somewhat tendential comment, assuming an authority for the Bible that has been made the distinctive of more conservative schools of thought, it is not. To the extent that a given organization or church claims to be Christian, it should be able to show its relationship to the constituting document of Christianity, the Bible.

3. There also is a commendable honesty in recognizing, acknowledging, and addressing the difficulties their view must face. Thus, each proponent attempts to wrestle with, not merely ignore, the Scriptures that seem to teach a view contrary to theirs, namely, that some persons will be eternally lost.

4. There is an attempt to relate their overall doctrinal system to the issues involved in the question of eternal salvation. Thus, for example, the doctrine of God and his attributes is brought to bear upon the question of future destiny, as is also true of the understanding of human nature as that relates to freedom and divine action. In other words, these men strive to do genuinely *systematic* theology.

5. There is, especially in Robinson, a more perceptive understanding of the dynamics of freedom and sovereignty than one often finds. Instead of the simplistic conception that divine initiative and human initiative must somehow be in competition and conflict with one another, the possibility of a genuine interaction is explored.

Negative

There are, however, a number of points where we must express reservation. In so doing, we will try to be as specific as possible, and to deal with the concrete arguments advanced by these men, rather than with some more general form of universalism.

1. Each of the attempts to deal with the contrary or exclusivist passages of Scripture contains some problematic features. For example, Dodd's response is to interpret the teachings of Paul in

terms of the development of his thought. Thus, while his early writing may have been more exclusivistic, reflecting his Jewish background, his later writings show a much more open stance. The assumption is that the later passages are to be treated as more authoritative. That in itself might be questioned, but even if the development is considered to be genuine progress, why does one assume that the progress must stop there, so that authority is attached to the latest passages? What if Paul changed his views subsequent to the latest writing we have, but did not commit those later views to writing, or at least, we do not now have them? Or might Paul have changed his views, had he lived longer, so that the last writings we have would have been superseded?

A somewhat different problem attaches to Robinson's treatment. If the approach is to regard the two counterthemes of the last judgment and the salvation of all as myths, how really does one choose between them? It appears that the former is taken somewhat more literally, and the latter is demythologized or interpreted more existentially. Similarly, the former is said to be the truth as it is for God, and the latter the truth as it is for us, the subjects facing decision. But how do we know the truth as it is for God? Must we not say that it is the truth as it is for God, as it appears to us? Apparently, by designating the former as the truth from God and treating it more literally, Robinson has given it preference. Yet it is doubtful whether he has really justified this choice.

Ferré has developed his position by choosing from among what he considers three conflicting themes on the basis of which fits best with his grand theme of Scripture, the love of God. Yet it appears that Ferré's understanding of God's love is itself somewhat a priori. It certainly is not drawn from Scripture as a whole, for it conflicts with certain passages. What, then, really is its basis? It appears that rather than criticizing, modifying, and adapting his basic motif on the basis of the full thrust of Scripture (even as delivered by critical studies), Ferré has made this the criterion for evaluation of Scripture. It appears likely that in the final analysis, one's own experience (such as his experience with the question of the lost) is the final authority.

2. The other major criticism pertains to the analysis of the problem of human freedom, and as such applies especially to Robinson's thought, because he is the one who has gone furthest with this issue. What Robinson in effect does is to introduce an epistemological dualism, as Kierkegaard, Brunner, and others have done.

Thus, while scientific matters can be examined using objective methodology and logic, matters such as this, dealing with human freedom, can be resolved only using subjective means. This, however, fails to recognize that there are different levels of discourse. To be sure, human personality and issues related to it and to interhuman relationships are different from matters of the physical universe. Yet there is, in addition to the nature of the subject matter itself, the question of reflection and discourse on that subject matter. This is quite a different thing, and it does not follow from the fact that the former is subjective that the latter must be also. For example, emotions are different from molecules, but it does not follow that the psychologist studying emotions should be emotional about the subject matter he is studying. Because of a confusion of these levels, the possibility of more fully understanding the problem of human freedom is forfeited.

There is one further difficulty concerned with Robinson's approach. It is fine to invoke paradox as the final word in a matter of this type. There are several different forms that paradox might take, however. That is to say, more than one position could be declared paradoxical. What is the reason for selecting this one? To fail to give further grounds for such a choice opens the door to numerous different options, and ultimately provides no defense against subjectivism; consequently no view is wrong, but no view is right either.

5

Twentieth-Century Pluralism

In the latter half of the twentieth century, the thinking of some Christian theologians on the nature and extent of salvation has taken a new turn. This view, known as pluralism, holds that Christianity is not the one true religion, or even superior in any significant way to other religions. This change in thought has resulted from a number of factors, one of which is the growing awareness of the variety of religious views extant in our world today. Pluralism has been an especially popular view in religion departments of universities, and with the growth of such departments and programs, this particular view has also grown rapidly. What is needed, in light of this understanding, is not the conversion of those of non-Christian religions to Christianity, but mutual dialogue among members of different religious groups, in which each learns from the other.

Varieties of Christian Attitudes toward Other Religions

One pressing issue of our times concerns the Christian attitude toward other religious faiths. What are the options? What shall be our stance? Probably the most vocal and prolific recent Christian advocate of pluralism, John Hick, observes that the traditional view was formed during a period of substantial ignorance of the wider religious life of humankind. More recently, however, the church has been thrown into a ferment of rethinking by greater and more widespread knowledge. Hick observes that there have been three phases thus far in the development of the Christian attitude toward the other world religions. These classifications and interpretations are useful in revealing where Hick and other pluralists see themselves relative to the historical development of Christian attitudes.

Total Rejection

The first phase was that of total rejection. This view, once virtually universally accepted among Christians, is the idea that the non-Christian is consigned to hell. Hick recognizes both a Roman Catholic and a Protestant version of this view. The medieval Catholic Church defined Christians as those who acknowledged the authority of the Catholic Church, especially the pope. While the Catholic Church has today passed decisively beyond that mind-set, it still lives on within evangelical-fundamentalist Protestantism. Hick considers the main difference between these two varieties of rejection to be that whereas the former group defined Christians as those who submit to the pope, the latter questions whether the pope and his followers are Christians at all.[1]

Hick sees this view as strongly correlated with ignorance of other faiths. During the medieval period there was contact between Christianity and Islam, but it was of a military type, rather than a religious dialogue or mutual exploration of one another's spirituality. When one encounters an adherent of another faith at the end of a sword, one is not likely to be impressed with the quality of that person's spirituality. The growth of contact with and awareness of other religions has made this orientation less tenable. Today, of course, this type of ignorance is less common, even on the part of extreme evangelical Protestants, who have missionary contact with Islam and access to a vast body of literature about the world religions. Rather, what lies behind the rejection of other religions by such persons is the blindness that comes from dark dogmatic spectacles that prevent them from seeing good in any religious devotion outside their own group.[2]

As Hick sees it, the major weakness of this attitude of rejection lies in the doctrine of God that it presupposes. If this view is correct, then the vast majority of those who have ever lived have lived and died without any possibility of being saved. "To say that such an appalling situation is divinely ordained," says Hick, "is to deny the Christian understanding of God as gracious and holy love, and of Christ as the divine love incarnate. Thus the attitude of total rejection, expressed in the dogma that outside Christianity there is no salvation, implies a conception of God radically questionable from the standpoint of Christian faith."[3]

1. John Hick, *God Has Many Names* (Philadelphia: Westminster, 1982), pp. 29–30.
2. Ibid., pp. 30–31.
3. Ibid., p. 31.

Early Epicycles

The second phase, which Hick terms the phase of the early epicycles, arose out of Catholic thinkers' contact with other religious persons, leading them to conclude that there was genuine religious faith among these people, first among Protestant Christians and then among devout persons of other religious faiths. This was a gradual development in the Catholic Church, in which the traditional formula was retained but was, at the same time, at least partially negated by the attachment of a rider, reversing its practical effect. Thus, while continuing to maintain that only Catholics may be saved, this approach declared that more persons may be Catholics than the Church initially realized. These individuals are Catholics, not empirically, but metaphysically. This paradox is likened to the dogma of transubstantiation, where the elements empirically remain bread and wine but metaphysically have been converted into the body and blood of Christ. So, there are persons who sincerely believe themselves to be Protestants, Hindus, Jews, and so on, because that is their affiliation and they remain such, but who are actually Catholic Christians. They belong to the invisible, not the visible church. They are invincibly ignorant of the Catholic faith and thus are not culpable; they are so disposed to it that they would accept it if they genuinely encountered it; or they have implicit, rather than explicit faith; or they have baptism by desire, that is, they sincerely desire the truth, even though they do not know what that truth is.[4]

Hick refers to these supplementary concepts as epicycles because they strongly resemble the concept of the epicycles that was added to the Ptolemaic view of the universe to accommodate the growing knowledge of the planets' paths. All the heavenly bodies were supposed to revolve around the earth, but as astronomical knowledge grew it became clear that the planets' paths did not fit this knowledge in a simple way. To explain this discrepancy, smaller supplementary circles, called epicycles (or circles upon the circles) were added. The planets moved in these paths, which had their centers on the major circle. In theory it was possible to continue this process indefinitely, adding epicycles upon epicycles, to reconcile the theory that the earth was the center of movement of these bodies with the observed facts. Eventually, however, the theory became so complex and contrived that it was abandoned in favor of the simpler Copernican view that the sun is the center of the planetary system. Hick considers the theory that insists that salvation is only in Christianity but then develops complex rationalizations of how professing non-Christians are actu-

4. Ibid., pp. 31–32.

ally Christians to be a theological equivalent to this astronomical theory. While it is logically possible to continue such maneuvers, they exact an unacceptable price.[5]

Later Epicycles

Hick's third stage is that of the later epicycles. This represents the period of the past few decades, especially Vatican II and since that time, in the Catholic Church. Here theological ingenuity goes to extremes to maintain simultaneously the two propositions that outside Christianity there is no salvation and that outside Christianity there is salvation. If the concept of salvation is given any experiential content, such as human renewal, liberation, becoming a new creature, or achieving authentically human existence, it must be conceded that such is found outside Christianity as well as inside it. Consequently, the former proposition, that outside of Christianity there is no salvation, has to be considerably redefined, especially by altering what it means to be a Christian. Hick maintains, however, that the orbit of some of the epicycles, such as that of Hans Küng, is now so wide that it is in danger of flying off out of the Ptolemaic frame.[6] Another variety, found more in liberal Protestant than in either Roman Catholic or evangelical fundamentalist views, is the idea of all persons accepting Christ sooner or later, and if this does not happen within this life, it must occur in the life to come.[7]

Hick does not find any of these proposed epicyclical solutions satisfactory, however. He believes that a growing number of Christians have lost confidence in these theological epicycles and are open to a genuinely Copernican solution to the problem. The Copernican revolution in theology would consist in a radical transformation of the understanding of the universe of faiths and the place of our own religious tradition within it. He says, "It must involve a shift from the dogma that Christianity is at the center to the thought that it is *God* who is at the center and that all the religions of mankind, including our own, serve and revolve around him."[8] As he has noted, it is possible to go on indefinitely thinking Ptolemaically. We must, however, realize that it is possible to have a Ptolemaic view of the universe of faiths from the standpoint of any religion, just as residents of Mars or Jupiter, if there be such, could develop a Ptolemaic astronomy in which the planets were considered to revolve around their own. So, the epicycles of Ptolemaic Christianity can be used to maintain a Ptolemaic Hinduism or Buddhism, or any

5. Ibid., pp. 32–33.
6. Ibid., pp. 33–35.
7. Ibid., p. 35.
8. Ibid., p. 36.

other religion. This points up the correlation between place of birth and religious commitment.[9] Hick, as we shall see in the following exposition, thinks that a much better solution is to abandon the Ptolemaic theology in favor of a thoroughly Copernican revolution.

Arguments for Pluralism

Several lines of argument have been advanced in support of pluralism. In the preface to *The Myth of Christian Uniqueness*, the editors classify these arguments into three groups that they refer to as three bridges, by which the respective authors are crossing over from exclusivism or inclusivism to pluralism. These are the historico-cultural bridge, or relativity; the theologico-mystical bridge, or mystery; and the ethico-practical bridge, or justice. While there is a certain amount of overlap among these three bridges, and a given thinker may present more than one type of argument, the classification nonetheless is helpful.

The Historico-Cultural Bridge

This set of considerations is used to argue that it is simply not possible to establish the objective truth of any one religion in such a way as to make it incompatible with other religious competitors. This contention stems from an awareness of the historical and cultural limitations of all religious beliefs. John Hick, whose background is in Christian faith and theology of a very conservative sort, has presented this type of argument most extensively and in several varieties.

The first argument is the phenomenological similarity of the worship found within the several religions. Hick came to this awareness through both his contact with other religious communities in Birmingham and his academic study of religion. He examines the religious and worship literature of several religions, and notes their similar experience and expression.[10] Indeed, if one were to read them to a typical group of Christians, they would probably not be able to detect that these were not Christian expressions. What, then, are we to make of such similarities? Are these worshipers in church, synagogue, mosque, gurdwara, and temple worshiping different gods or are they worshiping the same God? "Are Adonai and God, Allah and Ekoamkaar, Rama and Krishna different gods, or are these different names for the same ultimate Being?"[11]

There would seem to be three possible explanations of the phenomenon. The first is that many different gods exist ontologically. This,

9. Ibid., pp. 36–37.
10. Ibid., pp. 62–66.
11. Ibid., p. 66.

however, conflicts with each worshiper's claim that his god is the creator or the source of the world. The second possibility would be that one of these groups of believers worships the true God, while the others worship false gods, the products of their imaginations. Even within Christianity, however, a variety of overlapping mental images of God can be found, such as the stern judge and predestinating power, and the gracious and loving heavenly Father. Are these different groups worshiping different gods or the same God, under these differing images? And the samples of worship drawn from various religions suggest a considerable overlap between Christian images and these non-Christian views. This leaves a third—and most probable—possibility in Hick's judgment: that "there is but one God, who is maker and lord of all; that in his infinite fullness and richness of being he exceeds all our human attempts to grasp him in thought; and that the devout in the various great world religions are in fact worshipping that one God, but through different, overlapping concepts or mental icons of him."[12]

Hick's second major argument is cultural relativity, although he does not use this expression. He observes that although it is not always taken into account by theologians, it is evident to ordinary people that in the great majority of cases, say perhaps 98 or 99 percent, the religious belief and membership of a person depend on where he was born. Thus, someone born to Muslim parents in Egypt or Pakistan is very likely to be a Muslim. If his parents were Buddhists in Sri Lanka or Burma, it is highly probable that he is a Buddhist. A child of Hindu parents in India is very probably a Hindu. A native of Europe or the Americas born into a Christian family is almost certainly a Christian. The one most common factor involved in whether one is a devotee of one of these religions or is a Marxist or a Maoist is geographical location of one's birth, whether he is a fully committed or a merely nominal adherent of that faith. Hick's conclusion is that

> Any credible religious faith must be able to make sense of this circumstance. And a credible Christian faith must make sense of it by relating it to the universal sovereignty and fatherhood of God. This is rather conspicuously not done by the older theology which held that God's saving activity is confined within a single narrow thread of human life, namely that recorded in our own scriptures.[13]

A third argument is Christianity's relative lack of success in relationship to the other world religions. Christianity is growing numerically,

12. Ibid., pp. 66–67.
13. Ibid., p. 61.

although not necessarily at a rate equal to that of the worldwide population. Most of the success of the Christian worldwide mission is downward, however. That is to say, it is winning its converts from tribal religions. It really is not succeeding over against the other major world religions. Indeed, in some cases, other religions are winning more converts from Christianity than vice versa. Christianity is a minority religion, and becoming ever more so. If, however, Christianity is the one true religion, should not truth triumph? Should not this truth be reflected in a special success in relationship to the other religions?[14]

Hick's fourth argument has an individual and a social version. Both are pragmatic arguments, concerning Christianity's effect when adopted and practiced. In the individual form, this argument examines the relative quality of the spiritual life of adherents of different religions. It has been popular to contend that Christianity is true because of the difference made in the spiritual quality of those who accept and practice its teaching. Yet this hardly serves to establish its uniqueness, in Hick's judgment. Indeed, striking parallels to Christian piety can be found in all the world's religions. A most notable example would be Gandhi within Hinduism. This raises a question for this type of argument. Hick says,

> But if human salvation, or liberation, has any concrete meaning for men and women in this world, it must include the kind of transformation of human existence seen in Gandhi and, in varying ways and degrees, in the saints of all the great traditions. But this transformation, with its further influence upon other individuals and through them, more remotely, upon societies, is manifestly not confined to the Christian areas of the world. There are persons who have in varying degrees given themselves to God, or to the ultimate Reality, within each of the great traditions.[15]

The other variety of this argument is the collective or social outworking of the different faiths. Christians sometimes assume that Christian countries in the Northern Hemisphere are relatively affluent, just, peaceful, and democratic, whereas in the Southern Hemisphere we find relatively poor, backward, violent, undemocratic societies, held back by non-Christian faiths. This picture, however, must be deconstructed on several levels, according to Hick. On the one hand, these benefits are not restricted to the Christian countries. It simply is not possible to say

---

14. Ibid., pp. 60–61.
15. John Hick, "The Non-Absoluteness of Christianity," in *The Myth of Christian Uniqueness: Toward a Pluralistic Theology of Religions*, ed. John Hick and Paul F. Knitter (Maryknoll, N.Y.: Orbis, 1987), p. 24.

that Buddhist-Shinto Japan, Muslim Saudi Arabia and the other Gulf states, and Hindu India are poor and technologically backward. While social injustice is endemic in these countries, it is also in various kinds of countries.[16]

Conversely, the negative social problems sometimes pointed out in non-Christian countries are found in large measure in Christian countries as well. Poverty, social injustice, and political violence can be found in varying degrees in such predominantly Christian nations as Latin America, South Africa, Ireland, and Lebanon, and the Amnesty International Report, *Torture in the Eighties*, identified Christian countries where this was a problem, along with Muslim, Hindu, Buddhist, and Jewish societies.[17]

Hick's fifth argument is from biblical studies. He has correctly observed that much of the issue of Christian uniqueness hinges on the nature and status of Jesus. If he is indeed the one and only instance of God entering the human race, then Christianity is unique and could perhaps be the only means of salvation. Until three or four generations ago, it was commonly accepted among biblical scholars that Jesus claimed to be God the Son and had a unique consciousness of his divinity. Thus, the doctrine of the incarnation was believed to rest on Jesus' self-consciousness and teaching regarding himself. That, however, is no longer generally held. Rather, this transfer of titles and ideas to Jesus took place at the hands of the post-Easter community of believers. Hick quotes approvingly from Wolfhart Pannenberg to the effect that "Today it must be taken as all but certain that the pre-Easter Jesus neither designated himself as Messiah (or Son of God) nor accepted such a confession to him from others."[18]

Hick advances one final argument. He concedes that there are indeed differences among the conceptions found in the different religions. This is taken by those of the Ptolemaic variety of Christianity to be evidence for the uniqueness and the superiority of Christianity, and its being the only channel of salvation. Yet, Hick notes, there are also considerable variations of belief and practice among different segments of Christianity.[19] If this type of variation does not preclude their being essentially the same, why should the variations between religions?

16. Ibid.
17. Ibid., pp. 24–25.
18. *God Has Many Names*, p. 73; from Wolfhart Pannenberg, *Jesus—God and Man* (Philadelphia: Westminster, 1968), p. 237.
19. Hick, *God Has Many Names*, p. 66.

The Theologico-Mystical Bridge

The first set of considerations focuses attention particularly on the historical relativity of our means of religious perception; this approach focuses instead on the object of that perception, and emphasizes the infinite nature of that object, as a consequence of which it exceeds all our forms of understanding.[20] This particular type of argument is found in a number of manifestations.

One of these is presented by Stanley J. Samartha, an Indian Christian and former Hindu. He maintains that in India's history of developing religious tolerance, it is essential to note the profound sense of mystery, which he terms the ontological basis of that tolerance. This Mystery, he says, is "the transcendent Center that remains always beyond and greater than apprehensions of it or even the sum total of those apprehensions. It is beyond cognitive knowledge (*tarka*) but is open to vision (*dristi*) and intuition (*anubhava*)."[21] This emphasis on Mystery, he maintains, means that the rational is not the only way to do theology. Rather, the mystical and the esthetic must be taken into account and allowed to make their contribution. The true nature of this Mystery must be correctly understood; "Mystery is an ontological status to be accepted, not an epistemological problem to be solved."[22] In other words, it is not a question of inadequate knowing ability on the part of the knower, but a result of the very nature of the object known.

This Mystery is related to meaning, which is a matter of the human response to the Mystery. The doctrines of Christianity, for example, are the attempts of Christians to make sense of the particular revelations that have come to them at specific times and places. These responses are many and varied, even sometimes within the same religious community, due to varying cultural and historical conditions. Each of these responses has a normative claim upon the followers of that tradition, but "the criteria derived from one response cannot be made the norm to judge the responses of other traditions."[23]

This, then, means the relativity of the particular doctrines or traditions of each religion. These must now be understood, not as divinely revealed truths, but as particular, conditioned, responses to the Mystery. This would be true, for example, of the Christian understanding of Jesus:

> That Jesus is the Christ of God is a confession of faith by the Christian community. It does remain normative to Christians everywhere, but to

20. See *Myth of Christian Uniqueness*, p. x.
21. Stanley J. Samartha, "The Cross and the Rainbow," in *Myth of Christian Uniqueness*, p. 75.
22. Ibid., pp. 75–76.
23. Ibid., p. 76.

make it "absolutely singular" and to maintain that the meaning of the
Mystery is disclosed *only* in one particular person at one particular
point, and nowhere else, is to ignore one's neighbors of other faiths
who have other points of reference. To make exclusive claims for our
particular traditions is not the best way to love our neighbors as ourselves.[24]

If these doctrines are to be seen as relative, then so also are the various experiences of salvation. It is not a question of whether there may
be plural ways of salvation. In multireligious situations, the fact is that
there *are* plural ways of salvation. This is not surprising, because these
are different experiences and articulations of salvation. Different religious traditions understand the human predicament, from which salvation is the deliverance, in different ways. While Christians understand it as sin, Hindus describe it as ignorance and Buddhists as
sorrow. Further, many persons today, even within the Christian tradition, understand the problem as oppression. These alternative views of
the way of salvation have provided meaning and purpose for millions
of persons in varied cultures. It is therefore presumptuous to claim that
the Christian way of salvation is the only answer for all persons in all
places. Saying this is not a matter of denying the validity of the Christian experience of salvation in Jesus Christ, but rather contesting its
claim to exclusiveness. Lest we should misunderstand him, Samartha
says, "The nature of Mystery is such that any claim on the part of one
religious community to have exclusive or unique or final knowledge becomes inadmissible."[25] He points out several unfortunate results of an
exclusivist approach to salvation and to religion in general:

1. It puts fences around the Mystery.
2. It creates dichotomies between the divine and the human, between humanity and nature, and between different religious
   communities.
3. It leaves little room for the nonrational elements of religious
   life.[26]

For such reasons as these, there must be a rethinking of the meaning
of Jesus' uniqueness. He is not to be equated with God, for that would
be to make him the tribal deity of Christianity, as contrasted with those
of other cultures. We must not elevate Jesus to God, which is Jesusol-

24. Ibid.
25. Ibid., p. 77.
26. Ibid., pp. 77–78.

ogy, or limit Christ to Jesus of Nazareth, which is Christomonism. Instead, what is necessary is a theocentric Christology, which emphasizes the priority of God rather than Jesus, as indeed the Bible and Jesus himself do.[27]

What Samartha has said is expressed in somewhat different but equally emphatic fashion by Wilfred Cantwell Smith, one of the pioneers in twentieth-century Christian pluralism. His treatment is in terms of a discussion of idolatry. He notes that Christians have generally been quite harsh in their assessment of the use of idols by adherents of other religions. They believe the worshiper is worshiping the idol, the actual physical object itself. As an example of this attitude he cites Bishop Heber's hymn, particularly the line "The heathen in his blindness bows down to wood and stone." Smith objects to that line, for it represents a misunderstanding of the role of idols, and thus, the missionary, not the national, is blind. The worshiper does not worship the object, but what the object represents. Smith had written earlier, "No one has ever worshipped an idol. Some have worshipped God in the form of an idol; that is what idols are for." Similarly, he remarks that cow-worship is misnamed, since "the Hindu reveres the cow that he sees, not the cow that we see."[28] In other words, the normal role of an idol is to represent the thing worshiped, not to be an object of worship in itself. Christianity has been disdainful of the use of idols, in large part, he believes, because it has failed to recognize the transcendent dimension involved in the worship of the person who bows down before an idol. It has failed to see that anything spiritual was going on at all in the worship of those who employed images.[29] Samartha became aware of this distinction when he lived for some years in India and observed ceremonies in which the objects were consecrated or sacralized. Prior to this ceremony, they are regarded merely as material objects. In the ceremony, the god or goddess is invited to take up a presence in the object. The image then serves the worshiper as a locus of the presence of the god. There also is a ceremony of desacralization, after which the object can be discarded.[30]

A second stage of Smith's argument comes when he notes that Christianity has often been disdainful of the metaphysical views of other religious practitioners.[31] Yet he received a fundamental insight from the

27. Ibid., p. 79.
28. Wilfred Cantwell Smith, "Idolatry in Comparative Perspective," in *Myth of Christian Uniqueness*, p. 53.
29. Ibid., p. 54.
30. Ibid., p. 55.
31. Ibid., p. 54.

Hindu teaching that the transcendent, or what Christians would call God, is basically formless; the only form is our knowledge of him. Every theological system or idea is a response to this revelation by God of himself or herself. Yet it can be a means by which one who ponders it is introduced to the reality that it represents. Thus, theologies are conceptual images of God, just as what we call idols are physical images of him.[32]

If this is the case, then we must look intensively at how we regard these doctrinal beliefs. Exclusivism is the attitude that one's own religion's doctrines are true, while those of other religions that conflict with these beliefs are false. To hold this, however, is to regard the doctrines, not as our construction, our response to God's revelation, but as God's construction, which is idolatry, in the bad sense of the word. Smith does not doubt that people, in constructing their belief systems, are helped by God, or in Christian terminology, by the Holy Spirit. That is quite different, however, from identifying one's own religion or tradition with God, or with absolute truth. That would be to regard it as divine, rather than as a channel to the divine.[33] Smith says:

> For Christians to think that Christianity is true, or final, or salvific, is a form of idolatry. For Christians to imagine that God has constructed Christianity, or the Church, or the like, rather than that He/She/It has inspired us to construct it, as He/She/It has inspired Muslims to construct what the world knows as Islam, or Hindus what is miscalled Hinduism, or inspired Bach to write the B Minor Mass or Ramanuja to write his theological commentaries, or Pancapana (if it was indeed he) to build Borobudur—that is idolatry.[34]

Smith is here using "idolatry" in the pejorative form, of exclusivist claims for one's own doctrinal beliefs.

The Ethico-Practical Bridge

The final set of arguments comes from those that contend that by their very nature, absolute or exclusivist views, or for that matter, inclusivist views, of Christianity contribute to injustice. This has been argued by a number of theologians in the general cluster of theologies broadly referred to as liberation theologies, but perhaps most of all by feminist theologians. Marjorie Suchocki is representative of them.

Suchocki states her thesis at the very beginning of her presentation: "Universalizing one religion such that it is taken as the norm whereby all other religions are judged and valued leads to oppression, and hence

32. Ibid., p. 56.
33. Ibid., p. 59.
34. Ibid.

falls short of the norm that liberationists consider ultimate—the normative justice that creates well-being in the world community."[35]

This view might seem to face some problems, however. First, does not the use of the norm of justice reintroduce universalism in a different form, and thus possess the potential of perpetuating oppression? Second, who defines human "well-being"? Justice is closely allied with religious convictions, and hence participates in the cultural conditioning of those convictions. Finally, if these first two problems cannot be adequately answered, do we not fall into a situation of religious relativism, wherein there are no norms of discernment to be applied to religious positions?[36]

Because she contends that absolutizing one religion clearly parallels sexism, Suchocki sketches a feminist critique of sexism and its effects on women, following two routes. The first consists of pointing out the way in which masculine experience is universalized and made the defining criterion for what is fully human. In such a framework, women's experience is either treated as nonexistent or subsumed under humanity. Men's experience is presented as the norm, on the basis that women's experience is included within it. To be fully human, on this basis, means that women must emulate men. The second is an opposite approach, but with similar consequences. Instead of subsuming women's experiences under those of men, they are kept separate, and women are then assigned all those negative or problematic characteristics of dependence, emotionality, sensuality, and weakness. Because she possesses these negative characteristics, woman must be assigned to the care of a man. If, on the other hand, these qualities come to be positively valued by culture, then woman is exalted by recourse to what Suchocki calls the "pedestal syndrome"—woman is too good for the roughness of the world of public life. Although the rationale is different, both subvarieties of the second approach lead to the exclusion of women from full participation in the human community, as does the first approach.[37] Not only are there the unfortunate consequences in the treatment of women, but male experience is also distorted. Human characteristics are divided into one group considered feminine, such as tenderness, and another group thought of as more masculine. Males who display some of these former qualities are thought of as "feminine," which leads to a truncation and distortion of what it means to be masculine.[38]

---

35. Marjorie Hewitt Suchocki, "In Search of Justice: Religious Pluralism from a Feminist Perspective," in *Myth of Christian Uniqueness*, p. 149.

36. Ibid., pp. 149–50.

37. Ibid., pp. 150–51.

38. Ibid., p. 151.

Suchocki now advances the thesis of her chapter: "Just as the universalization of male experience functions either to absorb women within the masculine norm or to ascribe to women those characteristics that men are not willing to name clearly as belonging to themselves, even so the universalization of one religion leads to similar distortions."[39] Using Hans Küng's popular work, *On Being a Christian*, she shows the parallels. Küng points out the negative characteristics of other religions, without applying the same criteria to Christianity, Suchocki claims. Although decrying any sort of "cheap superiority," he nonetheless presses the question of truth, using the essence of Christianity as the criterion of judgment. She summarizes her charge thus:

> Parallels with sexism can be drawn in that the norm of Christ is applied to other religions regardless of norms that may be generated from within those religions. Just as the norm of masculinity is applied to women regardless of women's protestations that their own experience of humanity is sufficient to generate their own norms, even so Christian norms are projected uncritically upon non-Christian religions. Also, just as women are measured and judged by masculine experience, even so Küng measures and judges other religions by Christian experience. Further, the form of sexism that separates reprehensible qualities within men and projects them upon women is also operative in Küng's treatment. The qualities which he specifically names as negative in other religions have parallels within Christianity. These parallels are not acknowledged.[40]

Paul Knitter approaches the issues from a somewhat broader perspective. He contends that two major problems challenge the churches today: "the experience of the *many poor* and the experience of the *many religions*." Two of the most vital expressions of Christian life and thought today are the respective responses to these two experiences, namely, liberation theology and theology of religions. Knitter raises the question of how these two theological camps can get to know each other and work together.[41] His chapter is to a large extent an exploration of this question.

Knitter affirms, in agreement with Arnold Toynbee, that religion is necessary to overcome society's selfishness and warring tendencies. He further claims that this implies that the liberation movement requires not merely religion, but religions. The task is simply too large for any

39. Ibid., pp. 151–52.
40. Ibid., p. 153.
41. Paul F. Knitter, "Toward a Liberation Theology of Religions," in *Myth of Christian Uniqueness*, p. 178.

one religious group to undertake. In fact, if it is really to take root in Asia, liberation theology must engage in dialogue with other, non-Christian, religions. Knitter says: "A purely Christian theology of liberation, in other words, suffers the dangerous limitation of inbreeding, of drawing on only one vision of the kingdom."[42]

Knitter then proposes as a basis for interreligious dialogue the employment of several insights of liberation theology. First, we must utilize a hermeneutics of suspicion, in which one is very much aware of the extent to which a given scriptural or doctrinal interpretation can become a means to promoting one's own interests at the expense of those of others.[43] Second, choosing a preferential option for the poor enables one to bypass the complex questions of the common ground or common essence of all religions.[44] Third, choosing a soteriocentric approach shifts dialogue from conversation about ideological differences to an actual step in the direction of realization of God's justice.[45]

Rather than a common ground of several religions, Knitter proposes a common approach or a common context. While coming from differing theological perspectives, the participants in such religious dialogue would focus on the common concern of working for and with the victims in the world.[46] He suggests that the evolution of Christian attitudes toward those of other faiths that he had earlier proposed must now be extended another step:

> If Christian attitudes have evolved from ecclesiocentrism to christocentrism to theocentrism, they must now move on to what in Christian symbols might be called "kingdom-centrism," or more universally, "soteriocentrism." For Christians, that which constitutes the basis and the goal for interreligious dialogue, that which makes mutual understanding and cooperation between the religions possible (the "condition of the possibility"), that which unites the religions in common discourse and praxis, is *not* how they are related to the church (invisibly through "baptism of desire"), or how they are related to Christ (anonymously [Rahner] or normatively [Küng]), nor even how they respond to and conceive of God, but rather, to what extent they are promoting *Soteria* (in Christian images, the *basileia*)—to what extent they are engaged in promoting human welfare and bringing about liberation with and for the poor and nonpersons.[47]

42. Ibid., p. 180.
43. Ibid., p. 182.
44. Ibid., p. 183.
45. Ibid., p. 188.
46. Ibid., p. 185.
47. Ibid., p. 187.

In the classic expression of liberation theology, orthopraxis takes precedence over orthodoxy.

The ethico-practical bridge appears to contain two components. The first, the negative, is the claim by Suchocki and others that the attitudes of superiority and of exclusive possession of truth by one religion inevitably lead to oppression and mistreatment of other religions. The second, the positive, advanced by Knitter, is that religions, despite their differing beliefs, can work together for the alleviation of injustice in the world.

A bit of analytical observation regarding these three types of bases or arguments for pluralism is in order. To some extent, we can regard them as examples of the three different conceptions regarding the nature of religion: that it is primarily belief; or feeling/experience; or action. From the time of Immanuel Kant's three critiques, religion has tended to be construed on one or the other of these models. The first of the types of arguments we have examined, the historico-cultural bridge, dealt primarily with arguments regarding the truth claims of the several religions, emphasizing the intellectual or belief character of religion. The second, the theologico-mystical, conceived of religion primarily on the model of feelings or experience. The third, the ethico-practical bridge, defined religion especially in terms of its ethical activity. Each sought to show the commonality, or at least equal validity, of the several religions to one another.

Evaluation

Let us now attempt some evaluation, both positive and negative, of this position. A number of strengths can be noted.

Positive

1. This theory correctly points out the considerable similarity of the experiences of practitioners of various religions. It is of course difficult to get within the emotional experience of another, but Hick's examples point out some clear similarities of experience.
2. This approach has the value, whether intended or not, of pointing out the vulnerability of much popular Christianity to psychological criticism. This is particularly true of those forms of Christian practice that emphasize the emotional component of Christianity to the depreciation of its intellectual or doctrinal content.
3. This approach rightly recognizes the quality of moral and spiritual life found in some persons in religions other than Christian-

ity. The older conception of the "heathen" is frequently based on a selection of the worst examples, not the best or even the typical variety.

4. A great deal of cultural conditioning, including geographical, historical, political, and racial factors, is present in views that are held, as pluralism has properly pointed out.

Negative

While not disregarding the positive values noted above, we must also express reservations about this view on a number of grounds.

1. There is inadequate grappling with the problem that inspired so much discussion and debate in the nineteenth century, namely, the essence of Christianity. The emphasis of the theologico-mystical approach is placed primarily on emotional experience. The third approach, the ethico-practical, sees religion primarily as praxis. Is either of these, however, the only, or even the primary, characteristic of Christianity, or for that matter, of religion in general?

2. There also is insufficient consciousness of the possible presence of the genetic fallacy, namely, that if one has explained how a particular view came to be held one has accounted for its truth or falsity. The discussion of the correlation of belief with one's place of birth seems to be an instance of this.

3. Hick himself exemplifies the fallacy of the cultural conditioning factor. On the grounds of his theory, he, born in England, should be an Anglican, if anything. Yet this is not the case. He has undergone a series of changes, first to a fundamentalist type of Presbyterianism and then to a broader, pluralistic sort of Christianity. How can this be? What this seems to point out is that the initial religious identity of a person can be accounted for by this theory, but that when a person matures to a point of more critical thought, other factors enter in. If this is not the case, then we must go to a more complex type of cultural conditioning, but to the extent that this ploy is successful, it will also succeed in neutralizing the truth status of the theory itself. For then one must say that Hick holds to pluralism not because it is true and supported by compelling evidence, but because these more complex conditioning factors are present. Eventually, not only religious pluralism, but philosophical pluralism must also be followed. To put it another way, the same factors that account for one being a Buddhist, Christian, and so on, also account for one being pluralist, inclusivist, exclusivist, or whatever.

4. Insufficient justification is given for the particular soteriological approach described by Knitter and advocated by himself, Suchocki, and others. Is there universal agreement on what constitutes salvation? They assume agreement on the very basic level of physical means of life. If one grants this, however, there is the further question as to which means of providing this promotes the greatest overall good for the human being. One of the differences between conservative and liberal political theory concerns the value of human freedom and initiative versus entitlement, or, in another form, the work ethic versus the entitlement ethic. Another closely related issue is the importance attached to preserving individual human identity.

   Underlying some of the positions, however, seems to be the assumption that human life consists entirely of physical life here and now. One strong element in Christian tradition is a life hereafter, which is supremely valuable. Salvation, on such a scheme, consists of eternal life. This assumption should be faced forthrightly and either justified or admitted as being an assumption.

5. Hick cites with approval Pannenberg's argument about authenticity and Jesus' self-consciousness. Yet, despite this, Pannenberg holds to the unique deity of Jesus, based on the resurrection. In other words, other features of Jesus' life argue for this deity. Hick does not really seem to have considered such phenomena.

6. There is a tendency to slide over differences among religions, in favor of what may actually be superficial similarities. This is the type of argument found within Frazer's noted *Golden Bough*.[48] Yet upon closer examination, there are some rather significant differences among religions. This was the experience of the man whom C. S. Lewis described as "the hardest boiled of all the atheists I ever knew," who came into Lewis's room and said, "Rum thing. All that stuff of Frazer's about the Dying God. Rum thing. It almost looks as if it had really happened once."[49] The argument regarding the resurrection of Jesus is perhaps the most emphatic of these characteristics of the uniqueness of Christianity.

7. Hick has come with an a priori, namely, the similarity of the different religions' experience and thus their equivalence. What if he began with the opposite assumption: the hypothesis of Jesus' uniqueness? He should have explored that possibility, not only as a relatively new Christian but as a mature scholar. He does not wrestle with the arguments of any major recent Christian apologist.

48. James George Frazer, *The Golden Bough: A Study in Magic and Religion* (New York: Macmillan, 1951).

49. C. S. Lewis, *Surprised by Joy: The Shape of My Early Life* (New York: Harcourt, Brace and World, 1955), pp. 223–24.

6

Roman Catholic Inclusivism

We observed, in an earlier chapter, that the official Roman Catholic position for many years was "outside the church, no salvation." By this was meant not only that one had to believe the Christian set of doctrinal beliefs to be saved, but also that one had to be a communicant member of the Roman Catholic Church, connected with it in such a way as to receive the benefits of its sacramental system. Yet, as we also noted, the effects of this system were gradually modified, so that while the official formula was maintained, those whose ignorance was deemed to be invincible were not considered culpably guilty. In this chapter we wish to examine the further development of this more inclusive position.

Statements of Inclusivism

In many ways, this development can be dated especially to the Second Vatican Council and certain subsequent writings. Yet, a decade or more before, an incident took place within American Catholicism that resulted in a ruling departing from the traditional position. In 1949 the rector of Boston College dismissed three lay teachers for maintaining that all who are not expressly members of the Catholic Church will be damned. This was, of course, the strict interpretation of the *extra ecclesiam*. They were publicly defended by Father Leonard Feeney, a Jesuit who from 1942 had been in charge of the center for Catholic students at Harvard University. Despite numerous warnings and penalties, he refused to desist from this action and this position, and was finally excommunicated on February 13, 1953.[1] Thus, ironically, one who held that there is no salvation for those outside the church was himself excluded from that church.

As part of the process, the Holy Office in Rome sent a letter to Cardinal Cushing, archbishop of Boston, dated August 8, 1949. In this letter the pope stated that "for someone to obtain eternal salvation it is not always demanded that he is in fact (*reapse*) incorporated as a member of the Church, but what is absolutely required is that he should adhere to it by wish and desire." This wish need not always be explicit and conscious, for "where a man labours under invincible ignorance God also accepts an *implicit wish*, as it [is] called, for it is contained in that good disposition of the soul whereby a man wishes to conform his will to the will of God."[2] While the statement did not elaborate the meaning of invincible ignorance, it did state that the wish or desire must be informed by perfect charity.

That letter mentions Pope Pius XII's encyclical on Christ's mystical Body, written in 1943, which speaks of "members of the Church" as only those who belong effectively to her through baptism and communion with their bishops in union with the Apostolic See. Those who do not belong to her, but do not lack "justness" and therefore have supernatural faith and charity and are entered on the way of salvation, are referred to as "related to the mystical Body of the Redeemer." Such persons "have dispositions which can make them Christ's saved ones, members of his Body, but they do not belong effectively to that Body inasmuch as it is visible and recognizable on the earth, that is, identical with the Church."[3] To use a distinction more familiar to Protestants, this seems to say that they are members of the invisible, but not the visible, church. While the 1949 letter, written by a different pope, did not go as far as we might wish in elaborating the position, it did say enough to enable us to see that a new principle had been opened within the church's position. The agenda of the church in the years to follow would include clarification of this principle.

Yves Congar

One Catholic theologian who published on this subject prior to Vatican II was Yves Congar. In a chapter entitled "No Salvation outside the Church?" in *The Wide World, My Parish*, he traces the history of interpre-

---

1. Yves Congar, *The Wide World My Parish: Salvation and Its Problems*, trans. Donald Attwater (London: Darton, Longman and Todd, 1961), p. 102, n. 1.

2. *The Teaching of the Catholic Church as Contained in Her Documents*, prepared by Josef Neuner and Heinrich Roos, ed. Karl Rahner, trans. Geoffrey Stevens (Staten Island, N.Y.: Alba, 1967), p. 244.

3. Congar, *Wide World*, pp. 102–3.

tation of the *extra ecclesiam* principle. While there are equivalents of this formula in the New Testament, the first real occurrence of it in its present form dates from about the year 250, from Origen and St. Cyprian. St. Fulgentius, bishop of Ruspe and a disciple of Augustine, was more explicit in enumerating who were referred to in this formula: pagans, Jews, heretics, and schismatics, who die outside the Catholic Church. All such, he said, "will go to that eternal fire which has been prepared for the Devil and his angels." While these men, says Congar, were not harder-hearted than we are, they were trying to honor the principle that there is no salvation except through Christ, and they could find no other way to do this than to exclude from salvation those who either had not known Christ or had rejected the means of salvation Christ had provided. He says, "The whole question turns on this point: is there or is there not another way of honouring the principle of the oneness of the mediator of salvation?"[4] It is apparent that to him that principle is nonnegotiable.

Congar observes that the Fathers and the Christians in the Middle Ages knew that there were people beyond the regions in which the church had taken root. They did not, however, for the most part, have curiosity or disquiet about those people. They were little disturbed about the ultimate fate of these "others." He notes that even St. Bernard of Clairvaux, a sensitive and high-souled man, was not much concerned about such matters. How could this be, he asks? He attributes it to "the conspicuousness of the Church and her far-flung triumph," which were so great as to weaken the consciousness one might have of what lay outside Christendom.[5]

A change occurred when, following the great geographical discoveries of the late fifteenth and early sixteenth centuries, Christian missionaries, especially Jesuits, made one anthropological discovery after another of previously unknown persons who were both civilized and good. Consequently, Congar states, Catholic theology has kept the formula "outside the Church, no salvation," but now gives it a meaning very different from that of its originators. Briefly, he says, it is no longer a question of applying the formula to any concrete person whatever, but rather of emphasizing that the church is commissioned and qualified to carry salvation to all persons, and that she alone is so commissioned and qualified. The formula is therefore no longer to be regarded as answering the question, "Who will be saved?" but rather, the question, "What is it that is commissioned to discharge the ministry of salvation?"[6]

4. Ibid., p. 95.
5. Ibid., p. 96.
6. Ibid., pp. 97–98.

Congar notes that there are stages in attaining faith. He finds very instructive the distinctions drawn by P. A. Liégé among levels in the church, to which the duties of ministry correspond. These are instructional community, community of faith, eucharistic community, and, beyond death, community of glory. He observes that we are no longer living in a unanimous Catholic society, but in a society in which there are numerous unbelievers, many of whom are good men and some of whom are feeling their way toward faith. There are also a large number of the indifferent or nonpracticing believers, even among the baptized. Finally, there are several other moral and religious worlds in addition to the Catholic one. Adherence to Christ can no longer be looked at in a simple, monolithic fashion. Congar says, "When faced by implicit Christianity, states of preparation, progress in the right direction but its object not yet fully attained, we shall have more and more to look on them as moments of faith before Faith."[7] He finds examples of this in the Gospels, in such a person as the man born blind, whom Jesus healed. These preformations of faith and charity, as Congar calls them, take shape in us through choices about a truth concerning God and Jesus Christ; this truth is veiled and presents itself not in itself, but in other forms and under other names. The man believed in Jesus virtually or implicitly, although he did not know him and had not realized who he was. Now, asks Congar, "If the blind man had died before Jesus met him the second time, would he not have been numbered among the saved, even though he had not expressly recognized his Saviour?"[8]

There is, then, an implicit faith. This is not exactly in the sense that the medieval Scholastics spoke about, of logical implicitness, where a truth or idea is held unrecognized within another idea already held, but of a real implicitness, analogous to what is hidden in every living seed. He notes that Augustine referred to this kind of prechurch, a church before the church and on its threshold, formed by a beginning of faith. Using Cornelius before his baptism as an example, Augustine speaks of the inchoations of faith, which can be compared to the conception of a child. To reach eternal life, however, says Augustine, it is not enough simply to be conceived, but one must also be born. Congar comments, "And it is through baptism that we are born in that birth which makes us citizens of God's kingdom (cf. John iii.5)."[9]

Congar is much impressed with Jesus' parable of the last judgment and of the sheep and the goats. Here were persons who had served and obeyed the Lord without knowing it. He asks how far this principle can

7. Ibid., p. 103.
8. Ibid., pp. 106–10.
9. Ibid., p. 110.

be extended, speaking of the realm of "God in disguise." Here he is really met, the dialogue is really with him, but he does not call himself God and the one encountering him does not know that it is he. Congar states that theology has now "cleared up any misgivings about the element of unconsciousness that there can be in the supernatural implication, and it is no less unanimous in envisaging the spheres of God's 'disguises' and of a Christian implication very widely."[10] He inquires about very general conditions in which a disguise can be God's and an implication can be a Christian one.

Congar affirms that necessarily when we are invited to encounter God without knowing, the object of our attention should have a certain absolute character that may be recognized and respected as such.[11] That in itself is not sufficient, however; this absoluteness must go further. It must make us go beyond ourselves, and therefore give ourselves. Congar's comment is, "when a man goes out of himself, when he gives himself to some good that surpasses himself, when there *really* is love, then there is the possibility of meeting, in the form of an absolute, the hidden God who wants to draw us to himself and save us."[12] It need not be that God is explicitly and consciously recognized, but he may be at work and encountered, nonetheless: "May it not be thought that when there is love—whatever its object, but a true selfless love, and one cannot 'love' just anything thus—there is grace from God, an initial giving in relation to life and the meaning of the world, whose complete fulfillment will be in Paradise?"[13] There is the mass of men who know nothing of God or whose knowledge of him is absurd or even repulsive. They are not excluded from relationship with God, either, according to Congar: "The meeting with God could take place under the form of one of those master-words that stand for a transcendent absolute to which they may have given their love, words that are often written with a capital letter: Duty, Peace, Justice, Brotherhood, yes, and Humanity, Progress, Welfare, and yet others."[14] This is a paradoxical sign of God, in relation to which men can manifest their deepest commitment, namely, the neighbor. Congar concedes that the persons mentioned in Matthew 25 knew Christ but simply did not know that it was he whom they had met when they had helped the hungry, ragged, and imprisoned. There is, nonetheless, he says, "still the recognition of a *real* im-

10. Ibid., pp. 120–21.
11. Ibid., p. 121.
12. Ibid., pp. 121–22.
13. Ibid.
14. Ibid., p. 124.

plication in their actions, surpassing all implication of knowledge. We shall be judged on what we have done, not on what we have known."[15]

The Second Vatican Council

Vatican II elaborated, enunciated, and gave this position the sort of status that comes from adoption by a council. The beginning position of the council is the unity of the human race. God created the entire race to be one; after the scattering of his children, he decreed that they should again be united. This was the reason for his sending his Son into the world. There is in the whole earth only one people of God, which of course is the meaning of the idea of catholicity. This quality of universality is considered a gift from the Lord himself. Each individual part of the church contributes to the good of the other parts and to the good of the whole church.[16] Yet in spite of this universality and unity, there is a diversity among the members, because the church has different ranks and diversity of ministry. The church encompasses all persons throughout the world, and yet these people are related to the church in varying ways. Here is the first hint of the crucial distinction that is to be elaborated—the degrees of membership in the church: "All men are called to be part of this catholic unity of the People of God, a unity which is harbinger of the universal peace it promotes. And there belong to it or are related to it in various ways, the Catholic faithful as well as all who believe in Christ, and indeed the whole of mankind. For all men are called to salvation by the grace of God."[17]

The council then turns its attention first to the "Catholic faithful," those who are professing and practicing communicants of the Roman Catholic Church. It reaffirms the principle of *extra ecclesiam nulla sallus*: "It teaches that the Church, now sojourning on earth as an exile, is necessary for salvation."[18] The explanation of this principle is interesting, however. Because Christ is held to have affirmed the necessity of faith and baptism, as well as of the church, "whosoever, therefore, knowing that the Catholic Church was made necessary by God through Jesus Christ, would refuse to enter her or to remain in her could not be saved."[19]

These Catholic faithful are said to be "fully incorporated into the society of the church." They "possess the Spirit of Christ, accept her entire system and all the means of salvation given to her, and through union

15. Ibid., pp. 125–26.
16. *The Documents of Vatican II*, ed. Walter M. Abbott (New York: Guild Press, 1966), p. 32.
17. Ibid., p. 32.
18. Ibid.
19. Ibid., pp. 32–33.

with her visible structure are joined to Christ, who rules her through the Supreme Pontiff and the bishops." This joining is effected by "the bonds of professed faith, of the sacraments, of ecclesiastical government, and of communion." Those who, though part of the body, do not persevere in charity, are not saved. Such remain in the bosom of the church, but, as it were, only in "bodily" manner and not "in the heart." Indeed, such will be the more severely judged. Catechumens who seek with explicit intention to be incorporated into the church are by that very intention joined with her.[20]

A second category of membership is those who are said to be "linked" to the church: non-Catholic Christians. They honor sacred Scripture, taking it as a norm of belief and action, and show a true religious zeal. They lovingly believe in God the Father Almighty, and in Christ, Son of God and Savior. They are consecrated by baptism, through which they are united with Christ. They also receive other sacraments, and in many cases follow much of the rest of the Catholic faith and practice. They do not, however, profess the faith in its entirety, and do not preserve unity of communion with the successor of Peter. However, "in some real way they are joined with us in the Holy Spirit, for to them also He gives His gifts and graces, and is thereby operative among them with His sanctifying power." The Holy Spirit arouses in all disciples the desire to be united as one flock, and prompts these to pursue this goal. The Mother Church never ceases to pray, hope, and work that they may gain this blessing. While these are not as fully incorporated into the church as are practicing Catholics, they are, in their appropriate way, also part of it.[21]

The third group consists of those who have not yet received the gospel, of whom it is said that they "are related in various ways to the People of God." The first subclass of these is the Jews, those to whom the covenants and promises were given and from whom Christ was born. "On account of their fathers," says the council's statement, "this people remains most dear to God, for God does not repent of the gifts He makes nor of the calls He issues (cf. Rom. 11:28–29)." A second subclass are those who acknowledge the Creator and who are also included in the plan of salvation. These include the Moslems. Professing to hold the faith of Abraham, they adore the one and merciful God. God also is not far from others, "who in shadows and images seek the unknown God."[22] He gives to all men life and breath and every other good gift (cf. Acts 17:25–28), and as Savior wills that all men be saved (cf. 1 Tim. 2:4). This

20. Ibid., p. 33.
21. Ibid., pp. 33–34.
22. Ibid., p. 35.

second subclass also includes those who "through no fault of their own do not know the gospel of Christ or His Church, yet sincerely seek God and, moved by grace, strive by their deeds to do His will as it is known to them through the dictates of conscience." They also can attain to everlasting salvation. Finally, there is a third subclass of those "who, without blame on their part, have not yet arrived at an explicit knowledge of God, but who strive to live a good life, thanks to his grace."[23] Whatever goodness and truth are found among them are regarded by the church as a preparation for the gospel, having been given by him who enlightens all men so that they may finally have life. The statement says of them, "Nor does divine providence deny the help necessary for salvation to [such]."[24]

The Vatican Council has therefore made completely explicit what was relatively implicit in the immediately preceding statements we have heard. If the principle is "outside the Church, no salvation," then this must be understood in light of the full meaning of being inside the church. There are indeed degrees of membership in the church. Each of these groups participates in the grace of God, but to varying degrees and with varying experience and enjoyment of that grace. The task of the church is to proclaim the gospel to all persons, so that they may fully experience that Gospel's grace.[25]

Karl Rahner

Because of his views on these matters, Karl Rahner has probably attracted more attention than any other recent Roman Catholic theologian. His major contribution to the subject came in a discussion of the Second Vatican Council, under the title, "Anonymous Christians." He begins by observing that it is now almost two thousand years since Christ gave his commission to the church to go and preach the gospel to all nations to the end of the earth. Those limits of the world have now been marked out. We may ask how the church has done in this endeavor. In the ancient cultures of Asia, Christianity has never really gained a foothold, and in the West, where it became one of the historical roots, it is still steadily losing its importance and influence. This is the situation in which believing Christians find themselves, and it seems safe to assume that the future will only bring an accentuation of this trend.[26]

23. Ibid.
24. Ibid., pp. 34–35.
25. Ibid., pp. 35–37.
26. Karl Rahner, *Theological Investigations*, trans. Karl and Boniface Kruger (Baltimore: Helicon, 1969), 6:390.

Two principles of the Christian's belief must be maintained conjointly. The first is the necessity of holding the Christian faith, and indeed, of being a member of the church. The other is God's declared desire to see everyone saved. How, then, can the Christian believe that the overwhelming majority of persons who have ever lived or ever will live are in principle and unquestionably denied salvation and condemned to eternal meaninglessness? Rahner says, "He must reject any such suggestion, and his faith is in agreement with his doing so." Scripture tells us of God's universal salvific will (1 Tim. 2:4). God's covenant of peace with Noah has never been abrogated, in fact, the Son of God sealed it with his self-sacrificing love that embraced all men.[27]

How are these two principles of Christian belief to be maintained and kept joined together? Rahner declares that this can really only be done in one way: by acknowledgment that there is some way in which all persons are capable, really capable, of being members of the church. This in turn must lead us to the conclusion that there are degrees of membership in the church: ascending degrees from baptism to the realization of holiness, as well as descending degrees from the explicitness of baptism into "a non-official and anonymous Christianity which can and should yet be called Christianity in a meaningful sense, even though it itself cannot and would not describe itself as such."[28] If the person who is the object of the church's missionary endeavor is on the way to salvation and finds it under certain circumstances, and if the only source of such salvation is the salvation of Christ, then it must be possible to be an anonymous Christian. But how is such a relationship to be conceived?

Such a relationship is not and cannot be simply by virtue of being human, for that would negate grace as grace. To be sure, grace presupposes the creature, but it must be the case that this being has unlimited openness toward God, or spirit. There also must be some knowledge of his superiority over the world and of his personality. In other words, man must be not only capable of hearing a possible word from the hidden God, but also be positively expecting it. Every denial of one's being ordered to the "unsurpassably Absolute" would, in Rahner's judgment, implicitly affirm it, because it would speak with the "claim of absolute truth," be subject to the "demand of an indisputable good," and derive its force from the desire for a "final and definitive meaning."[29]

The further question for Rahner is now, however, how this tendency toward God, which sometimes is quite implicit and incoherent

---

27. Ibid., p. 391.
28. Ibid.
29. Ibid., p. 392.

and yet always permeates man's being, includes a reference to the incarnate God, Jesus Christ. "If one takes it seriously that God has become man, . . . then it must be said that man is that which happens when God expresses and divests himself."[30] Man is accordingly that which God becomes if he sets out to express himself in the extradivine. Putting it another way: Man is the one who realizes himself when he "gives himself away into the incomprehensible mystery of God." Thus, "the incarnation of God is the uniquely supreme case of the actualization of man's nature in general."[31] Bestowal of grace and the incarnation are the two most basic modes of God's self-communication. They are beyond his ability to compel and yet as such also eminently fulfill the transcendence of man's being. Rahner refers to this self-communication of God to all as the "supernatural existential."[32]

Man, then, in experiencing his transcendence, his limitless openness, no matter how implicit, is also experiencing grace—not always expressly as grace, but its content is there. The expressly Christian revelation is the explicit statement of that continuous revelation of grace that man experiences implicitly in the depths of his being. If man accepts the revelation, he does so by supernatural faith. If, however, he really accepts himself completely, he also accepts this revelation, for it already speaks in him. Rahner says, "Prior to the explicitness of official ecclesiastical faith this acceptance can be present in an implicit form whereby a person undertakes and lives the duty of each day in the quiet sincerity of patience, in devotion to his material duties and the demands made upon him by the persons under his care." In accepting himself the person is accepting Christ "as the absolute perfection and guarantee of his own anonymous movement towards God by grace." This is not a human act, but a work of divine grace. Such a person is thereby an "anonymous Christian."[33]

It would not be correct, however, to declare every man an "anonymous Christian," irrespective of whether he accepts grace. On the contrary, "Anyone who in his basic decision were really to deny and reject his being ordered to God, who were to place himself decisively in opposition to his own concrete being, should not be designated a 'theist', even an anonymous 'theist'; only someone who gives—even if it be ever so confusedly—the glory to *God* should be thus designated."[34] Rahner gives the most specific definition thus far of the anonymous believer:

---

30. Ibid., p. 393.
31. Ibid.
32. Ibid., p. 393.
33. Ibid., p. 394.
34. Ibid., pp. 394–95.

Therefore no matter what a man states in his conceptual, theoretical and religious reflection, anyone who does not say in his *heart*, "there is no God" (like the "fool" in the psalm) but testifies to him by the radical acceptance of his being, is a believer. But if in this way he believes in deed and in truth in the holy mystery of God, if he does not suppress this truth but leaves it free play, then the grace of this truth by which he allows himself to be led is always already the grace of the Father in his Son. And anyone who has let himself be taken hold of by this grace can be called with every right an "anonymous Christian."[35]

Some might think this concept of the anonymous Christian is an act of desperation in a world where Christian faith is fast disappearing, to rescue for the church all that is good and human. It does offer encouragement and strength to Christians, who increasingly find themselves in a diaspora situation. This knowledge of the anonymous Christian does not in any way free the explicit Christian from caring and sharing the message with those who do not yet know the explicit message of the gospel. It does, however, free him from panic and help him practice patience.[36] It would be quite mistaken to think that this teaching regarding the anonymous Christian should in any sense lessen the importance of mission, preaching, the Word of God, baptizing, and so on. Such failure to understand him, Rahner contends, correctly demonstrates that his exposition has not been read with sufficient attention.[37] Indeed, what he has said on the subject is also materially taught in the *Constitution on the Church* of Vatican II.[38]

Hans Küng

Hans Küng's writings on this subject are the clearest of those setting forth the new Catholic inclusivism. He begins with the familiar story about the blind men and the elephant. He notes that tolerance is characteristic of a large number of persons, both Eastern and Western. He quotes Gandhi's statement: "I believe in the Bible as I believe in the Gita. I regard all the great faiths of the world as equally true with my own. It hurts me to see any one of them caricatured as they are today by their own followers." Küng finds in this statement a greater view of God than in that of those who allow him to be the God of only one party.[39]

35. Ibid., p. 395.
36. Ibid., p. 396.
37. Ibid., pp. 397, 398.
38. Ibid., p. 397.
39. Hans Küng, "The World Religions in God's Plan of Salvation," in *Christian Revelation and World Religions*, ed. Joseph Neuner (London: Burnes and Oates, 1967), pp. 25–26.

The church has, of course, over its long history, proclaimed the "outside the Church, no salvation" principle. Küng asks, however, whether we can continue to maintain that principle in light of a number of important considerations. The first is the current relative minority of Christianity. At the time of his writing, the population of the earth was 2.5 billion persons, of whom only 847 million were Christians and only 500 million were Catholics. In India, only 2.4 percent of the population are Christians, and 1.2 percent Catholics, whereas in China and Japan, Christians constitute only .05 percent of the total population. Even in Europe, only a fraction of those who call themselves Christians actively participate in the church. What is one to say, then, about the salvation of these millions who at the present time live outside the Catholic Church and completely outside Christianity?[40]

Turning from the present to the past, we encounter similarly sobering facts. The years of humanity's history before Christ's coming are probably not 5,200, as the Bible suggests, but perhaps as many as 600,000. What is one to say about these countless millions who lived in the past outside the Catholic Church and completely outside Christianity?[41]

The prospects for the future are even less encouraging. The statistics show that the non-Christian nations of Asia and Africa will numerically outstrip the Christian nations of the West. Just to maintain our present share of the world's population would require not just 500,000 converts annually to the Catholic Church, as is true at present, but 6.5 million. It is calculated that by the year 2000, China alone may number 1.7 billion people, 400 million more than the present population of Europe, the Soviet Union, North and South America, and Africa combined. What is one to say about the millions and billions of persons who will live in the future outside the Catholic Church and altogether outside Christianity?[42]

These, says Küng, are the facts, and we are familiar with them. We must, however, come to grips theologically with the fact that Christianity in general and the Catholic Church specifically is a small and insignificant minority. There are two additional aspects of the problem. One is that we are at the end of a particular period of world history, the "modern age." The period of Western domination of the world, and all that goes in the name of "colonialism," is over. The missionary situation was excessively linked to that system, but now, instead of being borne along by the current, it must swim against it. This requires a new justification of the church's mission. Küng says, "Contemporary history forces upon us an awareness that today it is less and less a matter of evangelizing the 'poor

40. Ibid., p. 27.
41. Ibid.
42. Ibid., pp. 27–28.

heathens,' but rather of bringing the Gospel to modern men in industrialized states with great and ancient cultures."[43]

The other facet relates to the fact that not only politically, socially, economically, and technologically, but religiously as well, the peoples of Asia and Africa are entering a new period of world history. Many Christians had expected that, confronted by Western culture and hence by the Christian religion, these other religions would slowly wither away. This, however, has not happened. While it is true that there is indifferentism in these religions as well as in Christianity, they have nonetheless passed over from a defensive to an offensive stage. These religions are reflecting on their traditions. This renaissance of the world religions leads, on the one hand, to an assimilation of the resources of Western thought and, on the other, to the development of a considerable missionary drive of their own. Consequently, the question being considered is not merely that of the individuals outside the church, but also of these religions that are outside the church. The issues are so urgent that they cannot be ignored.[44]

Küng proceeds to contrast two views: the ecclesiocentric view (outside the church there is no salvation) and the theocentric view (God's plan of salvation). The former, he acknowledges, has a long history in the church. It was the impact of the discovery of whole new continents with civilized and morally good inhabitants that finally effected a breakthrough. This led to a gradual softening of the principle, culminating in Pius IX's statement about the nonculpability of those whose ignorance is invincible. Küng contends that today no one disputes the fact that men are saved outside the Catholic Church. However, this principle continues to produce confusion and misunderstandings. The basic solution is to be found in a positive reassessment of the significance of the world religions in relation to God's universal plan of salvation.[45]

One way in which the apparent paradox of no salvation outside the church and yet of salvation outside the church has been handled is through expanding the meaning of the church to cover non-Christians as well. While Küng feels that the term can be extended to include Protestant Christians, he says that to stretch the concept of "church" to include persons who know nothing of Christ and wish to know nothing of Christ would mean a vague community of "men of goodwill." He rejects such a construction for four reasons: It does not accord with the New Testament and the Christian tradition; it is not necessary in order to see the possibility of the salvation of non-Christians;

---

43. Ibid., pp. 28–29.
44. Ibid., pp. 29–30.
45. Ibid., pp. 31–36.

it complicates the task of missionaries, who must preach to non-Christians about entry into the church while at the same time proclaiming that all men of goodwill are already within it; it is rejected by thinking non-Christians as theological speculation and as a somewhat dishonest evasion.[46] He proposes on the one hand that the expression be retained in dogmatic teaching, while simultaneously showing the limitations and liability to misunderstanding of such an expression, and emphasizing that salvation is given in Christ, whether those of goodwill ultimately find themselves inside or outside the visible communion of the believing and confessing church. On the other hand, Küng feels that in preaching the statement should as far as possible be set aside and not used, because it leads to more misunderstanding than understanding.[47]

In contrast to this approach, Küng offers the theocentric view, tracing the divine plan of salvation. He examines the Old Testament, Jesus' preaching, and the apostolic preaching. He finds a much more positive stance toward the world religions than has usually been thought, both by those inside and outside the church. His conclusions are as follows:[48]

1. Universalist testimonies pervade the Old and New Testaments, precluding the view that the Bible takes a purely negative attitude of exclusive intolerance toward other religions.
2. The Bible makes clear that the God of the Bible is not only the God of the Jews and Christians, but of all human beings.
3. The negative statements about the errors and sin of the pagan world refer to it insofar as it sets itself against God's saving will. These should be regarded as calls to conversion directed to pagans of the present day, with the fate of pagans of another day, or those who have not heard of Christ, being of only indirect interest to the Bible.
4. There are indications that there is an original, primitive communication of God to the whole of mankind. God is near to every human being.

The starting point, then, for any discussion of salvation is not to be the church, but God's will and plan. The question of what lies outside the church can be answered only with difficulty. The clear teaching of Scripture is that all men can be saved. "As to what lies outside *God* and his plan

46. Ibid., pp. 35–36.
47. Ibid., pp. 36–37.
48. Ibid., pp. 45–46.

of salvation, this is not a real question at all. If we look at God's plan of salvation, then there is no *extra*, only an *intra*; no outside, only an inside, for 'God desires *all* men to be saved and to come to the knowledge of the truth. For there is *one* God, and there is *one* mediator between God and men, the man Christ Jesus, who gave himself as a ransom for *all*' (I Tim. 2.4–6)."[49]

When Küng discusses the world religions, he acknowledges that despite whatever truth these religions possess concerning God, they are also at the same time in error. They proclaim the truth of Christ, although not recognizing him for what he really is, namely, the Truth. They do this when they recognize man's need of salvation, acknowledge God's graciousness, and listen to the voice of their prophets. Christianity proclaims a radical universalism, but salvation is in every case dependent on Christ's work. Every human being is under God's grace and can be saved. So, similarly, every world religion is under God's grace and can be a way of salvation, and we may hope that they all are.[50]

This latter point hinges on Küng's conception of the ordinary and extraordinary way of salvation. The church is the extraordinary way of salvation and the world religions can be called the ordinary way of salvation. God is the author both of the special salvation history of the church and of the universal salvation history of all mankind. Because God seriously and effectively wills that all men should be saved and none should be lost unless by his or her own fault, everyone is intended to find salvation within his own historical condition. Küng says, "A man is to be saved within the religion that is made available to him in his historical situation. Hence it is his right and his duty to seek God within that religion in which the hidden God has already found him. All this until such time as he is confronted in an existential way with the revelation of Jesus Christ."[51] By assigning the terms in the way in which he has, Küng gives the impression that those saved who are not conscious adherents of the Christian faith and especially the Catholic Church are the more numerous, in the judgment of John Hick,[52] with which interpretation of Küng I would agree.

Summary

We need now to summarize briefly the views we have been examining, giving some overview of the positions being described. Several tenets emerge:

49. Ibid., p. 46
50. Ibid., pp. 51–57.
51. Ibid., p. 52.
52. John Hick, *God Has Many Names* (Philadelphia: Westminster, 1982), p. 35.

1. There are stages in the development of faith, and thus it is appropriate to speak of degrees of faith.
2. Corresponding to these, there are degrees or types of membership in the church.
3. Faith may be implicit. It may not be necessary to know all of the details about the object of faith. In fact, it may not necessarily even be conscious faith in God.
4. There is a rather strong belief in immanence. This shows itself in two ways. On the one hand, the knowledge of God that the non-Christian religions have from nature is basically valid. On the other hand, one may be knowing God by way of knowing oneself. This does not mean, however, that it is merely by virtue of being human that one knows God. It is only the response of "openness" that constitutes this.
5. The quality of the relationship is what determines the object of the understanding. Those who are deeply receptive and responsive to God's working are those who are really related to God, whether they realize that or not.
6. In spite of all this, conscious rejection of the gospel and the church leaves one outside salvation and the church. These promises, whether of anonymous Christianity or of degrees of membership in the church, are to those who are not consciously within the church because, through no fault of their own, they have never heard the message.

Evaluation

Positive

There are several commendable features of the endeavor made by these modern Catholics.

1. These theologians are to be commended for their courage in being willing to consider positions that are in conflict with the traditional position of the Catholic Church. They have been willing to speak publicly what apparently was held privately by a number of theologians, clergy, and lay persons for some time.
2. This approach is consistent with, and even to some extent, implied by a number of conceptions that have been traditionally part of Catholic theology. One of these is the view of salvation. The key conception was that of sanctifying grace, which combines what in Protestant theology are two doctrines, justification and sanctification. In Catholic theology justification is not cate-

gorical and complete in one moment, but one is as justified as one is actually holy. This allowance for degrees of salvation then also fits well with the idea of degrees of membership within the church.

3. Another doctrine with which this approach is consistent is the Roman Catholic doctrine of general revelation. On that view, much of the essential truth of Christian belief is objectively present in general revelation, and it is possible to form a natural theology from this view. Thus, there is considerable possibility of persons being anonymous Christians or something of that type.

4. This approach fits with the fact that the restrictions in Scripture are oriented to one's relationship to Christ, rather than to the church. Thus, it takes more seriously one authority held by all Christians in some degree.

5. This view fits well with Jesus' statement, "I have other sheep which are not of this fold" (John 10:16), as well as other more inclusive statements in Scripture.

6. This approach also avoids the major difficulty of the problem of the salvation of those who lived before the establishment of the church, primarily Old Testament believers.

Negative

There are, however, a number of unresolved difficulties within this view, some of them unrecognized by the advocates of Catholic inclusivism.

1. There is a problem with the denotation of language. There seems to be such an elasticity of words, at least with respect to the meaning of "church," that virtually nothing is inconsistent with it. If this is the case, then we must also ask what really is being asserted and affirmed by the language.

2. Beyond this, however, one must ask in what sense the approach to life included here can be really called Christian, since it seems to be compatible with no belief at all.

3. Part of the problem here is that more basic questions have not really been addressed. One of these is the question of the nature of religion. Is it belief and content, or is it merely feeling or action? This issue, prominent in Christian and theological circles since the time of Schleiermacher, deserves some careful examination.

4. Closely related to this is the question of the objectivity and subjectivity of truth, which Kierkegaard so powerfully raised. The idea of truth as subjective is implied, but this is not overtly addressed.

5. Another doctrine intimately connected with this position is the immanence of God. To the extent that God is immanent, it is possible to know him anywhere and at any time. This view is more oriented to an immanental view of God than was the earlier theology, but that is not made explicit, it is not argued for, nor are its implications dealt with.

6. Certain portions of Scripture are not dealt with completely, particularly the more exclusivistic passages. In fact, one shortcoming of this view is the relative absence of scriptural treatment.

7

Protestant Inclusivism

We examined, in the preceding chapter, the changes in Roman Catholic theology in the past century or century and a half, from the "outside the church, no salvation" view to a more inclusive view of degrees of church membership or anonymous Christianity. A similar development in Protestant Christianity has approximately paralleled this change. Although the time period was somewhat later and more compressed and the nature of the view of inclusiveness is less extensive, there are definite similarities. Because conservative, orthodox, or evangelical Protestantism was more definitely exclusivist in nature than more liberal Protestantism, it is in the former group that the change is most clearly seen. We will consequently draw our sources from that constituency. The issue of the church was not as significant for Protestants as for Catholics. Thus, the focus is more strongly on the question of what it means to be correctly in the faith rather than what it means to be within the church. Correct belief, rather than correct affiliation, is the major issue. As we have seen, however, the redefinition of the church by Catholicism has tended to make the two views more similar than in the past.

Issues Involved

A number of issues are involved in this discussion. First is the meaning of salvation. Is salvation primarily juridical or forensic justification, or is it repentance and faith, or a living relationship of some kind? Does it involve spiritual redemption and transformation of the person, or does it also include physical healing and wholeness? A second issue is the nature of the requirements for salvation. What does one need to know and believe in order to be saved? Must one know about Christ and his atoning death, or is it sufficient to believe in a powerful, good, and holy God, to repent of one's sin, and cast oneself on the mercy of this God? And what about the time extent of the opportunity for entering into a saving relationship with God? Does death bring that opportunity to an end, or is there a possibility that after this life those who have never heard will be given a chance to hear and believe the gospel? A further question is the extent and efficacy of general revelation. How much is revealed through that channel? How capable are persons of knowing and understanding general revelation? What is the relationship between this understanding gained through general revelation and the nature of saving faith? Another important question, which in a sense is an implication of all these preceding questions is, how many persons will be saved? Will these constitute merely a small minority of the human race, or will they be many, perhaps even most, of those who have ever lived? If the latter, will this come to pass through the effective worldwide preaching of the gospel, or will the saving faith come about through some other means? Closely related to all of these questions is of course the issue of the relative sinfulness of humans, or the extent to which it can be said that persons are totally depraved rather than basically good. Finally, how are the world religions to be thought of? Are they alternative means of salvation, do their adherents have true but confused knowledge of divine truth, or do they simply represent idolatry? These are some of the many questions that enter into the discussion posed by the Protestant inclusivist position.

Earlier Inclusivist Theologians

Augustus Hopkins Strong

Like the Roman Catholic position, this more inclusive, or less exclusive, view did not simply burst on the scene overnight. It was partially foreshadowed by a gradually increasing openness to the idea of salvation in some way for those who had never heard. One early twentieth-century theologian who expressed this idea was Augustus Hopkins Strong, a Baptist theologian and seminary president, whose systematic theology textbook was a standard work for many years. He sees the possible salvation of the heathen as being on the basis of a faith like that of the Old Testament believers:

> The patriarchs, though they had no knowledge of a personal Christ, were saved by believing in God so far as God had revealed himself to them; and whoever among the heathen are saved, must in like manner be saved by cast-

ing themselves as helpless sinners upon God's plan of mercy, dimly shadowed forth in nature and providence. But such faith, even among the patriarchs and heathen, is implicitly a faith in Christ, and would become explicit and conscious trust and submission, whenever Christ were made known to them (Matt. 8:11, 12; John 10:16; Acts 4:12; 10:31, 34, 35, 44; 16:31).[1]

He contrasts his view with that of the Princeton theologians, who restricted faith to explicit hearing of the gospel. In particular, he objects to Charles Hodge's approach of restricting the operations of grace to the preaching of the incarnate Christ. Yet he quotes with approval Hodge's statement, which he refers to as inconsistent because it speaks of a presence and revelation of God to all men, through Christ, the eternal Word. He then elaborates his own position:

> Since Christ is the Word of God and the Truth of God, he may be received even by those who have not heard of his manifestation in the flesh. A proud and self-righteous morality is inconsistent with saving faith; but a humble and penitent reliance upon God, as a Savior from sin and a guide of conduct, is an implicit faith in Christ; for such reliance casts itself upon God, so far as God has revealed himself,—and the only Revealer of God is Christ. We have, therefore, the hope that even among the heathen there may be some, like Socrates, who, under the guidance of the Holy Spirit working through the truth of nature and conscience, have found the way of life and salvation.[2]

Strong believes that the number of such is so small as not to weaken at all the need of engaging in the missionary enterprise. There are basically two reasons, however, why he holds to this wider hope. The first is the intimations of such in Scripture. He cites such texts as Matthew 8:11–12; John 10:16; Acts 4:12; 10:31, 34–35, 44; 16:31. He also is impressed by the apparent cases, discovered by missionaries, of persons who had never had the gospel preached to them, but who nevertheless were apparently regenerated heathen.[3]

Norman Anderson

The person who up until about the late 1980s had probably made the largest impact on evangelicalism on this subject and still is widely quoted is Sir Norman Anderson, formerly professor of oriental laws and director of the Institute of Advanced Legal Studies at the University

---

1. Augustus Hopkins Strong, *Systematic Theology: A Compendium and Commonplace-Book* (Philadelphia: Judson, 1907), p. 842.
2. Ibid., p. 843.
3. Ibid., pp. 843–44.

of London. His book, *Christianity and the World Religions: The Challenge of Pluralism*, was published by InterVarsity Press, both in England and in the United States. He raises the question of special importance for us in a chapter entitled, "No Other Name?"

Anderson gives early consideration to the view of those who find the key in the idea that all will be judged by the light they have. Thus, Jews will be judged on the basis of the law of Moses, while non-Jews will be judged according to the requirements of the law "written on their hearts" (Rom. 2:14–16). He grants that the most elementary principles of justice would seem to require this. He does not believe, however, that it provides any sort of solution to the problem at hand. The reason is this: Just as no Jew has ever lived up to the demands of the Mosaic law, so no non-Jew has ever succeeded in living up to the standard of the moral and ethical principles by which he knows he should govern his life and conduct. This, therefore, does not provide any solution to the problem of salvation and damnation of those who do not have special revelation.[4]

The question, says Anderson, can then be stated in the following form: "Is there any basis on which the efficacy of the one atonement can avail those who have never heard about it?"[5] One answer that has been given is that of Wilfred Cantwell Smith: A Buddhist, Muslim, Hindu, or anyone who is saved is saved only because God is the kind of God whom Jesus Christ has revealed him to be, namely, a loving God. This, however, will not do, for the nature of God, as revealed in Scripture, is not that of a purely benevolent being, but is light as well as love, justice as well as mercy, and to concentrate on only one quality is to distort his character and caricature love's essence. As Anderson puts it, "God's hatred of sin is, in reality, the inevitable concomitant of his love for the sinner: the reverse side of the very same coin. . . . God 'desires all men to be saved and to come to the knowledge of the truth' (1 Tim. 2:4), but this can be only through the Saviour who is himself 'the propitiation for our sins, and not for ours only but also for the sins of the whole world' (1 Jn. 2:2)."[6]

Anderson recognizes that many Protestant theologians believe we must simply leave unanswered this question of the eternal destiny of all those who have never heard the gospel, inasmuch as the Bible gives no explicit solution to the problem. Others insist that the various New Testament references to saving faith seem to confine it to explicit faith in

4. Norman Anderson, *Christianity and World Religions: The Challenge of Pluralism* (Downers Grove, Ill.: InterVarsity, 1984), p. 146.

5. Ibid.

6. Ibid., pp. 146–47.

the Lord Jesus Christ. He acknowledges this, but the question is not simply a matter of faith, but also of grace, as for example, the problem of those who die in infancy.[7]

Anderson proposes an alternative that has been picked up by a number of others: We may find a glimmer of insight by looking at the situation of the Old Testament Jews. They "turned to God in repentance, brought the prescribed sacrifice . . . and threw themselves on his mercy."[8] Yet they did not earn that mercy by their repentance or obedience, nor did that animal sacrifice avail to atone for human sin. That repentance and faith "opened the gate, as it were, to the grace, mercy and forgiveness which he always longed to extend to them," and which was to be made available through Christ's death on the cross.[9] Indeed, that repentance and faith were themselves the result of God's work in their hearts. Their situation, he concedes, was somewhat different than the case in point, for they had a special divine revelation in which to put their trust. "But," says Anderson, "might it not be true of the follower of some other religion that the God of all mercy had worked in his heart by his Spirit, bringing him in some measure to realize his sin and need for forgiveness, and enabling him, in the twilight as it were, to throw himself on God's mercy?"[10]

In considering Romans 10:12–18, Anderson notes Calvin's comment, that while the preached word is in view in the passage, Paul cannot be made to say that this is the only means by which God can instill a knowledge of himself among men. While not claiming the authority of Calvin for his view, Anderson observes that God can, and indeed sometimes does, communicate directly with individuals. The Old Testament records instances where God "moved" men's hearts (e.g., Cyrus) or spoke to them, whether for their own good or that of others, through dreams (e.g., Abraham, Joseph, and Nebuchadnezzar), miracles (e.g., Naaman), visions (e.g., Belshazzar), or in some unspecified way (e.g., Balaam).[11]

These cases are, of course, instances of special revelation, and consequently of limited extent of opportunity, unless somehow preserved and transmitted to others. More pertinent to the discussion here is whether God may be known sufficiently through general revelation to bring about saving faith. He has always made himself known through the phenomena of nature (Rom. 1:19–20; 10:18–19). This cosmic revelation would in

7. Ibid., p. 148.
8. Ibid.
9. Ibid.
10. Ibid., pp. 148–49.
11. Ibid., pp. 149–50.

the natural state have produced in persons a knowledge of God's eternal power and divine nature that would have been swallowed up in "the darkness of humanistic philosophy, idolatry and even gross immorality," rather than leading them to worship and thanksgiving. But, asks Anderson, does God only awaken in persons some spark of his grace among them so that they may be without excuse, and without any possibility of salvation? May it not rather be compatible with both experience and Scripture, to "suggest that God sometimes so works in men's hearts by his grace that, instead of them 'holding down the truth,' he opens their hearts to it and enables them to embrace such of it as has been revealed to them"?[12]

Anderson also advances an argument from experience and observation. He says that his study of Islam, for example, convinces him that it is undeniable "that some of the great Muslim mystics have sought the face of God with a wholeheartedness which cannot be questioned."[13] He does not doubt that in some cases it was God himself that they were seeking, not self-justification or a mystical experience in itself. They would, of course, be saved by grace alone, but may they not have been responding to some initiative in that grace that was uniquely operative in the cross and resurrection of the one whose story they had never really heard?[14]

The question Anderson is posing is whether the numerous promises in the Scriptures to those who seek God should apply exclusively to Old Testament Jews who responded to God's grace under the old covenant and those who have heard and responded to the gospel. He points out items of similarity and points of difference between these Old Testament believers and the "unevangelized" today. Neither of these is ever saved by earning salvation through their religion, nor indeed are any others. The difference between the Old Testament Jew and the unevangelized person of today is that the former could put his trust in a special revelation, incomplete though it might be. Yet, Anderson asks, may there not also be a significant point of similarity between the two? The basis on which the believing Jew was accepted was not the animal sacrifices he offered or his repentance and abandonment of himself to God's mercy. Rather, it was the atoning work that God was going to do in his only Son on the cross. But the believing Jew had never heard of this. Similarly, the unevangelized today are dependent on whether God works in their hearts, "convicting them of sin and need, awakening a love of the truth, and quickening their faith in whatever he has shown

12. Ibid., p. 151.
13. Ibid., p. 152.
14. Ibid, pp. 152–53.

them of his 'purpose of mercy'—that they may be included in the efficacy of the atoning sacrifice, made by a Saviour about whom they have never heard, which was offered, in some sense at least, 'for the sins of the whole world' (1 Jn. 2:2)." We cannot be dogmatic about such matters, but must rest in the wisdom and knowledge of God.[15]

If such persons were to be presented with the gospel, Anderson is confident that they would then be among those of whom one sometimes hears on the mission field, who immediately welcome and accept it, saying, "This is what we have been waiting for; why didn't you come sooner?" There are of course those who have been brought the message they longed for, like Cornelius. Evidently, however, Anderson holds that Cornelius was already a believer and saved when he received the message. Anderson says, "But I myself cannot doubt that there may be those who, while never hearing the gospel here on earth, will wake up, as it were, on the other side of the grave to worship the One in whom, without understanding it at the time, they found the mercy of God."[16]

Anderson does not place much confidence in the theory of an afterdeath experience of God's love. He finds no scriptural warrant for such a theory, and also considers it superfluous. If as a result of the prompting of the Holy Spirit people cast themselves upon the mercy of God, that mercy will have already reached them.[17] Anderson does not, however, appear to consider this as a possibility for those who have not so responded to general revelation.

Finally, Anderson responds to the objection sometimes raised against views such as his that they would lead to a diminution of missionary urgency. First, we are under definite unambiguous orders to take the gospel message to everyone. Second, even persons such as he has described, who have responded on the basis of general revelation, may indeed have received that mercy but still lack some important elements of Christian experience: teaching, heart assurance, and a message they can communicate to others. Third, in our own experience it was hearing the message that led us to belief, so we should also take that message to others as well. Fourth, we cannot deny others the present experience of joy, peace, and power that comes only from a conscious knowledge of Christ and communion with him.[18]

15. Ibid., p. 153.
16. Ibid., p. 154.
17. Ibid.
18. Ibid., pp. 154–55.

Arguments of Contemporary Inclusivist Theologians

Among those who have most vehemently argued for some sort of wider hope, probably the most expressive of evangelicals, both in terms of frequency and quantity of expression and also of vehemence, is Clark Pinnock, professor of theology at McMaster Divinity School in Canada. Another whose teaching emphasis and writing have also dealt with this topic of the fate of the unevangelized is John Sanders of Oak Hills Bible College, a very conservative institution in Bemidji, Minnesota. Pinnock has written on this complex of issues off and on for approximately ten years. His most recent work, *A Wideness in God's Mercy*, indicates his present assessment of the situation.

Religious Pluralism

Pinnock begins his analysis of the need for this discussion by placing it in the current setting of religious pluralism. This, of course, is nothing new, for the gospel came into a religiously pluralistic world in the very beginning. There is, however, a different "feel" to the situation today, for in the past there was relatively little contact with persons of different cultures and religions. Today, however, the small world continues to shrink. Nations are compelled to formulate economic alliances with trading partners. Electronic communications bring us in contact with persons in far-off parts of the globe. It is essential that religions become truly global if they are to compete, or even survive. Like it or not, religions will not be able to survive in isolation from each other. While this contact with persons from other religions is not something new for persons in the other two-thirds of the globe, it is unusual for most of us in the West.[19]

The actual presence and contact with other religions are not the sole contributors to the pluralistic atmosphere, however. There is also a relativistic mind-set of late modernity, an ideology of pluralism, which celebrates choice in itself as a good no matter what is chosen. The only choice in this atmosphere that is not good and desirable is the mentality that holds that some actions are right and others wrong, some beliefs true and others false. That is considered intolerable in such a relativistic framework.[20]

In this climate, truth is not a correct reflection of the way things are. Rather, beliefs considered true by various peoples in times past are now understood as functions of a given culture. What appears true to some-

19. Clark H. Pinnock, *A Wideness in God's Mercy: The Finality of Jesus Christ in a World of Religions* (Grand Rapids: Zondervan, 1992), pp. 8–9.
20. Ibid., pp. 9–10.

one depends on where one was born. Customs and beliefs are the right ones for that culture, but not necessarily for others. Religious beliefs are human constructions or useful fictions created to help make life easier, but are not necessarily objectively true. Although Pinnock does not say so, underlying this conception is a pragmatist view of truth which maintains that truth is what works or is useful, rather than some objective description of reality. Religions tend to be thought of as equally valid responses to reality, equally valid routes to salvation. Utility is the criterion on which religious and other beliefs are evaluated.[21]

Pragmatic Contemporary Theology

Pinnock also points out the present situation in theology, in which the theological pot is boiling over this issue. The challenge of religious pluralism has given a new life to radical theology, such as it has not had since the 1960s. In light of this challenge, some have made doctrinal concessions, such as scaling down the lordship of Christ. Part of the problem stems from a characteristic of contemporary theology: Its tendency to be driven, not by the Bible or tradition, but by practical or ethical considerations. Examples of this can be seen coming from feminism, homosexuality, ecology, and so on. Thus, the idea of Christ as the sole mediator between God and humanity would not be acceptable in today's atmosphere, not because Christ did not claim it or because the church has not confessed it, but rather because, in the present cultural mood, it would be unthinkable and intolerable. It would not be fair or equal treatment. It promotes intolerance. It is not politically correct.[22]

Both Pinnock and Sanders are very clear about the status of Jesus Christ among the world religions. Their view is by no stretch of the imagination universalism, in which all persons are saved. It is not pluralism, in which all religions are merely alternate routes to salvation. They are emphatic about the indispensability of Jesus Christ for salvation. Anyone who is saved is saved on the basis of Jesus Christ's atoning work. There can be no whittling down of his nature or his work. He is Lord of all.[23]

Luke's Openness

Pinnock takes his cue from Luke's writing and attitudes as revealed in the Book of Acts. In particular, his theology on this matter stems

21. Ibid., p. 10.
22. Ibid., p. 11.
23. Ibid., pp. 13–14; idem, "The Finality of Jesus Christ in a World of Religions," in *Christian Faith and Practice in the Modern World: Theology from an Evangelical Point of View*, ed. Mark A. Noll and David F. Wells (Grand Rapids: Eerdmans, 1988), p. 157; John Sanders, *No Other Name: An Investigation into the Destiny of the Unevangelized* (Grand Rapids: Eerdmans, 1992), p. 215.

from the combination in Luke of the finality of Christ and a remarkable openness to people of other faiths. He is not trying to use Luke anachronistically, but rather as reflecting a certain perspective and attitude. He is using Luke only to give his remarks focus, but drawing on other Scriptures to prove his case as well.[24]

Pinnock calls attention to Luke's handling of the account of the conversion of Cornelius as an example of this openness. A further instance would be the account of Paul's speech at the Areopagus. The problem then becomes how Luke can combine such an openness with his commitment to the finality of Jesus. He believes this can be comprehended if we understand two presuppositions that Luke possessed.[25]

General Revelation

One of these presuppositions is that Luke believed in a form of revelation accessible to all persons, which then served as a point of contact for evangelism. Contrary to Barth, says Pinnock, the knowledge of God is not limited to those places where biblical revelation has penetrated. There are numerous examples of those who had this broader source of knowledge. Melchizedek is an example, according to Pinnock, who apparently believes that Melchizedek came to his status through general revelation. Evidently God had more plans afoot than the plan he shared with Abraham. Failure to recognize this "Melchizedek factor" keeps many believers from recognizing the breadth of God's working. Pinnock says: "It seems to me that the reason traditional Christians often refuse to recognize genuine piety outside the church is because they persist in ignoring the scriptural truth symbolized by Melchizedek, and this creates in them a brittleness, rigidity, and narrowness in the presence of non-Christian people."[26]

Sanders emphasizes that inclusivists see general revelation as one means by which God mediates his saving grace. They insist that general revelation is salvific because its source is the saving God. The knowledge of God is always saving knowledge. It is, of course, not general revelation that does the saving. That is the work of God. Can God save through this means, or is this only a means by which he condemns? Sanders quotes with approval from Dale Moody, who questions what kind of a God would make enough known about himself to make persons guilty, but not to save them. Rather, people can be saved or lost, depending on their response to general revelation.[27] Among the texts

24. Pinnock, "Finality of Jesus Christ," pp. 153–54.
25. Ibid., p. 158.
26. Ibid., p. 159.
27. Sanders, *No Other Name*, p. 233.

that bear witness to God's existence and power are Acts 14:17; Psalm 19:1; and Romans 10:18.

Inclusivists place a number of qualifications on the extent and efficacy of general revelation, according to Sanders. First, they in no way are seeking to demean special revelation. Rather, this is not the only instance of revelation, and the other should not be ignored. Second, the knowledge of God obtained from general revelation is not simply the accomplishment of human reasoning. It is through God's instruction that they know him (Rom. 1:19). In other words, this knowledge is an obtainment, not an attainment. Third, inclusivists are clear that no one is saved by his or her own efforts. Just as no Jew ever lives up to the law given by special revelation, no pagan ever lives up to the law given within by God. The Gentiles who acknowledge God and do his will (Rom. 2:14–16), do so not by good works, but on the basis of general revelation come to a place of repentance and anguish for their sins. Fourth, inclusivists do not deny the universal sinfulness of humanity. The depictions of the ungodliness of all persons, in Romans and elsewhere, are taken seriously.[28]

Pinnock also makes much of the Noachic covenant, which was made with all flesh (Gen. 9:17). According to Jewish theology this universal covenant "expresses itself in the conscience, in certain basic moral commandments being written on the heart."[29] Surely this is behind Paul's statement in Romans 2:14–16, about the law written on the heart. The Old Testament underscores God's liberality toward other people, such as Amos's statement from God likening his treatment of Israel to that of the Philistines and the Syrians. Evangelicals, however, have tended to conceal God's generosity, being uncomfortable with the fact that Daniel expected Nebuchadnezzar to know and respect the God of heaven, and the fact that the pagan sailors on Jonah's boat feared God and sacrificed to him. Supposedly to protect the uniqueness of God we have suppressed the positive witness to the universal revelation. We find it difficult to say that Jesus is the light that lightens everyone coming into the world, as John asserted in John 1:9.[30]

There still is a major problem, according to Pinnock. A large percentage of the human race has lived its life with only general revelation. If one assumes, as he does, that Christ provided redemption for such persons, how does that become effectual for them? He mentions the contention of some that God is within his sovereign rights to judge these people on the basis of their sins. He is not impressed with this argument, for this is not

28. Ibid., pp. 234–36.
29. Pinnock, "Finality of Jesus Christ," p. 159.
30. Ibid., pp. 159–60.

the issue. The problem is this: God indicates that he desires to save these, as well as all other humans. How can he save them, if there is salvation only where the gospel is effectually preached?[31]

The issue first is whether anyone can be and is saved on the basis of this general revelation. It appears to Pinnock that evangelicalism has been inclined to grant the reality of general revelation, while at the same time showing great reluctance to acknowledge that someone could be saved through it, the idea that it could do anyone any good or was intended to. He finds this appalling and is offended by the idea that a God who loves sinners and desires to save them merely tantalizes them with truth about himself that does not lead them to salvation, but only to great condemnation.[32] On this subject, he declares frankly that he finds the statements of Vatican II more evangelical than the overcautious or even niggardly comments of his fellow traditional Protestants. In fact, this tradition has a great deal to answer for in terms of turning multitudes away from listening to the Good News.[33] It seems strange to him that evangelical theologians have been willing to engage in conversations with non-Christian philosophers in building up their categories, but have not similarly welcomed conversations with persons of faith from the world religions. He asks, "Why do we look so hopefully to Plato and expect nothing from Buddha?"[34]

What is the actual benefit of this general revelation? Pinnock insists that God does have regard for faith in him, "even when it is forced to rely upon defective and incomplete information." This is indicated by Hebrews 11:6, which says that "God rewards them that diligently seek him." God is able to take account of faith, even if it arises in a person in a pagan context. Among those in this classification Pinnock mentions Abraham, Melchizedek, Jethro, Job, Abimelech, Naaman, and Balaam. All of these had faith in God even though they lived outside the range of Israel's revelation. If this was the case, then Pinnock asks, should not we so understand people who today stand spiritually "before Christ," even though they are chronologically "Anno Domini"? He endorses the position of Anderson regarding the possibility of a saving faith "in the shadows." He says, "Just as the Jews before Christ were saved in the context of shadows of the true and on the basis of a redemption yet to be revealed, so these others with so much less information to rely on can have called out to God to save them."[35]

31. Ibid., pp. 162–63.
32. Ibid., p. 160.
33. Ibid., p. 161.
34. Ibid., p. 159.
35. Ibid., p. 163.

Pinnock claims that this is what Paul is saying in Romans. To be sure, on the basis of that writing it is clear that persons possess enough knowledge of God so that they are without excuse and thus are justly condemned if they reject it. The converse is also true, however. They possess enough light so that it is possible for them to renounce their sin and seek God, even if ignorant of Christ's provision for their sins. The text does say that on the day of judgment their consciences may "accuse *or perhaps excuse* them."[36]

The Melchizedek Factor

One of the most vigorously put elements in Pinnock's argument is the "Melchizedek factor." He criticizes those like J. I. Packer, who conclude that if any good pagan came so far as to throw himself on his Maker's mercy for pardon, it would be grace that had brought him there; God would surely save anyone whom he had brought that far, but we cannot be certain whether God actually saves anyone in that way. Pinnock's response to the data is quite different: "For my part I am bold to declare that on the basis of the evidence of the Melchizedek factor I referred to earlier God most certainly does save people in this way. I do not know how many, but I hope for multitudes."[37] His objection to the traditional Protestant treatment of general revelation is that it overlooks the Melchizedek factor and places most or all of its emphasis on the negative side of the ledger. We must, however, says Pinnock, remember that Melchizedek worshiped the true God before meeting Abraham, and that Jethro, a Midianite priest, knew God and even instructed Moses before he learned of Israel's commission. Pinnock comments that God is known throughout the whole world because of his mighty acts in creation, and the supreme revelation in Christ is not the sole revelation of God.[38]

Pinnock does issue a cautionary word, however. He feels that it is possible to let this insight get out of hand. He would call Jethro a pre-Christian believer, but not an anonymous Christian. We cannot say, from the evidence, that Jethro enjoyed the benefits of knowing Christ and had no need of ever meeting Christ in a fulfilled relationship. He feels that Karl Rahner has gone much too far in endorsing the other religions as channels of salvation. He says, "We cannot say anything that would create the impression that there are some who do not need to repent and believe the gospel."[39]

36. Ibid., pp. 163–64.
37. Ibid., p. 164.
38. Ibid.
39. Ibid., p. 165.

The Hermeneutical Role of Control Beliefs

In his most recent book, Pinnock ostensibly takes his approach from the perspective of hermeneutics. Actually, he gives considerable play to one of the control beliefs that governs much of his interpretation of the Bible. He states, "The foundation of my theology of religions is a belief in the unbounded generosity of God revealed in Jesus Christ."[40] Here, as in so many areas, the doctrine of God is fundamental. What kind of a God is he? Is he the kind that can sit back while large numbers perish, or is he the kind to seek them out patiently and tirelessly? Does he take pleasure and get glory from the damnation of sinners, as some traditions maintain, or is he appalled and saddened by the prospect? Pinnock believes the issue is quite clearly dealt with in Scripture. Three passages are especially determinative. Peter says in 2 Peter 3:9, "[God] is patient with you, not wanting anyone to perish, but everyone to come to repentance." Two references from Paul are equally clear and unequivocal: "[God] wants all men to be saved and to come to a knowledge of the truth" (1 Tim. 2:4); "For God has bound all men over to disobedience so that he may have mercy on them all" (Rom. 11:32).

Pinnock interprets the various portions of Scripture in light of this control belief. He contends that people may come to Scripture with fundamentally an optimistic or a pessimistic attitude, which will go far toward determining the nature of their understanding of the Bible. God, in Pinnock's judgment, is committed to full racial salvation. The God in whom we have placed our trust will not be satisfied until there is a healing of the nations and an innumerable host of redeemed people around the throne. Biblical grounds for such optimism are found in passages such as Revelation 7:9; 21:24–26; and 22:2–6.

Various features of the doctrine of God are found in the Old Testament passages, leading to the conclusion of the universality not only of his love but of his redemptive work. In addition, the New Testament gives abundant evidence of this breadth of God's concern. Jesus is the cosmic Christ (Col. 1:16–17). He is the last Adam, representing the human race in his redemption as the first had done in his sin, and thus being the Savior of the whole world. His resurrection gives life to all (1 Cor. 15:22). The picture of the culmination of history is breath-taking, with God making all things new (Rev. 21:24–30).[41]

What, however, of the problematic passages? How are they to be handled within a hermeneutic of this type? One of these is the Book of Romans, especially the early portions, which seem to conflict with Acts. That

40. Pinnock, *Wideness in God's Mercy*, p. 18.
41. Ibid., pp. 33–34.

may not be so, however, according to Pinnock. It would be if we read it on a pessimistic basis, but that may not be necessary. Note what Paul does say in that book. In 1:19–20, he emphasizes that God has made his power and deity known to all men. In 2:14–16, he adds that God has made his moral law known to all, through writing it on their hearts. Paul is insisting that all have access to the truth. He is also teaching that no one is able to save himself apart from God's redemptive work. It would be wrong, however, to conclude that he is denying that there have been many Jews and Gentiles in the past who have responded positively to God on the basis of this light, as Luke intimates in the Book of Acts.[42]

The other seemingly difficult passage is Matthew 7:14, which appears to contend that few will be saved and emphasizes the narrowness of the way and the difficulty of entering it. Pinnock says we must recognize that Jesus was urging his disciples to avoid speculation, and to choose the hard and unpopular path. At this time, of course, they were but few in number. We cannot take these passages alone, however. We must bear in mind that Jesus gave his disciples many other promises about the largeness of the hope. Thus, this text cannot be used to cancel out the many texts that speak of God's generosity.[43]

Evaluation

Positive

This position has attracted some strong reaction, both positive and negative. We note that there are a number of very perceptive and helpful aspects of this system.

1. In the thought of Pinnock and Sanders, in particular, there is conscious awareness of the role that a central theological theme plays in the approach to interpretation of the Bible and to theological construction. Certainly, where there are ambiguous passages, or one must choose which of two or more competing passages to emphasize, our basic theological convictions come into play, whether consciously or unconsciously, to the degree that we attempt to be logically consistent. The virtue of these men's work is that they are conscious of their "control beliefs," as they term them, and the role these beliefs play in their hermeneutical and theological constructions. To be conscious of this factor is to limit its illegitimate or uncontrolled influence.

42. Ibid., p. 33.
43. Ibid., p. 154.

2. This theology takes seriously the concept of those who have not heard the gospel nonetheless being "without excuse," as Paul put it in Romans 1:20. Some exclusivists seem to formulate their view in such a way that persons are held responsible for something over which they had absolutely no control. On both textual and logical grounds, this presents real difficulty. The inclusivists have endeavored to take such considerations into account.

3. This is a definite effort to give a theological basis for the salvation of all who according to Scripture are saved. This particularly applies to the Old Testament believers, at least some of whom certainly experienced redemption, yet without having very detailed knowledge of the one who was the object of their faith and the basis of their salvation.

4. This approach is consistent with the principle frequently followed elsewhere in theological interpretation by numerous theologians, that the amount that must be believed is proportionate to the amount known.

5. There is a correct critique of the use sometimes made of the exclusivist passages. In some cases, as these theologians have pointed out, the Scripture simply says that those who believe on the Lord Jesus Christ are saved, but does not say that these are the only ones saved. The latter statement is sometimes illegitimately inferred from the former statement.

Negative

Some significant problems remain for this approach.

1. The principle of control beliefs is not sufficiently scrutinized. There is a tendency to allow it not simply to shed light on ambiguous passages, but also to control the interpretation of those passages that would otherwise be interpreted quite differently. There is no really critical discussion of how and why one adopts a given control belief, or under what conditions one modifies such a belief or even replaces it with another principle or motif. Thus, instead of being integrating or interpretive principles, these control beliefs may actually come to be distorting principles.

2. A specific instance of this is concerned with the nature of divine love. The concept of persons being condemned without having been exposed to the specially revealed gospel is abhorrent to Pinnock. This assumes a certain conception of divine love that needs to be made explicit and argued for at length.

3. There is in the thought of both Pinnock and Sanders a failure to distinguish between possibility and actuality, in a certain sense. They both seem to assume that if something can happen, sooner or later it must happen, or that, vice versa, if something does not happen it must be because it is impossible. That, however, is an inadequate analysis of the factors. While these men may be right, the issue should be overtly faced, dealt with, and their position argued for, rather than, in effect, simply assuming their view.

4. Closely related to this question is a failure to distinguish two separate issues: how people are saved and how many are saved. So Sanders, for example, expresses surprise that exclusivists expect large numbers to be saved, while questioning the authenticity of the inclusiveness of those inclusivists who wonder how many, if any, will be saved. These are two distinct questions, and the failure to distinguish between them contributes to the confusion displayed within this theology.

5. The question of how Melchizedek came to belief in the God of Israel is glossed over. By citing him as an evidence for the wider hope through general revelation these theologians commit themselves to the idea that his knowledge of God came through that means. Yet it is at least logically possible that God manifested himself to Melchizedek, just as he did to Abraham, but that we simply have no biblical record of that. Such an issue is not really dealt with. As it turns out, the position taken is an instance of question begging.

6. There also is a problem with the status of Cornelius, the other major biblical character cited in support of inclusivism on the basis of general revelation. These inclusivists insist that Cornelius was already a believer before talking to Peter. Yet Peter, in recounting the story in the following chapter, quotes the angel as saying to Cornelius, "He [Peter] will bring you a message through which you and all your household will be saved" (Acts 11:14). This would suggest that he was not a saved person prior to the conversation with Peter. In addition, the angel's appearance to Cornelius certainly must be considered special revelation. Sanders is aware of these objections, yet does not really give an adequate response, nor does Pinnock. Sanders' response in effect maintains that all "God-fearers" were saved. Those "God-fearers," however, had already been exposed to special revelation, and "God-fearers" also seem to be required to take some additional action.

7. There is considerable ambiguity regarding the signification of the biblical concept of salvation. Both Pinnock and Sanders wish to

treat it in a broad sense, including more than what many modern evangelicals believe by it. So Pinnock, for example, deals with Acts 4:10–11 by understanding salvation there to include physical healing. The text does not say that, however. In response to the question by what power or in what name they have healed, Peter responds with the statement about Christ. Not all who were healed physically were saved (in the spiritual sense of regeneration and justification), and not all who were saved in this latter sense were healed. Neither here nor elsewhere in Scripture, such as in Jesus' ministry, are these declared to be inseparable. To equate them has the effect of enlarging the problem of evil, for there are many otherwise devout believers who are not delivered from physical ailments. Pinnock seems to endorse the idea that atonement includes healing as well as spiritual salvation,[44] but without dealing with the considerable difficulties associated with that view.

8. There are logical leaps in the argument at a number of places. One of the most glaring comes in the treatment of Melchizedek. By claiming him as a case of salvation through general revelation, Pinnock argues for the salvation of some who have never heard the gospel explicitly. He then, however, leaps to the hope for a multitude being saved this way, but without offering evidence for the transition from one to many.

9. A number of issues connected with the role of general revelation are not adequately treated. There is a tendency to assume that if there is a valid general revelation, persons will arrive at a knowledge of God through it, or in more technical terms, natural theology will result from general revelation. This, however, requires a number of additional premises or assumptions, such as the integrity of the human personality, despite sin, and the correspondence of the human knowing mechanism to the world, which is the locus of general revelation. These are simply not dealt with adequately.

10. Carl F. H. Henry has contended that the analogy of the salvation of persons in our time who do not hear the gospel to the Old Testament believers overlooks the fact of the latter's benefit from special revelation. This particular point is not sufficiently responded to by these inclusivists.[45]

44. Pinnock, "Acts 4:12—No Other Name under Heaven," in *Through No Fault of Their Own? The Fate of Those Who Have Never Heard*, ed. William V. Crockett and James G. Sigountos (Grand Rapids: Baker, 1991), p. 109, n. 6.

45. Carl F. H. Henry, *God, Revelation, and Authority*, vol. 6, *God Who Stands and Stays* (Waco, Tex.: Word, 1983), p. 369.

11. There is at times a disturbing ad hominem treatment of those who are not similarly inclusivist. So, for example, Pinnock questions the legitimacy of the designation of evangelical for "those who seem to want to ensure that there is as little Good News as possible."[46] The assumption is that the evidence for the wideness of grace is so indisputable that it must be sheer unwillingness on the part of these theologians to allow anyone else to be saved. The possibility of a genuine disagreement over what the Bible teaches is ignored in favor of such an accusation.

46. Pinnock, *Wideness in God's Mercy,* p. 163.

Part **3**

The Issues

8

General Revelation

The topic of general revelation is an important consideration for deciding between the positions of exclusivism and inclusivism. Both views consider the Christian religion normative and the only basis of salvation. This means that there must be at least some minimal knowledge of Christianity's content, sufficient for a faith that would enable one to receive God's grace. The first issue, then, is how much of Christian truth can really be known from general revelation, apart from special revelation. The second issue, to be examined in the following chapter, is how much must one know and believe in order to be saved.

It is apparent that special revelation will not come to everyone, if for no other reason than that it has not come to everyone who has lived up until the present time. If, however, general revelation is, as its definition would seem to indicate, available to everyone, then is it possible that through general revelation some who do not have special revelation may be saved? This of course raises a number of questions about the relationship of special revelation to general revelation. What does special revelation do or supply that general revelation does not? Are there cases where special revelation is not needed?

Views of General Revelation

Natural Theology

A variety of positions with respect to general revelation have been held over the years. The classical Roman Catholic position, deriving from Thomas Aquinas, divides reality into two realms, nature and grace. Reason deals with the realm of nature, whereas faith relates to the realm of grace. In the lower realm of nature are certain tenets that can be proved by reason to any rational person willing to examine the evidence, including such matters as the existence of God and the divine origin of the Catholic Church. Other matters, however, are the object of revelation, such as the doctrines of the Trinity and the incarnation. These cannot be discovered or proved by reason, but must be taken by faith.

Christomonism

A radically different position is that of Karl Barth, who insisted that any revelation is in effect redemptive. There is not, and cannot be, any revelation independent of Jesus Christ. If that were the case, then it would be possible to know something about God independent of the revelation in Christ, and that knowledge would have redemptive effect. It would also be the accomplishment of the person who possesses it. Consequently, the principle of salvation by grace would be, at least to a small degree, compromised.

Spectacles of Faith

John Calvin's position is intermediate between these two. According to his understanding, there is an objective, genuine, rational, general revelation, present whether anyone perceives and responds to it or not. Sin, however, has obscured humans' ability to recognize the truth that is present. Faith and salvation, however, restore the ability to perceive the truth. Calvin speaks of the "spectacles of faith," which enable a person to see clearly that which sin had obscured.

Eternity in Their Hearts

A more recent variety of understanding is the "eternity in their hearts" view. This is an empirically based theory, derived from observation of actual humans, who have never heard the gospel or received special revelation but nonetheless hold a belief quite similar in many features to the Christian message. This belief does not include the exact details of the gospel with the correct identification of the Son of God as Jesus of Nazareth, however. When presented with the gospel, these people respond, often with an exclamation such as, "This is what we have been waiting for," or "Why haven't you come sooner?" It is not necessarily held that such persons were already saved or regenerated prior to hearing the gospel. This internal knowledge of God is believed to be excellent preparation for the biblical message, however.

Implicit Faith

Another relatively recent interpretation of the doctrine of general revelation is known as "implicit faith." According to this theory, it is possible, on the basis of general revelation, to come to a knowledge of the outlines, or the contours, of the gospel. This would mean, for example, that there is a God, that he is a powerful and holy God, and that he expects the same sort of holiness from us. Such an understanding would include the belief that one was a sinner. Given that understanding, one would then, presumably, throw oneself upon the mercy of God. Salvation would be granted, but on the basis of Christ's work. In such a pattern, there is no question of salvation by works. Even the discovery of the truth is not one's own doing. Both this and the justification of the sinner are wholly of grace.

Several types of evidence are appealed to in seeking to determine how much can be known from general revelation. The first is biblical teachings. Here the major passages are the nature psalms, such as Psalm 19 and 104; Acts 14 and 17; and Romans 1 and 2. The second type of data includes biblical case studies of persons who seem to have become believers prior to exposure to special revelation. A third type of argument consists of inferences from other doctrines, the most prominent being the nature of divine love as requiring that all be given some means to saving faith, and the idea of justice, that unless people could believe, there is no just basis for their being condemned. The fourth area of evidence is empirical cases encountered especially by missionaries of persons who already seem to have a belief in the same God found in the Bible.

Biblical Passages

Nature Psalms

The logical place to begin is the biblical teachings themselves. One set of passages often consulted as helpful in this matter consists of a number of psalms, such as Psalm 19 and Psalm 104, generally referred to as "nature psalms" because of their reference to God's presence and action in the creation as revealing his nature. The major significance is their indication of what they set forth about God, namely, his power, glory, and creative and providential working. Their usefulness for our purposes is somewhat limited, however. The reason is that they are subjective expressions of praise for God's nature and acts, on the basis of the knowledge of him from general revelation, rather than discussions of the phenomenon of general revelation as such. Further, they are expressions by persons who, as believers, are probably acquainted with special revelation. Thus, it is not really possible to deduce from this what a person who has never been exposed to God's special revelation would find in the creation. We will not, therefore, examine these psalms in detail.

Acts 14:15–17

A major passage bearing on our concerns is Paul's speech to the people of Lystra in Acts 14. Based upon the miracle that Paul and Barnabas had worked, these Lycaoanian-speaking residents took them for gods. When Paul and Barnabas heard what was going on, they protested vigorously that they also were human beings with similar feelings. They indicated that they had come to bring the good news to these people. They then set this in context: "In past generations [God] allowed all the nations to go their own ways; yet he did not leave himself without witness, for he did you good, sending you rain from heaven and seasons of fruitfulness, satisfying you with food and rejoicing" (vv. 16–17). Here Paul and Barnabas indicate that God had permitted what sounds to be a common reaction, of going their own way, failing to heed his testimony and his appeal. Even throughout this, God continued to give a witness to himself, which here is especially identified with his providential regular working in providing for their needs: through sending rain and fruitful harvest, giving them food and rejoicing. Note here that the major substance of the revelation appears to be the goodness of God.

Acts 17:22–31

Another expression in a speech by Paul is found in his remarkable address at the Areopagus in Athens, as recorded in Acts 17. Here Paul takes note of the large numbers of deities these persons worshiped, including one called "the unknown God." This caused Paul great distress (v. 16). He then proceeds to tell them about this God, the creator of everything (v. 24) and the one from whom all humans receive life, breath, and everything (v. 25). He is sovereign over the affairs of nations, appointing the times and places of various nations and peoples (v. 26). He is spiritual, not dwelling in temples made with hands (v. 24). He also is not dependent on humans for anything. He accepts service from them, but not because of a need on his part (v. 25). Paul assumes that they have correctly identified the true God, but that they have not really known him. This is, as their label indicates, "the unknown God." They are in need of instruction regarding this one. There is a point of reservation in Paul's statement, however, revealed in the grammatical usage. His statements about this God are in the neuter rather than the masculine gender, "what" rather than "who." Bruce sees in this a qualification of any endorsement of their unknown God as equivalent to the God whom Paul intends to declare to them. Bruce says,

> This God whom they venerated, said Paul, while they confessed their ignorance of his identity, was the God whom he now proposed to make known to them. But he did not express himself quite so personally, as if

unreservedly identifying the "unknown god" of the inscription with the God whom he proclaimed. He used neuter, not masculine, forms: "what therefore you worship as unknown, this I proclaim to you" (RSV). Since they acknowledged their ignorance of the divine nature, he would tell them the truth about it.[1]

Romans 1:18–32

Romans 1:18–32 is especially pertinent. Here a positive teaching is inserted in a passage that is primarily speaking of God's judgment. It should be noted that the whole context is one in which the framework is oriented to the objective character of things. This is true, for example, of God's wrath. Note, says Barclay, that Paul never speaks of God being angry, but of the wrath of God as something objective. This is despite the fact that he speaks of God's love and his being loving, his fidelity and his being faithful, and his graciously giving. Paul is saying that if we look at the world, suffering follows sin. Whenever one breaks God's laws, negative results follow. If you break the laws of agriculture, the harvest fails; if you break the laws of architecture, your building collapses; if you break the laws of health, your body suffers.[2]

It appears, furthermore, that the witness possesses a clarity, sufficient in itself. If there is any problem with the perception of the witness, it is not with the witness itself. Calvin, for example, said, "We must, therefore, make this distinction, that the manifestation of God by which He makes His glory known among His creatures is sufficiently clear as far as its own light is concerned. It is, however, inadequate on account of our blindness. But we are not so blind that we can plead ignorance without being convicted of perversity."[3]

Verse 19 refers to that which may be known (τὸ γνωστὸν). Most generally this word refers to what can be known, but in the New Testament it usually refers to what actually is known. If it bore that meaning here, however, it would constitute a tautology, saying, in effect, that what is known is known. Thus, it probably should be rendered here as what can be known. It is plain "in them." This, of course, might be understood as an inward revelation, as in chapter 2. The "manifest in them" is not to be confused with the reference in chapter 2. This is simply the fact that understanding takes place within human beings, rather than that they are the locus of the revelation. There is another dimension to Paul's use of this preposition. Paul uses it a great deal; in fact, 988 of the 2,713 New Testament uses are in Paul's writings, although his material con-

---

1. F. F. Bruce, *The Book of the Acts* (Grand Rapids: Eerdmans, 1988), p. 336.
2. William Barclay, *The Epistle to the Romans* (Philadelphia: Westminster, 1975), pp. 25–28.
3. John Calvin, *Commentaries on the Epistle of Paul to the Romans and the Thessalonians,* trans. Ross Mackenzie (Grand Rapids: Eerdmans, 1961), p. 31.

stitutes only 215 pages out of 895 pages in the New Testament Greek text. Thus, 36.4 percent of the occurrences are in Paul's writings, although those are only 24 percent of the corpus. The relative frequency of his use of the preposition is 50 percent higher than the overall frequency or 80 percent higher than the usage in the rest of the New Testament. From this, Leon Morris draws the conclusion that Paul's heavy usage should lend us some interpretive insight. He says: "He seems to use it almost from habit, and we cannot always insist on a precise meaning. Since the grammarians usually regard it here as equivalent to the dative case, we should accept *to them* as the meaning."[4]

These things are then said to be made clear. The words φανερόν and ἐφανέρωσεν speak of what is outward or made clear. It is objectively present. There is an open or public notice, according to Bauer. He says of this adjective, "visible, clear, plainly to be seen, open, plain, evident, known."[5] It refers to what is outward or obvious, as contrasted with what is not so self-evident, the interior things.[6] Paul seems to be saying that the things that cannot be seen or observed are (or have been) clearly perceived. This means to perceive or grasp with the reason the things that in themselves cannot be observed with the physical eye of perception.

What is it, however, which is thus perceived? It is God's power, which is a specific attribute. The word used here for God's nature is an unusual one, appearing only here in the New Testament. Sanday and Headlam say it "is a summary term for those other attributes which constitute Divinity."[7] Leon Morris says of this statement, "Paul is laying it down that what is revealed is God himself. In nature we see something of nature's God."[8]

This revealing activity is general or universal. It is not, unlike special revelation, just to a few persons at a particular time and place. Rather, it is to all people. E. H. Gifford explains this grammatically: "The sentence, '*For the invisible things of him . . . are clearly seen. . . ,*' is an explanation of the statement **God manifested it unto them**; and as the mode in which this manifestation *was made to them* is the mode in which it *is made* to all men, at all times, the explanation is put in the

4. Leon Morris, *The Epistle to the Romans* (Grand Rapids: Eerdmans, 1988), p. 80.

5. Walter Bauer, *A Greek-English Lexicon of the New Testament and Other Early Christian Literature,* trans. William F. Arndt and F. Wilbur Gingrich (Chicago: University of Chicago Press, 1979), p. 852.

6. Aída Besançon Spencer, "Romans 1: Finding God in Creation," in *Through No Fault of Their Own? The Fate of Those Who Have Never Heard* (Grand Rapids: Baker, 1991), p. 126.

7. See Morris, *Romans*, pp. 81–82.

8. Ibid., p. 82.

most general and abstract form (Present Tense and Passive Voice), without any limitation of time or persons."[9]

There is not a positive response to this revelation, however. Instead, the recipients of this revelation fail to respond to, accept, acknowledge, or live up to this knowledge. They should have glorified and thanked God because of this knowledge. Rather, they transformed the means or channels of revelation into idols. They took the things that conveyed him and put those in the place of God himself (v. 23).

This reaction to general revelation results in judgment. Three times Paul says that God "gave them over": "in the sinful desires of their hearts to sexual impurity for the degrading of their bodies with one another" (v. 24); to "shameful lusts" (v. 26); "to a depraved mind, to do what ought not to be done" (v. 28). God, in other words, abandoned them to the ways they had chosen. Thus it is that "the wrath of God is being revealed from heaven against their wickedness" (v. 18).

There is debate over whether the judgment is to be understood as the result or the purpose of the manifestation. The Greek expression in verse 20 is εἰς τὸ plus the infinitive. This is a characteristic expression of Paul. According to Moulton, the expression appears three times in Matthew, once each in Mark, Luke, and Acts, twice each in James and 1 Peter, eight times in Hebrews, and forty-three times in Paul. It seems to require the idea of purpose rather than result unless there is good contextual basis (as in 12:3) for seeing it as result.[10] Here, the expression can be interpreted to mean that Paul is saying that if they turn away they are without excuse (result); Paul is not referring to God's purpose that they be guilty.

By way of summary, then, it appears clear that Paul is teaching that there is available, clearly and distinctly, to every person, a manifestation of God's existence and something of his nature. Yet, at least so far as his statement here is concerned, it seems to result only in rejection and suppression of the truth. Indeed, the very truth itself is distorted and perverted. The impression given is that this is universal, although the description does not seem to fit literally all persons' behavior. What is missing from the passage is any reference to persons coming to saving knowledge on the basis of general revelation. There may be those who respond positively, but Paul makes no mention of them.

Romans 2:14–16

In Romans 2:14–16 Paul speaks of Gentiles who do not have the law but do by nature the things required by the law. They are, he says, a law

9. E. H. Gifford, *Epistle of Paul to the Romans* (London: John Murray, 1886), p. 63.
10. Morris, *Romans*, pp. 82–83, n. 225.

for themselves, even though they do not have the law. They show that the "requirements of the law are written on their hearts" (v. 15). What are we to make of these statements? Do they indicate that it is possible that some Gentiles, even though they do not have the law of Moses, are saved by works, because they fulfill the requirements of that law that is conveyed to them inwardly?

It would seem, based on examination of other statements of Paul, that this view cannot be maintained. It seems simply impossible to square such statements with anything he writes on the subject elsewhere, such as Romans 3:20a, 28; 4:5; Galatians 2:16; 3:1–14, especially verse 11. That verse says, "Clearly, no one is justified before God by the law, because, 'The righteous will live by faith.'" The thrust of these several references seems to be that no one, not even those who have the Mosaic law, are or can be saved this way, that is, by fulfillment of the law.

If the idea that these are Gentiles who fulfill the law is not sustainable, what about the interpretation that this passage is referring to Gentile Christians? They do the law, but without having the formal law. Douglas Moo objects to this interpretation on several grounds, one of which is that this "doing by nature" is contrary to how a believer fulfills the law. While Gentile Christians certainly fulfill the law (Rom. 8:4), they do it through the Spirit, not "by nature" (φύσει), a word which Moo maintains "alludes to natural, inborn capacities."[11] Moo, however, fails to wrestle with the problem of the syntax of the sentence, on the basis of which a number of commentators such as Bengel hold that Paul is saying that the Gentiles are by nature without the law.[12] Morris feels that we must leave the matter open.[13]

Moo also contends that this interpretation requires us to assume that what Paul really means by people being saved by doing good or obeying the law is that they are saved by their faith, which is manifested or proved by their doing good. This, however, is a big assumption, because Paul appears to be saying that it is the doing itself that is the criterion for God's judgment.[14] This may be sufficient for an exegete or biblical theologian. A systematic theologian, however, must ask how to deal with the same type of problem in the scene of the great judgment in Matthew 25:31–46. If we do not adopt such an interpretation there, we seem to be in direct contradiction to the clear statements of Paul re-

11. Douglas Moo, "Romans 2: Saved Apart from the Gospel?" in *Through No Fault of Their Own? The Fate of Those Who Have Never Heard*, p. 141.

12. John Albert Bengel, *Gnomon of the New Testament* II (New York: Revell, 1866), pp. 227–28.

13. Morris, *Romans*, p. 124, n. 80.

14. Moo, "Romans 2," p. 141.

ferred to above, to the effect that no one is saved by works. Yet, having said all this, the Gentile Christian interpretation appears somewhat strained, to say the least.

The final major interpretation of this passage is what is often referred to as the hypothetical view. This interpretation notes that Paul is dealing with the question of the standard by which God judges persons in the eschatological judgment. He is not trying to tell us how a person is saved, but his aim is to demonstrate the righteousness of God's judgment. On this basis, the passage is not asserting that anyone ever fulfills the law. Rather, it may be that some Gentiles, even though they do not have the full and formal law of Moses, at points fulfill it. They cannot plead their excuse for failure to fulfill it completely on the basis of not having the law. This, then, is a hypothetical situation. If those who did not have the law were to fulfill it nonetheless, they could, in the judgment, pass judgment on the Jews who do have the law. This is not actually the case, however. Paul is not saying that any actually do this.

We must take a closer look at what is being asserted in this passage, and evaluate it in the light of other theological considerations, as found in other passages of Scripture, and in particular, other affirmations by Paul. We must ask the meaning of the "conscience" referred to in verse 16. F. F. Bruce points out that this is not a classical Greek term; rather, it appeared in the language only shortly before the New Testament. He says, "It meant 'consciousness of right or wrong doing,' but Paul uses it (and perhaps he was the first to do so) in the sense of an independent witness within, which examines and passes judgment on one's conduct. In Christians this examination and judgment are specially accurate because their conscience is enlightened by the Holy Spirit (cf. ix:I)."[15] Bruce seems to be saying that this is a matter of moral consciousness, that is, an awareness of the moral dimension or moral consideration of the judgment.

Is this, then, an inward knowing of the content of the law, that is, of what the law specifies to be right and wrong? It does not appear that Paul is saying anything this definite. Rather, it may be merely that the person possesses a consciousness of right and wrong, that is, the sense of there being an objective difference between the things that are right and the things that are wrong. This means that the difference between right and wrong is something other than merely what is expedient and what is inexpedient. Something is wrong when it is contrary to the way things ought to be, whether one suffers any adverse effects or not.

---

15. F. F. Bruce, *The Letter of Paul the Apostle to the Romans: An Introduction and Commentary* (Grand Rapids: Eerdmans, 1985), p. 91.

This contention also fits the data of anthropology. Here we do not find universal agreement on what is right and what is wrong among and across societies. While anthropologists differ greatly regarding the extent of agreement of different societies' moral codes, it is apparent that rather significant differences are present. What we do find, however, is a universal impulse of the sense (the consciousness) that there is such a thing as right and wrong, and that one ought to do the right and avoid the wrong. This explains the universal constructing of moral codes. The only real exceptions to this tendency to make moral judgments and codes would be psychopaths and sociopaths, persons who lack any real moral consciousness, being somehow defective in their personalities or characters. This, however, is not evidence against the universal possession of the moral consciousness, any more than the fact that a few persons are born without two legs negates the contention that the possession of two legs is normal for human beings.

We must ask, further, what is the real purpose or function of the law, as described in Scripture? It is not to save, for Paul seems to make clear that no one, not even the Old Testament saints, is saved this way, simply because no one can fulfill the law. Rather, according to Paul in Galatians 3:24, the law is a παιδαγωγός, given to bring us to Christ. It does this by showing us our own insufficiency, inability, and so on. If the inward impulse to the doing of the right tells one that he or she falls short, or fails to fulfill the law, then that is the indication that the person knows the law's requirement of doing right. This would not serve to make one just or aware of his or her justness. It would, rather, simply make one aware of the need of doing something in response to this sense of sin or of shortcoming.

If this is the case, then the inner moral impulse, the law written within, could serve the same function as the Mosaic or written law. That would, properly speaking, be to bring about repentance. What the law requires is perfect obedience, and, lacking that, repentance. It would, in that sense, bring an awareness of the need of divine grace, and might also cause one to cast oneself upon the mercy of God. How much one would have to know and believe for that mercy to become effective in one's life is not discussed in this passage, and will have to be the subject of a subsequent chapter. Note also that Paul does not in this passage tell us whether anyone does actually come to this state or response. He speaks of how their consciences bear witness, "their thoughts now accusing, now even defending them" (v. 15). This, he says, "will take place on the day when God will judge men's secrets through Jesus Christ," as his gospel declares (v. 16). While this seems to suggest that some are defended by their thoughts or their consciences, it is not fully clear whether this defense results in justification of the person.

Two Recent Arguments

Empirical Cases

Let us now return to examine somewhat more closely two recent positions on general revelation, in light of this exposure to the pertinent biblical texts. One that most surely deserves such scrutiny is the position of Don Richardson in his *Eternity in Their Hearts*. Richardson's appeal is not primarily to Scripture as such, but to empirical case studies of persons whom missionaries have discovered on the mission field. These persons possess a tradition that prepares them for the gospel message. Their faith is a monotheistic faith. They respond eagerly and in great numbers when the message of Christianity is brought to them.

Richardson gives a number of examples of these types of cases. One is the Karen people of Burma, who had a tradition of a book that had been lost for a long time. Their tradition also included the idea that a white man was going to bring this lost book back to them. This white foreigner was to come from the west with "white wings" (white sails). When a Karen man then came to Adoniram Judson, he became convinced that the missionary's Bible was the lost book. When George and Sarah Boardman launched a mission to southeast Burma, that convert, Ka-Thah-byu, a former robber, went to the Karen villages and preached the gospel in each of them. He urged those who wanted to learn more about the lost book and its story to go to hear Boardman speak. Huge numbers of the Karen, as well as other peoples such as the Kachins who had a similar tradition, turned to faith in Christ. It was, as a missionary to the Nagas once put it in my hearing, as if these people were prewired for the gospel and the missionaries simply "plugged in" the gospel to that circuitry.[16]

There are also customs or practices of native people that may be utilized in the presentation of the gospel message. Richardson relates his own missionary experience among the Sawi tribe in New Guinea, one of only five or six tribes in the entire world who practice both headhunting and cannibalism. Presenting the message to them was difficult because of their admiration of "masters of treachery," deceivers who put on a facade of friendship while "fattening" their victims with that friendship for a day of slaughter, which would come as a surprise to those victims. Because of this value structure, their hero worship led them to mistakenly identify Judas Iscariot, Jesus' betrayer, as the hero of the story. Jesus was a dupe taken in by Judas, and there-

---

16. Don Richardson, *Eternity in Their Hearts* (Ventura, Calif.: Regal, 1984), pp. 73–102.

fore to be laughed at. Richardson, however, discovered that the Sawi had an unusual way of making peace and forestalling outbreaks of treachery. If a Sawi father offered his son to another group as a "Peace Child," past grievances were thereby settled and future instances of treachery were prevented. This would be true, however, only so far as the Peace Child remained alive. Richardson and his wife presented Jesus Christ as the ultimate Peace Child, appealing to such biblical texts as Isaiah 9:6; John 3:16; Romans 5:10; and Hebrews 7:25. This enabled the meaning of the gospel to break through to the Sawis. When they realized that Judas had betrayed a Peace Child, they no longer viewed him as a hero, for this was, in their value system, the worst possible crime.[17]

The major point Richardson seems to emphasize in his book is the importance of being willing to utilize concepts and practices within the religion of native people as a point of contact, rather than rejecting them as totally false and as something those people must therefore abandon in order to accept Christianity's message. His contention is that God has given all people a witness of himself through general revelation in nature and in their moral makeups, which contain elements of the message of special revelation, or parallels or similarities to it.

Holy Pagans

One major component of Richardson's argument is the "Melchizedek factor." This is the idea that there are those who, on the basis of general revelation, have already become believers in the God of special revelation. These cases of the first half of the book are believed to be instances of that general revelation. The second part of the book deals with what Richardson calls the "Abraham factor," those who have special revelation available to them. He distinguishes special revelation primarily as "always associated with an inspired canonical record."[18] If the first part of the book is concerned to show how God has prepared the world for the gospel, then the second part is a demonstration of the fact that God has prepared the gospel for the world.

This Melchizedek factor also plays a prominent part in the theology of both Clark Pinnock and John Sanders. Both feel that Melchizedek, together with other believers from outside the covenant nation of Israel, such as Abimelech and Jethro, were saved on the basis of general revelation. Another example is Cornelius. Here was a Gentile "God-

17. Ibid., pp. 111–12.
18. Ibid., p. 156.

fearer," who was already a saved believer, although not a Christian, when he came to Peter.[19]

We need to evaluate and synthesize the data we have examined regarding what some term "holy pagans," beginning with an analysis and assessment of the "Melchizedek factor" or the case of Cornelius. The problem with attempting to utilize Melchizedek is that we do not really know enough about him to assign a status to him and his testimony. Pinnock, Sanders, and Richardson all claim that he possessed a knowledge of God (presumably saving) through general revelation, but without offering any evidence to that effect. How do we know that this knowledge was through general revelation rather than special revelation? May it not be that God appeared to him as he did to Abram? That God may not have appeared to him is of course also a possibility, but the point is that we do not know from the biblical text which was the case. Certainly, if this is to be used as evidence for the possibility of persons knowing Christ, there should be some clear indication of that fact.

The same problem pertains to Cornelius. Here again the inclusivists we have cited consider this a case of an outsider to the Abrahamic covenant, and as a Gentile, this is surely true. From this they draw the conclusion that he was savingly related to God on the basis of general revelation. Sanders makes much of the argument that Cornelius was already a saved person, but not a Christian, prior to his conversation with Peter, evidently considering this a crucial issue. He even quotes exclusivists such as Calvin to the effect that Cornelius was already a believer.[20] Three observations need to be made, however. The first is that Cornelius is described as a "God-fearer," a technical term in Acts for a Gentile who attended synagogue services, but was not a full proselyte, not having been circumcised. This, however, was a result of being exposed to the Jews and their beliefs. In other words, Cornelius was a recipient of the same special revelation that the Jews had as the basis of their salvation. Epistemologically, his status was the same as that of the Old Testament believers. Unless, therefore, one is prepared to say that no Jews were saved prior to hearing of Christ, one would have to say that this is not salvation on the basis of general revelation, any more than with those Jews.

The second observation is that prior to Cornelius's meeting with Peter, an angel appeared to him. To be sure, what that angel said to him seems

19. Clark Pinnock, *A Wideness in God's Mercy: The Finality of Jesus Christ in a World of Religions* (Grand Rapids: Zondervan, 1992), pp. 175-76; John Sanders, *No Other Name: An Investigation into the Destiny of the Unevangelized* (Grand Rapids: Eerdmans, 1992), p. 222.
20. Sanders, *No Other Name*, pp. 223–24.

to indicate that he had already been accepted. Such an appearance would certainly be a special revelation. It is clear, however, from this incident, that a special appearance to a Gentile was not unheard of. If this is the case here, we cannot exclude the possibility of similar prior appearances to him or to other Gentiles. In short, we can hardly make Cornelius a paradigm of saving faith exclusively through general revelation.

The final observation about Cornelius is to note Peter's recounting of the message the angel had given to Cornelius, as presumably Cornelius had told it to him. Peter says, "He told us how he had seen an angel appear in his house and say, 'Send to Joppa for Simon who is called Peter. He will bring you a message through which you and all your household will be saved'" (Acts 11:13–14). It is difficult, if this report is considered accurate and authoritative, to understand how one can maintain that Cornelius was already saved. While Pinnock does not discuss this issue, Sanders' response is that salvation has many meanings in the New Testament, and that here it means "fullness of salvation as experienced in a relationship with Christ."[21] Without further substantiation, however, this seems to be a case of begging the question. In any event, it would seem wise for Sanders not to refer to Cornelius in this same context as "saved but not yet a Christian." Even if Sanders is correct on this point, however, this is still scarcely a case of someone coming to salvation through general revelation alone.

One other person frequently mentioned as an example of general revelation is Abimelech.[22] Yet, note that God appeared to Abimelech in a dream (Gen. 20:3–7), which is generally identified as one of the modalities of special revelation.[23] Thus, Abimelech cannot be considered an instance of general revelation either.

What is interesting about Richardson's statement is that he seems to admit this while ostensibly denying it. He insists that Melchizedek is a case of general revelation. Yet he concedes that God revealed himself to men, and the enumeration of persons, description of God's action, and listing of the content of the revelation sound very much like what is usually referred to as special revelation.

> Clearly the Abrahamic covenant did not mark the first time God revealed Himself to men. Adam, Cain, Abel, Seth, Enoch, Noah, Job, and no doubt many others right on through to Abraham's contemporary, Melchizedek, had received direct communication from God. God even revealed Himself through a dream to Abimelech, a Philistine king (see Gen. 20:6). All

21. Ibid., p. 66.
22. Pinnock, *Wideness in God's Mercy*, pp. 26, 92, 94, 96; Sanders, *No Other Name*, p. 153; Richardson, *Eternity in Their Hearts*, p. 155.
23. Bernard Ramm, *Special Revelation and the Word of God* (Grand Rapids: Eerdmans, 1961), pp. 45–46.

of these prior revelations center around (1) the fact of God's existence; (2) creation; (3) the rebellion and fall of man; (4) the need for a sacrifice to appease God and the crafty attempts of devils to make men sacrifice to them; (5) the great Flood; (6) the sudden appearance of many languages and the resulting dispersion of mankind into many peoples; and finally (7) an acknowledgement of man's need of some further revelation that will seal man back into a blessed relationship with God.[24]

Richardson continues to use the term "general revelation" of this type of person. Yet it should be noted that direct appearance, such as he describes here, is ordinarily understood to be special revelation. The difficulty appears to lie in his definition of special revelation. He identifies special revelation as that which is associated with canonical Scriptures. This, however, confuses revelation and inspiration and fails to note that it is possible to have one without the other. Thus, if special revelation is defined as a particular manifestation to a specific person, then there is, as John 21:25 indicates, revelation that is not incorporated in Scripture because no biblical author was inspired to record it, assuming that the works of Jesus constituted special revelation. There also are statements of ungodly men recorded in Scripture by inspiration, which were not specially revealed to them. Where these are erroneous statements, they do not even constitute correct derivations from general revelation. We therefore conclude, with Tiénou, that Richardson has incorrectly defined special revelation.[25] Tiénou also is correct in accusing Richardson of inconsistency, because on Richardson's own (incorrect) definition of special revelation, Melchizedek should be considered an instance of special rather than general revelation, inasmuch he is included in Scripture.[26]

Conclusions

Certain conclusions can now be drawn from the investigation we have made.

1. According to Scripture, there exists a genuine, valid, objective, rational revelation of God, independent of his special revelation of himself. It has not been obliterated by the fall or by ongoing sin.
2. What can be known of the Lord is primarily his power and glory, his greatness. His moral goodness can also be discerned from the

24. Richardson, *Eternity in Their Hearts*, p. 155.
25. Tite Tiénou, "Eternity in Their Hearts?" in *Through No Fault of Their Own?*, p. 212.
26. Ibid.

law written within, and by inference one can therefore know one's own moral and spiritual standing, as being in a state of sin.

3. Rather commonly, the Scripture seems to indicate, sinners fail to know God correctly and accurately from general revelation, instead distorting and confusing what is revealed there. The effect of sin on human noetic capability is everywhere presupposed. Passages such as Romans 1:18–20; 1 Corinthians 1:18–2:5; and 2 Corinthians 4:4 teach that one effect of sin on the human is to cloud the understanding, making spiritual truth difficult to perceive and understand. This would apply to general revelation as well as to special revelation.

4. There are no unambiguous instances in Scripture of persons who became true believers through responding to general revelation alone. Scripture does not indicate how many, if any, come to salvation this way. We know too little about persons such as Melchizedek to know whether their faith was the product of general revelation alone, or whether it may have been induced by exposure to special revelation.

5. Even in Romans, the letter in which he most extensively addresses the question of general revelation, Paul urges preaching of the specially revealed gospel to all persons (chap. 10). This seems to suggest that ordinarily, general revelation is insufficient to bring persons to salvation.

6. In Scripture, the evangelistic strategy with respect to those who have some faith in God without having been exposed to the gospel appears to be to regard them as prepared for, but still in need of, the gospel.

9

Postmortem Evangelism

There is another step in the argument regarding whether those who have never heard will be saved. Perhaps, say some, those who have never heard the gospel explicitly within this lifetime will yet have a chance to hear and believe, but in the future. Perhaps there will be an opportunity beyond death, when the message will be presented. This view, which goes by various names, but will here be identified simply as "postmortem evangelism," has had something of a resurgence of interest in recent years.

Although this view has had a fairly long history, only recently has it had any sort of popularity. For much of its earlier history, it existed virtually on the fringes of Christianity. Only in the past two or three decades has there been any real interest in it within what would ordinarily be called orthodox or evangelical Christianity. It generally appears as an alternative not only to the orthodox approach, but also to the implicit faith position. It agrees with the former that faith must be explicit, that is, that faith must require a conscious understanding and acceptance of Jesus Christ. It agrees with the latter that God would be unjust and unloving to condemn anyone to eternal punishment who has not had an opportunity to hear of Christ's redemptive work. Two major types of arguments are advanced in support of this hypothesis. Some of these are presented alone as evidence for the view under consideration here. Others are components in the argument, requiring additional elements for their force.

Death Not the End of Opportunity

The consideration that death is not necessarily the end of the opportunity for salvation is arrived at in part through the "preaching in Hades" idea with respect to Christ, but also as an inference from other concepts.

Doctrine of Hell

Donald Bloesch holds and has expounded this idea, which largely grows out of his doctrine of hell. According to his view, hell is part of God's loving plan. It is exclusion from communion with God, but not from his presence. It is to be thought of as "a sanitorium of sick souls presided over by Jesus Christ."[1] Bloesch's concept of election, which draws on Karl Barth's doctrine, enters into consideration, for he contends that "Even those who dwell in unbelief are elected by God in Jesus Christ, though not to salvation as such but to the exposure to salvation."[2] While hell is not to be considered a matter of purification in the sense advocated by Nels Ferré, Bloesch does not absolutely exclude the idea that some might be transferred ultimately from hell to heaven:

> We do not wish to build fences around God's grace, however, and we do not preclude that some in hell might finally be translated into heaven. The gates of the holy city are depicted as being open day and night (Isa. 60:11; Rev. 21:25), and this means that access to the throne of grace is possible continuously. The gates of hell are locked, but they are locked only from within.[3]

Hell is not outside the sphere of God's mercy or his kingdom. It is to be conceived of as the sinner's last refuge. Bloesch professes something of an agnosticism about the future state of unbelievers: "Edward Pusey voices our own sentiments: 'We know absolutely nothing of the proportion of the saved to the lost or who will be lost; but this we *do* know, that none will be lost, who do not obstinately to the end and in the end refuse God.'"[4] This way of putting the matter and the insistence that "Even the despised and reprobate are claimed for Jesus Christ in some way or other"[5] leaves the impression that only eternally persistent rejection of the offer of grace excludes one from heaven.

---

1. Donald G. Bloesch, *Essentials of Evangelical Theology* (San Francisco: Harper and Row, 1978), 2:225.
2. Ibid., p. 228.
3. Ibid., pp. 226–27.
4. Ibid., pp. 227–28.
5. Ibid., p. 228.

Probably the person who historically has exerted the strongest influence for this concept, even among conservative interpreters of Scripture, is John Peter Lange in his commentary on the First Peter passage. He writes, "Holy Scripture nowhere teaches the eternal damnation of those who died as heathens or non-Christians; it rather intimates in many passages that forgiveness may be possible beyond the grave, and refers the final decision not to death, but to the day of Christ."[6]

John Sanders identifies several of these passages. Although he does not indicate that these are his own arguments, he elsewhere says that "I also see many strengths in the concept of eschatological evangelization, particularly theological plausibility of its account of universal evangelization."[7] Because he cites several supporting texts without naming any advocates and does so in the passive voice, it appears that he shares the view that he reports:

> Several texts are customarily cited in defense of this assertion: "He has fixed a day in which He will judge the world in righteousness through a man whom He has appointed [Jesus]" (Acts 17:31); "I know whom I have believed and I am convinced that He is able to guard what I have entrusted to him until that day" (2 Tim. 1:12); "in the future there is laid up for me the crown of righteousness, which the Lord, the righteous Judge, will award to me on that day; and not only to me, but also to all who have loved His appearing" (2 Tim. 4:8); and "we may have confidence in the day of judgment" (1 John 4:17; see also John 5:25–29). In addition, it is pointed out that Jesus said that "many shall come from east and west, and recline at table with Abraham, and Isaac, and Jacob, in the kingdom of heaven" (Matt. 8:11/Luke 13:29) and that the gates of the heavenly Jerusalem will never be closed (Rev. 21:25). These texts are taken to mean that God still invites sinners from all areas of the globe and all periods of history to repentance in the afterlife.[8]

Sanders notes that many evangelicals object to this concept of opportunity after death on the basis of the parable of Lazarus and the rich man, which they believe to be evidence that humans' destinies are fixed at death. He responds, however, that "so literalistic an interpretation is by no means generally accepted in the scholarly community, especially in light of the fact that the point of all three parables in Luke 16 is to instruct us about the use of wealth, not about eschatology."[9] He feels that the issue is which view "makes best sense of God's universal salvific will

---

6. John Peter Lange, *First Epistle General of Peter* (New York: Scribner, 1868), p. 75.

7. John Sanders, *No Other Name: An Investigation into the Destiny of the Unevangelized* (Grand Rapids: Eerdmans, 1992), p. 283.

8. Ibid., p. 191.

9. Ibid., p. 191, n. 32.

and the other guiding themes of Scripture." He claims that the verses typically cited in support of the view that human destiny is fixed at death can easily be handled by the advocates of postmortem evangelization, and that, at the very least, they can argue that the biblical witness is not clear-cut in this matter.[10]

Some Whose Fate Is Not Fixed at Death

Clark Pinnock contends that Scripture does not require us to hold that death slams shut the door of opportunity. He bases this assertion at least in part on the idea that while the fate of some may be fixed at death, for others that is not the case. Babies who die in infancy are a major example. The question then becomes whether others are also enabled to qualify for special treatment. Yet, having said that, he goes on to assert that it is not so much a matter of qualification as of disposition: "Humanity will appear in its entirety before God and God has not changed from love to hate. Anyone wanting to love God who has not loved him before is certainly welcome to do so. It has not suddenly become forbidden. No, the variable is the condition of the human souls appearing in God's presence."[11]

Pinnock seems to assume that if one responded to God with love at this point, it would be accepted and would therefore result in the person's receiving eternal life. But is that the case? The question cannot be settled simply by asserting that it is not a question of qualification but of disposition. What is under dispute at this point is whether there is still opportunity, whether there can still be qualification.

God's Need to Discern Persons' Responses

For Pinnock, there is another logical point. He contends that the logic behind postmortem encounter "rests on the insight that God, since he loves humanity, would not send anyone to hell without first ascertaining what their response would have been to his grace. Since everyone eventually dies and comes face to face with the risen Lord, that would seem to be the obvious time to discover their answer to God's call."[12] This contention by Pinnock in turn rests on another feature of his own theology: that God does not know what we will do, until we do it, how we will choose, what we will believe. This in turn is an inference from Pinnock's view of freedom. Whereas Arminians customarily regard God as foreknowing what we will freely choose to do, Pinnock

10. Ibid., p. 209.
11. Clark H. Pinnock, *A Wideness in God's Mercy: The Finality of Jesus Christ in a World of Religions* (Grand Rapids: Zondervan, 1992), p. 171.
12. Ibid., pp. 168–69.

rightly sees that for God to be able to know our actions, it must be certain what we will do. That, however, is incompatible with the usual Arminian understanding of freedom. Consequently, Pinnock has abandoned belief in divine omniscience.[13] Some have advocated the solution of "middle knowledge," whereby God knows what persons' decisions would have been. Pinnock, however, does not find middle knowledge acceptable as a resolution of the difficulty.[14]

Comparative Religions/Consummation

Gabriel Fackre states his view of the postmortem encounter and opportunity in two contexts, that of comparative religions and that of the consummation of the world and history. In his *Christian Story* he suggests that three themes—reconciliation, revelation, and redemption— are crucial because they represent features of classical Christian faith and are also in the foreground in theological negotiations about the relation of Christianity to other religions. By the three themes he means, respectively, the deed in which God acts to bring into being the divine benefits; God's disclosure of truth integral to the divine actions; and our present participation in the benefits made possible by the source action of God.[15] He notes in connection with each of these the dimensions of universality and particularity. For example, there is a general revelation to all persons and yet the particular revelation in Jesus Christ.[16] Similarly, redemption is particular in having been worked out through the specific acts of Jesus Christ, but is universal, including deliverance from all that makes for death and the release of the grace that makes for life.[17] This means that Fackre cannot be a pluralist in the sense in which we have defined that term. He will have to be some sort of inclusivist.

Fackre develops this concern in somewhat more detailed fashion in *The Christian Story*. In his desire to find a way to combine these two dimensions of redemption he examines the view of those who advocate implicit faith, including Karl Rahner's concept of the "anonymous Christian." He says, however, that "the texts of the New Testament on this subject overwhelmingly assert faith to be an explicit confession and not a covert one," and then proceeds to list 177 texts. This, in his judgment, precludes the implicit faith or judgment in the light of conscience

13. Clark Pinnock, "God Limits His Knowledge," in *Predestination and Free Will*, ed. David Basinger and Randall Basinger (Downers Grove, Ill.: InterVarsity, 1986), pp. 146, 157.

14. *Wideness in God's Mercy*, pp. 160–61.

15. Gabriel Fackre, "The Scandals of Particularity and Universality," *Mid-Stream* 22.1 (January 1983):33.

16. Ibid., p. 45.

17. Ibid., p. 47.

position.[18] He takes note of a theme that made its way into the church at an early time, which gave its attention to the saving work of Christ that continues beyond death. This was the descent into Hades theme of the Apostles' Creed, based on 1 Peter 3:19–20 and 4:6, as well as related passages in Ephesians 4:8–9; John 5:25–29; Matthew 8:11; 12:40; Luke 13:28–30; Hebrews 9:15; Romans 10:7; and Revelation 21:25.[19] Fackre notes that both the early church and some nineteenth- and twentieth-century theologians working out of a missionary context sensitive to other cultures and religions (such as the "Andover theory") followed this approach. He says,

> They believed that the wideness and length of God's mercy would deny no one the hearing of the Gospel, a word of invitation extended even by the glorified Christ to those who have been reached by the earthly Body of Christ. That offer is made by the same vulnerable Love that does not force its will and way upon anyone, and thus in the eschatological encounter grants the right to respond with a No as well as a Yes.[20]

Thus, he makes clear that he does not believe in universalism, although there is and must be universal opportunity of exposure to the gospel.

Inadequate Opportunity to Hear

A further consideration is the inadequate opportunity some have to hear the gospel. One who argued from these grounds was Joseph Leckie. Leckie believed that a person must have explicit knowledge of Christ in order to be saved. Some, of course, do not have the opportunity to obtain such knowledge. Therefore, because judgment must be fair and equitable, there must be something such as postmortem evangelism. As biblical evidence he cites the now familiar passages in 1 Peter 3:19 and 4:6, as well as Ephesians 4:8–10. He says of the former texts, "St. Peter almost certainly meant to teach that Jesus in the interval between death and resurrection went down into the lower world and there proclaimed good tidings."[21] He believes that the early church favored such an interpretation, and that the New Testament nowhere excludes such a consideration.

The theological arguments are the most conspicuous and influential, however. The first is the idea that many do not really have an adequate

---

18. Gabriel Fackre, *The Christian Story: A Narrative Interpretation of Basic Christian Doctrine* (Grand Rapids: Eerdmans, 1984), pp. 232–33.

19. Ibid., pp. 233–34.

20. Ibid., p. 234.

21. Joseph Leckie, *The World to Come and Final Destiny*, 2d ed. (Edinburgh: T. and T. Clark, 1922), p. 91.

opportunity to consider, evaluate, and act on the gospel. Among these are those who die in infancy, those born with mental impairments, and those born into conditions in which thoughts of spiritual matters were not encouraged or likely.[22]

Leckie then goes on to ask about the status of this huge number of persons who die in infancy. He presents the idea that such mature in the future life and then are given an opportunity to hear the good news about Christ and accept him. He rejects three widely differing views for a common reason. The Roman Catholic view is of a limbo for infants; the Reformed view is that only elect infants are saved; the liberal belief is that all infants that die are saved. All of these, however, allow the salvation of infants without any sort of probation or acceptance of the Lord. This does not seem right to Leckie: "If the battle is the only path to victory, how can those who have never fought be counted among the conquerors?"[23] He also appeals to the practice of praying for the dead, which has early and widespread precedent. While the New Testament does not teach such a practice, it does not rule it out either, and the great majority of Christians throughout history have engaged in it. For such prayers to make any sense, the possibility of some sort of transformation after death must be assumed. This combination of arguments constitutes, in Leckie's judgment, a strong case for postmortem evangelism, both of those who die in infancy and those who have never heard the gospel during their lifetime.[24]

Salvation Offered to Some after Death

The second major argument is that Christ actually offered salvation to some dead persons. It should by now be apparent that the biblical texts, especially the references in 1 Peter to Jesus' descent and preaching, play a crucial role in this argument. Let us therefore examine those passages in somewhat greater detail.

Basis of the Contention

This view is generally related to a belief that Jesus, between his death and resurrection, descended into Hades and proclaimed the gospel to the persons who were enslaved there from Old Testament times. It finds its grounds in the statement in the Apostles' Creed, "he descended into Hades," and in certain biblical passages, such as Acts 2:31; Ephesians 4:9–10; and especially 1 Peter 3:18–20 and 4:6. Two steps are required

22. Ibid., p. 96.
23. Ibid., p. 97.
24. Ibid., pp. 99–101.

if we are to believe on biblical grounds that such an opportunity is given after death to all persons who have not heard during this life. It is first necessary to demonstrate that the 1 Peter passage indeed teaches that Christ preached the gospel to the persons in Hades during the interval between his death and resurrection, and that this was a genuine offer of salvation on the basis of belief. Second, it is necessary to demonstrate that the offer made to those Old Testament persons is also made available to all persons who live and die after that time.

It is worth noting that the presence of the clause in the Apostles' Creed, which undoubtedly was a major factor in inducing belief in the doctrine during the medieval period, does not occur until relatively late. It is not found universally in the creed until the eighth century, although it appears in some local versions as early as patristic times. It is included in the Athanasian Creed, composed about the middle of the fifth century and accepted by both the Eastern and Western wings of the church.[25]

The tradition of a descent of Christ into Hades goes back into quite early church history. Interestingly, however, it was not associated with the 1 Peter passage for some time. Selwyn says that "the outstanding fact in the Patristic evidence before A.D. 190 is that, despite the popularity of the doctrine of Christ's 'harrowing of hell,' I Pet. iii. 18ff. is never quoted as authority for it."[26] Loofs says Irenaeus, "who . . . regarded I Peter as authentic . . . never quotes the passage at all, nor, in dealing specially with the *Descensus*, does he even allude to it."[27] We find mention of the descent in relation to 1 Peter 3 in Clement of Alexandria, Origen, and Hippolytus. In Augustine we find the interpretation of Christ's preaching as being in his preexistent form to the people of Noah's day. Thus, three of the major interpretations of the passage (i.e., Christ preaching in Hades to men or to angels or preaching in the days of Noah) were held by some of the Church Fathers.

The passage in question reads as follows:

> For Christ also died for sins once for all, the righteous for the unrighteous, that he might bring us to God, being put to death in the flesh but made alive in the spirit; in which he went and preached to the spirits in prison, who formerly did not obey, when God's patience waited in the days of Noah, during the building of the ark, in which a few, that is, eight persons, were saved through water. (3:18–20)

25. Donald G. Bloesch, "Descent into Hell (Hades)," in *Evangelical Dictionary of Theology*, ed. Walter A. Elwell (Grand Rapids: Baker, 1984), p. 314.

26. Edward G. Selwyn, *The First Epistle of St. Peter* (Grand Rapids: Baker, 1981), p. 340.

27. Friedrich Loofs, "Descent to Hades (Christ's)," in *Encyclopedia of Religion and Ethics*, ed. James Hastings (New York: Scribner's, 1912), 4:659.

For this is why the gospel was preached even to the dead, that though judged in the flesh like men, they might live in the spirit like God. (4:6)

Issues in Interpretation of 1 Peter 3:18–20 and 4:6

Several issues are involved in the interpretation of this passage. Those questions and the major types of answers given are as follows:

1. Who did the preaching?
   a. Jesus (innumerable interpreters)
   b. Enoch[28]
   c. Noah, but Christ actually preaching through him by the Holy Spirit[29]
2. To whom was the preaching done?
   a. Fallen angels[30]
   b. Humans, in hell[31]
   c. Humans, who repented just before they died in the flood[32]
   d. People who lived during the time of Noah[33]
3. What was preached?
   a. The gospel: the Good News of the availability of salvation
   b. The triumph of Christ over death
   c. Judgment or condemnation[34]
4. When was the preaching done?
   a. In the days of Noah[35]
   b. Between the death and resurrection of Jesus
   c. After Jesus' resurrection but before his ascension[36]

---

28. J. Rendel Harris, "The History of a Conjectural Emendation," *Expositor* 6.6 (1902): 378–90. Cf. Edgar J. Goodspeed, *An Introduction to the New Testament* (Chicago: University of Chicago Press, 1937), p. 353; idem, "Enoch in 1 Peter 3:19," *Journal of Biblical Literature* 73 (1954):91–92.

29. Augustine, *Letter 164*, chaps. 15–17.

30. Selwyn, *First Epistle of Peter*, p. 199.

31. Bo Reicke, *The Epistles of James, Peter, and Jude* (Garden City, N.Y.: Doubleday, 1964), p. 109.

32. See William Joseph Dalton, *Christ's Proclamation to the Spirits: A Study of 1 Peter 3:18–4:6* (Rome: Pontifical Biblical Institute, 1965), pp. 29–30.

33. A. M. Hunter, "The First Epistle of Peter," in *The Interpreter's Bible*, ed. George Arthur Buttrick (New York: Abingdon-Cokesbury, 1957), 12:132–34.

34. R. C. H. Lenski, *The Interpretation of the Epistles of St. Peter, St. John and St. Jude* (Minneapolis: Augsburg, 1966), pp. 165–68.

35. Thomas Aquinas, *Summa Theologica*, part 3, question 52, art. 2, reply to obj. 3.

36. Theodor Schott, *Der erste Petrusbrief erklärt* (Erlangen: Andreas Deichert, 1861), pp. 218–40.

d. At the time of an "invisible ascension" of Christ on Easter
   Sunday morning, just after his appearance to Mary[37]
e. Throughout history, being symbolic of the universality of
   salvation, rather than a single literal occurrence[38]

Types of Interpretations

Taking into account all possible combinations, this would allow for
conceivably 180 different theories. Because the position taken on one
of these issues in many cases severely limits the available options on
other issues, however, the actual number is considerably less, basically
reducing to the following six general types of interpretation:

1. Christ "in spirit" preached through Noah during the time he was
   building the ark. This was a message of repentance and righteousness, given to unbelieving persons who were then on earth
   but are now "spirits in prison" (i.e., persons in hell).
2. During the period between his death and resurrection, Christ
   went and preached to humans in hell, giving them a message of
   repentance and righteousness, thus offering them a chance to believe and be saved, although they had not availed themselves of
   such an offer during their lifetimes on earth.
3. During this period, Christ went to people in hell and preached
   the message that he had triumphed over them and their condemnation was final.
4. During this time Christ proclaimed release to people who had repented just before the flood. He led them from imprisonment in
   purgatory to heaven.
5. Between his death and resurrection or between his resurrection
   and ascension, Christ descended into hell and proclaimed his triumph over the fallen angels who had sinned by mating with
   women before the flood.
6. The reference to preaching is not to be taken literally. It is symbolic, conveying in this graphic form the idea that redemption is
   universal in its extent or influence.

The examination of all the data of the passage requires much more
attention than can be given in the space of this chapter. We may deal

37. William Joseph Dalton, *Christ's Proclamation to the Spirits: A Study of 1 Peter 3:18–
4:6* (Rome: Pontifical Biblical Institute, 1965), p. 185.
38. Wolfhart Pannenberg, *The Apostles' Creed in the Light of Today's Questions* (Philadelphia: Westminster, 1972), p. 94.

with a few issues first, however, which should have the effect of narrowing considerably the number of viable options.

Examination of Alternatives

One issue basic to the question pertains to what was preached, and that centers especially on the meaning of the word κηρύσσω, in 3:19 and 4:6. According to views 3 and 5 above, this must mean preaching judgment or condemnation or declaration of triumph over the hearers. On views 1 and 2 it means the proclamation of the necessity of repentance and the possibility of forgiveness. In view 4 it means a declaration of forgiveness and liberation. Thus in views 1, 2, and 4, it is to be understood as "good news," while in views 3 and 5 it should be seen as "bad news." Which meaning is to be understood here?

The word used here is simply the broad word for proclamation. It is not necessarily restricted to evangelization or declaration of good news, or the message of salvation. If, however, the word here is to be taken as bad news, then it seems problematic on several grounds. For one thing, it is not really consistent with the rest of Jesus' preaching. While he certainly spoke words of harsh criticism and even condemnation of Pharisees, it is hard to find indications of Jesus "lording it over" persons who were already in prison and incapable of harming or misleading others. Further, the context does not seem to fit this interpretation well. The whole thrust of the argument seems to be concerned with the matter of bearing witness, giving an account of one's faith, and the like. In fact, verse 15 speaks of doing this witnessing "with gentleness and respect." This would hardly seem consonant with a depiction of condemnation or victory on Christ's part. This then appears to favor interpretations 1 or 2.

A further question relates to the recipients of the message. Who were they? Were they humans or angels? Much has been made of the idea of a parallel with the Book of Enoch, which speaks of Enoch going and preaching to the angels who were disobedient during the time of Noah. The claim is made that this tradition would have been familiar to Peter's readers and that he then merely modeled his argument along that line. There is a further claim that the "sons of God" in Genesis 6 were angels. Genesis 6 is then linked with 2 Peter 2:4 and Jude 6. Finally, 1 Peter 3:19 is associated with these several verses and with the idea of preaching to fallen angels.

There is much to commend this view because there was considerable interest in angels in the milieu of that time. Yet there are nonetheless problems with it. For one thing, there is no assurance that the correct interpretation of Genesis 6 is that which identifies the "sons of God" with angels. This is a highly disputed passage. Further, the idea of angels mating with humans to produce offspring seems to contradict

Jesus' statement in Matthew 22:30, although the latter passage could be interpreted as indicating that they do not marry, but do mate. That seems a somewhat remote interpretation, however.

What of the fourth view, that this was a declaration of deliverance to those who repented in the time of the flood, but too late to avoid perishing? There are several difficulties with this view as well. For one thing, the account of the flood contains no reference to such repentance. For another, this creates a special class for these persons, as compared with the rest of those who lived and died in Old Testament times. Why should this be? Presumably, if others in the Old Testament who repented were spared spiritually, these would be also, although they would perish physically in the flood. Why should this preaching then focus upon them?

Wolfhart Pannenberg holds the sixth view, that this passage is to be understood symbolically. In an exposition of the Apostles' Creed, he discusses the tradition in the early church of Christ's preaching in Hades and notes that this tradition is found in the New Testament in the only text to mention it clearly—1 Peter 3:19–20; 4:6. That he does not take this descent and preaching literally is indicated from his comment that the controversy between the Lutherans and the Reformed over whether it was the crucified or the risen Lord who descended into hell could arise only to the kind of mind that confuses the image with the thing itself.[39] This is made even clearer in his *Jesus: God and Man*, where he speaks of the "increasingly mythological conception of Jesus' preaching in the realm of the dead or in hell" that attached itself to the statements in 1 Peter. It ought rather to be thought of as "the expression of the universal significance of Jesus' vicarious death under the curse."[40] He explains this at greater length:

> The proclamation of the missionary message of primitive Christianity by Jesus himself in the realm of the dead is not, like the crucifixion, a historical event. The pictorial character of this concept is not simply a part of the mode of expression, as is the case with the resurrection which still is a specific, historically definable event. The symbolic language about Jesus' descent into hell and his proclamation in the realm of the dead is just what has been falsely asserted about Jesus' resurrection, namely, a statement about the real significance of another event, his death.[41]

It is difficult to ascertain the basis of Pannenberg's position. The status of the tradition involved in the Apostles' Creed and the nature of the

39. Ibid.
40. Wolfhart Pannenberg, *Jesus: God and Man* (Philadelphia: Westminster, 1968), p. 272.
41. Ibid.

biblical testimony relative to our belief are not made completely clear. In Pannenberg's theology neither biblical nor ecclesiastical tradition automatically carries defining authority. Thus, it is somewhat puzzling as to just why he feels that this should commend itself to us for belief. In the final analysis, it appears that this idea that appears in the Scripture is accepted as authoritative on extrabiblical grounds.

This leaves us with two major alternatives: views 1 and 2. The second interpretation appears to be the only one that really could serve as support for the idea of postmortem evangelization. Yet it faces some problems regarding whether the preaching was done just to the group from Noah's time, but not others. In other words, the contextual connection with the reference to those in the time of Noah seems strange on this theory. In addition, it seeks to draw support from other references, but on closer examination those are even more ambiguous. They either refer to God not leaving Jesus' soul in Hades or fit better with the idea of the second person of the Trinity descending to earth.

The first interpretation, of course, has difficulties both with the "spirits" in prison and with the preaching. The latter does not seem to be without parallel, however. For example, Luke speaks of the Holy Spirit speaking through the mouth of David (Acts 1:16; 4:25) and the expression, "the Word of the Lord came upon me, saying . . ." is virtually a paradigm for the Old Testament prophets. Regarding the spirits in prison, Selwyn argued that πνεῦμα is never used absolutely (i.e., without a "defining genitive phrase") to refer to human spirits, and thus must refer to good or evil angelic spirits,[42] but Grudem has shown that this is not the case.[43] Grudem further argues that the time question regarding "spirits in prison" may be understood from the time perspective of the writer.

Probably the most important issue between these two views is the context. The whole thrust of the passage seems to be faithful, gentle, respectful witness to one's faith, even in the face of opposition. This, plus the references to those in the time of Noah, seems to me to favor the first view, even though it has not been greatly in vogue of late. Very careful defenses of this position, taking into account the usual objections and pointing out well the weaknesses of the alternatives, have recently been advanced.[44]

The wider contextual issue, however, concerns the harmony of this teaching with broader doctrinal issues taught in the Scriptures. Here we

---

42. Selwyn, *First Epistle of Peter*, p. 199.

43. Wayne Grudem, "Christ Preaching through Noah: 1 Peter 3:19–20 in the Light of Dominant Themes in Jewish Literature," *Trinity Journal* NS 7.2 (Fall 1986):6–7.

44. Ibid., pp. 3–31; John S. Feinberg, "1 Peter 3:18–20, Ancient Mythology, and the Intermediate State," *Westminster Theological Journal* 48.2 (Fall 1986): 303–35.

should observe that evangelicals and conservatives generally have not held to a descent into Hades and a preaching by Christ. In the late 1960s, the chaplain of Wheaton College decided that a series of chapel messages on the Apostles' Creed would be a good thing. Members of the Bible department were asked to preach, each on a different phrase of the creed. No one, however, was willing to preach on "descended into Hades," because no one believed in it. That phrase was omitted from the series.

The major reason for hesitancy about this phrase and concept stems from the conviction that the Bible teaches that death ends all opportunity for decision for Christ, so that one's eternal destiny is sealed at death. This is argued for on the basis of several texts. One is the story or parable of Lazarus and the rich man. There has been considerable debate as to whether this is to be understood as a parable. If it is, it is the only parable in which one of the characters is named. Those who hold that it is a parable maintain that one cannot obtain doctrine from parables, but it should be noted that in Jesus' parables, even when the specific event referred to may not have been a historical occurrence, nothing in the details of the occurrence was untrue to life. Thus, regarding the events referred to in the parable of the prodigal son, although such an event may not have actually occurred to three specific members of one actual family, there is nothing in the parable contrary to the circumstances of life, nothing that could not have happened or nothing contrary to the culture of that time. The same will be found to be true of the other parables on closer examination. If, however, this passage is a parable, Lazarus and the rich man may not be actual persons and this incident may not have occurred, but if this is an inaccurate picture of the world beyond this, and of the state of persons following death, this parable is different from others.

It sometimes is also objected that the major point of the parable is not to teach eschatology. Sanders, for example, states that "so literalistic an interpretation is by no means generally accepted in the scholarly community, especially in light of the fact that the point of all three parables in Luke 16 is to instruct us about the use of wealth, not about eschatology."[45] This appears to be an instance of the common fallacy of assuming that the only lesson that can be drawn from a passage is the central one. That is an assumption severely in need of justification, however. For if the basic teaching is like the conclusion of a syllogism, then if the conclusion is to follow as true from the premises, those premises must also be true. Therefore, one may draw from the passage the premises as well as the conclusion.

45. Sanders, *No Other Name*, p. 191, n. 32.

Other passages as well seem to speak to the idea of death bringing the opportunity to an end. The thrust of much of Psalm 49 is that the sinner will go to the grave and perish there, with no indication of any possible release from that place. Revelation 20:11–15 contains the scene of the Great White Judgment Throne at which each person who wanted to be judged on the basis of his or her works is judged, and all are accounted guilty. There is no offer of any sort of salvation. In addition, the sequence of Hebrews 9:27, "Just as man is destined to die once, and after that comes judgment," seems to assume an invariable transition from the one to the other, with no mention of any additional opportunities for acceptance. To be sure, this may be labeled an argument from silence, but it would seem that the burden of proof rests on those who maintain that opportunity for deciding intervenes.

With respect to the interpretation of these verses, no one theory is completely satisfactory. We must be content with finding the one with the fewest difficulties. As a biblical exegete and theologian I find the first of these, the idea that Christ by the spirit spoke through Noah to those of his day, the least problematic, especially in terms of its context. When, however, I approach the passage as a systematic theologian, attempting to bring the entire biblical revelation together into a coherent whole, it is even more strongly preferable.

The Additional Premise

It should be noted that the argument for postmortem evangelism is not necessarily successful even if we accept the interpretation that says that Christ descended into Hades and offered salvation to the imprisoned sinners there. For even if that is achieved, that only takes care of those few people. It says nothing about others who have lived since that time or will live in the future. To be sure, the principle of no salvation beyond the grave, or death being the end of all opportunity, has been breached, but that gives no guarantee that others will be saved. That might have been a unique situation. It is necessary to establish an additional link in the argument, namely, that because Christ proclaimed and provided salvation for those imprisoned sinners, there will also be an opportunity for others to come. What support is offered for this particular premise?

Here we find an amazing absence of argumentation or even of apparent awareness of the issue. Sanders, for example, does not seem to see the point, moving quickly from the former to the latter. Bloesch also seems to identify the two, stating that "What the descent doctrine affirms is the universality of a first chance, an opportunity for salvation for those who have never heard the gospel in its fullness."[46] That, however, does not seem to me to be what the doctrine of the descent teaches. If interpreted in Bloesch's way, what the passages assert is that Jesus preached to and offered salvation to those persons in Hades at that time, not that everyone is guaranteed a first chance. Nor does Pannenberg offer much help here. He sees this as primarily symbolic, so that the truth is not to be identified with a particular occurrence. This, however, requires a fairly serious revision of the way in which we handle Scripture.

George Beasley-Murray takes a somewhat different approach. He evidently considers the key to the interpretation of the passage to be the fact that the generation referred to here is also regarded as the most wicked generation of history. Thus, as an extreme case it becomes an example of the truth that there is hope for all generations. He says:

> the primary reference of both statements [3:19 and 4:6] is the same, and the primary lesson in the writer's mind is to exemplify the universal reach of Christ's redeeming work and the divine willingness that all should know it. The preaching of Christ between his cross and his Easter is intended to prove that the wickedest generation of history is not beyond the bounds of his pity and the scope of his redemption, hence there is hope for *this* generation, that has sinned even more greatly than the Flood generation in refusing the proclamation of a greater Messenger of God and that faces the *last* judgment (4:7).[47]

One would wish for a bit more evidence and argument here, however. How does Beasley-Murray know that this was the writer's primary intention? A plausible explanation here has been transformed into a probable one, but with no further evidence than the theory itself.

For Clark Pinnock, the argument rests upon a certain logic, as he terms it. He sees scriptural warrant for the idea of a postmortem encounter in Christ's preaching in Hades. He seems to be making a similar assertion to that of Beasley-Murray when he says, "Could the meaning of the descent into hell be that the people who never encountered the Gospel in their lifetimes can choose to receive it in the postmortem situation? Such a possibility would make good the universality of grace and God's willingness that all should know it. It would make clear that the most wicked of sinners are not beyond the scope of God's mercy, and that God is patient even with them."[48] Could it be? Yes, most cer-

46. Donald Bloesch, "Descent into Hell," in *Evangelical Dictionary of Theology*, ed. Walter Elwell (Grand Rapids: Baker, 1984), p. 314.
47. G. R. Beasley-Murray, *Baptism in the New Testament* (London: Macmillan, 1962), pp. 258–59.
48. Pinnock, *Wideness in God's Mercy*, p. 169.

tainly that is a possibility. Is it true, however? That is the real question. Pinnock acknowledges that "the scriptural evidence for postmortem encounter is not abundant," but contends that "its scantiness is relativized by the strength of the theological argument for it."[49]

Conclusion

In conclusion, then, we are faced with whether to accept a view of postmortem evangelism for which there is no clear biblical teaching and which seems at points to contradict other, clearer, biblical teachings. The major biblical passage appealed to is one that Robert Mounce says is "widely recognized as perhaps the most difficult to understand in all of the New Testament."[50] It would seem strange to rest a doctrine about the eternal destiny of humans on such an obscure passage. The doctrine is based on a series of interpretations of Scriptures and philosophical and other assumptions which, by admission of the proponents of this view, are in many cases at best possibilities, and scant in number. When, however, a theory is based on a series of statements and inferences, each of which is of a rather low level of probability, the probability of the several steps or premises is not added but multiplied. Thus, in a four-step argument, each step of which is 75 percent probable, the probability of the conclusion is only 32 percent. The burden of proof for a view such as this, which at least on its surface conflicts with some other teachings of Scripture, rests on those who advance it. And here, it must be observed, the proof falls sadly short of demonstration.

49. Ibid.
50. Robert Mounce, *A Living Hope: A Commentary on 1 and 2 Peter* (Grand Rapids: Eerdmans, 1982), p. 54.

10

The Biblical Requirements for Salvation

The question that must now be asked concerns just what is involved in receiving salvation. While often treated as a self-evident matter or a superfluous question, in reality this is the basis of some of the disagreements among the persons involved in the debate. There are differences of understanding of the nature of salvation, as well as of the conditions for reception of it. In addition, even among those who hold that faith is the primary basis on which salvation is granted, the nature of faith is not unanimously agreed upon. It is necessary to examine in turn each of these issues and each of these positions.

The Importance of Works

Jesus' Teaching

A first position in effect minimizes the role of faith. It calls attention to the fact that in Scripture, works are frequently indicated as the criterion for awarding eternal life. This is a most important consideration for our purposes here, for if indeed judgment is on the basis of works, then the object of the faith of the one doing the works may be relatively unimportant. Conceivably, it does not matter whether any person is believed in at all. The most familiar of the passages appealed to is Jesus' teaching about the last judgment in Matthew 25:31–46. Here the reason given in each case for granting eternal life or for denying it is the persons' action during their lifetimes. Feeding the hungry, giving drink to the thirsty, showing hospitality to strangers, clothing persons in need of clothing, caring for the sick, and visiting those in prison are the grounds of the justification involved here. And, in the ultimate sense, it was not, of course, works done to the other person, but the fact that such works are actually done to Jesus, or at least regarded by him as works done to him, that makes the difference. Jesus did not say, "You have correctly believed," or, "Your theology was right." Works, pure and simple, constitute the basis of the judgment, so far as we can determine from this passage.

Nor is this the only such teaching in Jesus' recorded words. In the passage in which he challenged any would-be followers to take up their crosses and follow him, he added, "For the Son of Man is going to come in his Father's glory with his angels, and then he will reward each person according to what he has done" (Matt. 16:27). Jesus did not seem to base salvation on or at least to identify its criterion as being purely faith.

In a somewhat different form, Clark Pinnock seems to emphasize the role of works as equivalent to faith. He sees Jesus' parable of the last judgment as teaching that works done to needy people are treated as if they were works done to Christ himself. He then says:

> Such a reading coheres well with the principle in his teaching that good works manifest one's basic attitude to God and that noncognitive responses to God count as much as cognitive responses do. Surely the text picks up on the beatitude: "Blessed are you who are poor, for yours is the kingdom of God" (Lk. 6:20). Serving the poor embodies what the love of God is, and it is accepted as the equivalent of faith. . . . Those who confess Christ and those who do not are judged alike by the extent to which they walk in the way of the Son of Man.[1]

Paul's Writings

This is even found in the writings of Paul, the great champion of salvation by grace through faith. In the passage in which he discusses God's judgment, which leads to the statement about those who do not have the law being judged by a law they do have, namely, the law within, he says, "For he will render to every man according to his works: to those who by patience in well-doing seek for glory and honor and immortality, he will give eternal life; but for those who are factious and do not obey the truth, but obey wickedness, there will be wrath and fury. There will be tribulation and distress for every human being who does evil, the Jew first and also the Greek" (Rom. 2:6–10). There is no reference here to faith, but rather to works. Doing good or doing

1. Clark H. Pinnock, *A Wideness in God's Mercy: The Finality of Jesus Christ in a World of Religions* (Grand Rapids: Zondervan, 1992), pp. 164–65.

evil is the distinguishing factor. Is it possible that Paul's strong message of justification, of which so much has been made, is here instead directed to the question of the human decision for good or evil?

Even more pointed are some of Paul's other statements. For example, in Galatians 6:7–9 he writes, "Do not be deceived; God is not mocked, for whatever a man sows, that he will also reap. For he who sows to his own flesh will from the flesh reap corruption; but he who sows to the Spirit will from the Spirit reap eternal life. And let us not grow weary in well-doing, for in due season we shall reap, if we do not lose heart." In 2 Corinthians 5:10, a much-quoted text, he speaks more directly of the matter of judgment: "For we must all appear before the judgment seat of Christ, so that each one may receive good or evil, according to what he has done in the body." He wrote to the Colossians, "Whatever your task, work heartily, as serving the Lord and not men, knowing that from the Lord you will receive the inheritance as your reward; you are serving the Lord Christ. For the wrongdoer will be paid back for the wrong he has done, and there is no partiality" (3:23–25). To the Corinthian church, in which morality and lifestyle were so crucial, he wrote, "Now if any one builds on the foundation with gold, silver, precious stones, wood, hay, straw—each man's work will become manifest; for the Day will disclose it, because it will be revealed with fire, and the fire will test what sort of work each one has done" (1 Cor. 3:12–13).

This is an amazingly strong collection of texts from Paul, seemingly indicating an important role for works in the determination of one's future state. Even so staunch a Calvinist as G. C. Berkouwer comments on these passages:

> We can hardly say that such ideas form a subordinate line, a secondary and rather unimportant element of Paul's message. Quite the contrary. The utmost earnestness of the judgment and the appeal to man to consider his daily responsibility before the Lord of life sound clarionlike through his whole witness. It is not to be denied that for Paul, too, the works and affairs of man play a role in the final drama of God's judgment.[2]

While Berkouwer does not necessarily accept this argument, and has raised it only as an example of objections advanced in opposition to the orthodox view of salvation by grace through faith, he feels the force of these passages, which often are not taken into account by evangelicals in developing their doctrine.

2. G. C. Berkouwer, *Faith and Justification* (Grand Rapids: Eerdmans, 1954), p. 105.

Other Portions of Scripture

Lest we think that such witness is confined to Jesus and Paul, we may also note that this theme seems to run throughout Scripture. Note what Peter conveys on the subject: "And if you invoke as Father him who judges each one impartially according to his deeds, conduct yourselves with fear throughout the time of your exile" (1 Pet. 1:17). Old Testament authors repeat the same thought. David writes, "Surely you will reward each person according to what he has done" (Ps. 62:12). And the preacher concludes his book by writing, "For God will bring every deed into judgment, including every hidden thing, whether it is good or evil" (Eccles. 12:14). If one of the criteria of permanence or of the essence of the Christian message and belief is its presence in several authors and different kinds of material, and across different time periods and cultures, then this would surely seem to possess that kind of universality.

Faith and Works as Complementary

Traditionally, those who hold to justification by grace through faith have insisted that what we are dealing with here are not two opposed considerations, but rather two complementary lines of evidence. These two lines are profoundly in harmony with one another, not merely supplementing one another, so that justification is partially by faith and partially by works, but the latter is the demonstration of the reality, the actuality, of the former. Part of this is found in the fact that justification does not stand by itself. Justification is part of a larger package, which includes regeneration. Justification is forensic, involving imputation, rather than impartation, of righteousness and holiness. The person who is justified, however, is also regenerated. Consequently, he or she will not simply continue living as before. There will be a difference. Paul, after all, in the same passage in which he wrote about all appearing before the judgment seat of Christ to receive what is due them for the things done while in the body, went on to say, "Therefore, if any one is in Christ, he is a new creation; the old has passed away, behold, the new has come" (v. 17). Here is presumably the answer to the apparent incompatibility. The deeds done in the body are the evidence or the proof of the reality of being in Christ and thus being a new creation as well as being justified in him. Berkouwer says, "Paul does indeed set the righteousness of faith in contradiction to the righteousness of works—he could not have done it more definitely—yet he urges the necessity of works. The works he wants, however, are not the works of the law. These works are in close affinity with and are, in fact, embraced by faith-righteousness."[3]

3. Ibid., p. 107.

This can be seen in numerous places in Paul's writings, where the two factors are juxtaposed. So, for example, he urges his Roman readers to "present your bodies as a living sacrifice, holy and acceptable to God, which is your spiritual worship" (Rom. 12:1). In doing so, however, he urges this on them "by the mercy of God," and begins the exhortation with a "therefore," which follows a statement in which he speaks of God's mercy four times in three verses (11:30–32). That in turn comes at the conclusion of a passage in which he likens these Gentiles to a wild olive shoot that has been grafted in. The whole thrust of this central part of the letter is God's grace and mercy.

The textus classicus for salvation by grace through faith is Ephesians 2:8–9. When seen in context, however, it should be apparent that there is more to the picture than is seen if we stop with verse 9. For in the very next verse Paul goes on to say, "For we are his workmanship, created in Christ Jesus for good works, which God prepared beforehand, that we should walk in them." Thus, the works of the Christian life are inseparably linked with the grace and faith that are at the very heart and basis of justification. It could hardly be more clearly put than in 1 Thessalonians 1:3: "remembering before our God and Father your work of faith and labor of love and steadfastness of hope in our Lord Jesus Christ." Faith and works are so closely linked that even the works must be done in faith. Paul writes, "But he who has doubts is condemned, if he eats, because he does not act from faith; for whatever does not proceed from faith is sin" (Rom. 14:23).

Thus, it appears that in judgment all works are scrutinized and evaluated. The crucial factor is whether these works are done in faith, that is, whether they are works of faith or works of the law. Paul speaks of how his readers were called to be free, but are not to use their freedom as an excuse or occasion to indulge the sinful nature. They are rather to serve one another in love (Gal. 5:13). Thus, he contrasts the works of the flesh with the fruit of the spirit (vv. 16–26). The believer will live by the Spirit and the result will be "love, joy, peace, patience, kindness, goodness, faithfulness, gentleness, self-control" (vv. 22–23).

Peter also ties together the two factors of grace and works. So he writes, "And if you invoke as Father him who judges each one impartially according to his deeds, conduct yourselves with fear throughout the time of your exile. You know that you were ransomed from the futile ways inherited from your fathers, not with perishable things such as silver or gold, but with the precious blood of Christ, like that of a lamb without blemish or spot" (1 Pet. 1:17–19). As with Paul, the appeal to living in a way that will enable one's works to withstand God's judgment is derived from the fact of his or her redemption.

The same pattern can be readily discerned in Jesus' teachings, as reported in the Gospel accounts. He said to the Pharisees, "Either make the tree good, and its fruit good; or make the tree bad, and its fruit bad; for the tree is known by its fruit" (Matt. 12:33). He then went on to apply this to his hearers: "You brood of vipers! how can you speak good, when you are evil? For out of the abundance of the heart the mouth speaks. The good man out of his good treasure brings forth good, and the evil man out of his evil treasure brings forth evil" (vv. 34–35). He indicated that both profession and works must be joined together, if either is to be adjudged to be genuine. He said, "Not every one who says to me, 'Lord, Lord,' shall enter the kingdom of heaven, but he who does the will of my Father who is in heaven. On that day many will say to me, 'Lord, Lord, did we not prophesy in your name, and cast out demons in your name, and do many mighty works in your name?' And then will I declare to them, 'I never knew you; depart from me, you evildoers'" (Matt. 7:21–23). A similar saying appears in a different setting in Luke. There Jesus urges his hearers to make every effort to enter through the narrow door, because many will endeavor unsuccessfully to do so (Luke 13:24). Then he says, "When once the householder has risen up and shut the door, you will begin to stand outside and to knock at the door, saying, 'Lord, open to us.' He will answer you, 'I do not know where you come from.' Then you will begin to say, 'We ate and drank in your presence, and you taught in our streets.' But he will say, 'I tell you, I do not know where you come from; depart from me, all you workers of iniquity!'" (vv. 25–27).

Why is this whole matter of such importance for the issue now under consideration? If salvation can be received by works in themselves, then such salvation might be present within a number of religious contexts. A person might perform good works while holding a belief in a god different from that revealed in Jesus Christ. Thus, the problem of the salvation of the unevangelized cannot be resolved through this channel.

The Faith Principle

A different answer is given by Clark Pinnock, who holds that if God really loves the whole world and desires everyone to be saved, then everyone must have access to salvation. Yet some of these people have not heard of Christ. How, then, can they have salvation within their reach? Although the theory of universal accessibility is not a novel theory, it needs to be proven. How can this be done? How can it best be defended? Pinnock believes the answer is to be found in the faith principle.[4]

Faith and Belief

In using this principle, Pinnock is drawing a distinction between faith and knowledge, or some would say, between faith and belief. He says, "According to the Bible, people are saved by faith, not by the content of their theology. Since God has not left anyone without witness, people are judged on the basis of the light they have received and how they have responded to that light. Faith in God is what saves, not possessing certain minimum information."[5] He believes the statement in Hebrews 11:6 is clear on this matter, when it says, "And without faith it is impossible to please God, because anyone who comes to him must believe that he exists and that he rewards those who earnestly seek him."

Responsibility and Inculpable Ignorance

According to Pinnock, people can only respond to the revelation they have, not to that which they do not have, and will only be held responsible for what they know, not that of which they were inculpably ignorant. A person is saved by faith, even if the content of belief is deficient, and whose, after all, is not? The Bible does not teach that one must confess the name of Jesus to be saved. Job and David did not know it, nor do babies who die in infancy. The question is not whether the unevangelized know Jesus, but rather, whether he knows them. God does not care about the content of our theology, only the direction of our faith.[6] Pinnock feels that a number of theologians have held the position he is here espousing, from Justin and Clement, to Zwingli, Wesley, A. H. Strong, and Vatican II.[7]

Biblical Examples

Pinnock develops further his argument regarding the faith principle. He notes that Hebrews 11:6 is in a context that refers to Abel, Enoch, and Noah, indicating that people are saved by faith not primarily by knowledge. As an example, Abraham was accepted by God although he knew relatively little and merely believed that God would give him a son and heir. Pinnock summarizes this data by saying that "The fact that the information possessed by the unevangelized is slight

---

4. Clark H. Pinnock, *A Wideness in God's Mercy: The Finality of Jesus Christ in a World of Religions* (Grand Rapids: Zondervan, 1992), p. 157.
   5. Ibid., pp. 157–58.
   6. Ibid., p. 158.
   7. Ibid., pp. 158–59.

does not disqualify them from entering into a right relationship with God through faith."[8]

But if most Christians today would allow (as Pinnock thinks) that Job and others who have the desire for salvation will receive it, why do so many not allow for that same possibility today? Pinnock thinks this hesitation must be recognized for what it is and confronted. To Pinnock, there is no difference in the situation of a person just because of the passage of a few years of time. He says,

> Why would it make any difference if Job were born in A.D. 1900 in outer Mongolia? Why would God not deal with him the same way he dealt with him in the Old Testament? A person who is informationally premessianic, whether living in ancient or modern times, is in exactly the same spiritual situation. The same things apply to all such: "God will give to each person according to what he has done. To those who by persistence in doing good seek glory, honor, and immortality, he will give eternal life."[9]

Pinnock sees the fleshing out of the faith principle in the cases of the "holy pagans" in the biblical accounts. He describes these as "people saved by faith without any knowledge of the revelation vouchsafed to Israel or the church."[10] While we do not know how many of these there are in the world at any given time, we know that there are such because of the scriptural testimony. Pinnock describes these persons by saying that, "like Job and Abraham, there are those who, due to an inner voice, come to a fork in the road and turn to God in faith. There is always a way, whatever the path, wherever that path leads, to come to God. It is always possible to move closer toward God than farther away. Those who desire God will be led by his Spirit to closer communion with him."[11] He cites Abel, Noah, Enoch, Job, Jethro, the queen of Sheba, the centurion, and Cornelius as examples. He says of these, "No one can deny the fact that the Bible presents these holy pagans as saved by faith, even though they knew neither Israelite nor Christian revelation."[12] These are evidence, then, that "the grace of God touches people all over the world and that faith, without which it is impossible to please God, can and does occur outside as well as inside the formal covenant communities."[13] It appears that two assumptions are operating here: that the type of relationship these persons had with God constituted this

8. Ibid., pp. 159–60.
9. Ibid., p. 161.
10. Ibid.
11. Ibid., pp. 161–62.
12. Ibid., p. 162.
13. Ibid.

"pleasing of God" which would have to be considered salvation, and that being outside the formal covenant communities is equivalent to not knowing the Israelite or Christian revelations. These assumptions will need to be examined and evaluated at a later point.

Pinnock also cites several more categories of believers who give us insight into the nature of faith by their own situation. Among these are the following.

1. The Jews who lived before Jesus was born exercised saving faith, as did Abraham, and experienced forgiveness, as did David.[14]

2. While the interpretation of the parable of the last judgment in Matthew 25 that these are the missionaries Jesus sent out into the world may possibly be correct, it is likelier that these include Gentiles.[15]

3. Cornelius is the pagan saint par excellence of the New Testament. Pinnock rejects the view of John Stott and Calvin, that Cornelius was only relatively better than other pagans, but was not necessarily a saved person at this point. After all, Luke says that Cornelius's prayers ascended to God and that God guided him in a vision. Pinnock also rejects the idea that those who, like Cornelius, seek God will always be sent some Christian to witness to them. This implies that Cornelius was not already in a right relationship with God before becoming a Christian, and thus needed Peter to be saved from God's wrath. "But this is not true," says Pinnock. "As Job in the Old Testament story, Cornelius did not need a special messenger to make him a believer. He was a believer already and not hellbound."[16] What he needed Peter for was in order to become a Christian and to receive messianic salvation, including assurance and the Holy Spirit. Further, however, this theory is not adequate for the size of the problem. How is a Christian messenger supposed to show up among the Mongols in the fifth Christian century? Pinnock suspects that those who hold this theory do not think many such messengers will be needed because very few people call out to God for help.

4. Another category of the unevangelized are babies, whether baptized or not, who die in infancy, and the mentally incompetent. Most Christians today would hold that such persons will be saved. They are therefore prime examples of the unevangelized being saved apart from faith in Christ or even in God. How are

14. Ibid., p. 163.
15. Ibid., pp. 163–65.
16. Ibid., p. 166.

they saved? It is first through the fact that God reconciled the world to himself (2 Cor. 5:19) and this must include them. Ordinarily this reconciliation must be ratified by persons in history, "but if it cannot be ratified, one would expect this requirement to be waived or at least postponed. In the case of babies dying in infancy, the decision for God can come after death, since it could not have come before. This in turn may suggest that they are also given time to grow up and mature, so then a decision could be made. In this case, the salvation of all the unevangelized would not be certain."[17]

Pinnock believes that these considerations settle the important issue of the salvation of the unevangelized. He states categorically, "We have now refuted the restrictivist view that says that only those who actually confess Jesus in this life can be saved, be in a right relation with God, and be safe from eschatological wrath. On the contrary, the Bible teaches that many varieties of unevangelized persons will attain salvation. This will happen according to the faith principle."[18]

It is interesting to see how Pinnock works out this principle further. He says,

In the case of morally responsible persons confronted with the gospel of Christ in this life, they would surely turn to him in explicit faith. If they did not do so, it would prove that they had not been favorably disposed to God prior to that time, since Jesus is the culmination of divine revelation. Pre-Christian faith is valid up until that moment when Christ is preached, but not afterwards. When Christ is known, the obligation comes into force to believe on him. The unevangelized are expected to receive the Good News when it reaches them. God's offer becomes an objective obligation at that time, and refusal to accept that offer would be fatal. No hope can be offered to those declining God's offer to them in Christ.[19]

Evaluation of the Faith Principle

We must now examine and evaluate this view of the faith principle. A number of observations need to be made.

1. The definition of faith is important. Faith is contrasted with knowledge, or even with belief, in the usual sense of that word.

17. Ibid., p. 168.
18. Ibid.
19. Ibid.

Faith is not believing *that*, but believing *in*. Alternatively, one might conclude that what Pinnock is advocating is a believing that, but restricting greatly the content of what must be believed. Yet that does not seem to be the case. He does not argue for believing certain things, while contending that others need not be believed. The faith that he is arguing for is what has often been termed *fiducia* rather than *assensus*. It is trust in a person rather than assent to certain factual information. This has often been correlated with a view of special revelation as God's self-presentation as a person, rather than as communication of information.

There are certain problems with this theory, however. The first is that correct relationship with a person requires some conception of the person, if this is to be indeed a true relationship with that person, rather than someone else, or a false conception. If this is not the case, then the object of the faith becomes unimportant, and faith becomes purely a question of the inner subjectivity. That leads to the famous instance cited by Søren Kierkegaard in his *Concluding Unscientific Postscript*. Two men worship. One goes up to the house of the true God with a true conception of God, but prays in a false spirit. The other bows down to an idol, but with the full passion of the infinite. "Where," asks Kierkegaard, "is there most truth?" and then proceeds to answer his own question. "The one prays in truth to God though he worships an idol; the other prays falsely to the true God, and hence worships in fact an idol."[20] Surely Pinnock does not intend this point, but the question is whether sufficient elements are built into his theology to prevent it from slipping into this subjectivism. Sanders, however, quotes this very passage as an example of inclusivism.[21]

Further, the Bible specifies at least minimal content for this faith. Hebrews 11:6 states that "anyone who comes to him must believe that he exists and that he rewards those that earnestly seek him." The question then is not whether faith involves informational belief but the extent of that belief. The Old Testament prophets and other representatives of Jehovah also seemed to express considerable concern that their hearers place their trust in Jehovah, rather than in one of the other gods. Surely, the faith principle had to include enough knowledge about Jehovah to distinguish him from Baal or one of the other gods, regardless of the

20. Søren Kierkegaard, *Concluding Unscientific Postscript* (Princeton, N.J.: Princeton University Press, 1941), pp. 179–80.

21. John Sanders, *No Other Name: An Investigation into the Destiny of the Unevangelized* (Grand Rapids: Eerdmans, 1992), pp. 273–74.

name employed in either case. It was not simply belief in the supreme being. Presumably also there were other gods believed in by the persons surrounding Abraham or the "holy pagans" mentioned above. Each of these believers must have had enough knowledge to be able to distinguish Jehovah from these false gods.

2. A further problem pertains to Pinnock's identification of persons such as Abel, Noah, Enoch, and Job as "holy pagans." If he describes them as "people saved by faith without any knowledge of the revelation vouchsafed to Israel or the church," then there seems to be a serious problem here. Is he really saying none of these people had special revelation? If he is defining the revelation vouchsafed to Israel or the church narrowly, then this may be conceivable in the sense that these people antedated both Israel and the church. However, the revelation that Israel had included even the revelation that came to Abel and Noah, for example. It seems difficult to see how these individuals can therefore really be classified as holy pagans.

3. There also is a problem with the description of Cornelius as a God-fearing man. This appears to be an instance of the technical term, "God-fearer," which was used to refer to a Gentile who attended the synagogue services and practiced the law, but was not a full proselyte, not having been circumcised.[22] If this was the case, he was more like a Jew of that time than he was a Christian. Just as devout practicing Jews needed to be evangelized, so must God-fearing Gentiles. And Pinnock really gives no evidence or argument to support his contention that Cornelius did not really need Peter for salvation, being already a believer but not a Christian. He does correctly assert that Cornelius was outside the covenant community, but seems to make the illicit shift from this to the contention that he and others such as the queen of Sheba and the centurion "knew neither Israelite nor Christian revelation."[23]

4. The use of babies who die in infancy as an example of the unevangelized and an encouragement regarding the future status of the unevangelized is puzzling and possibly also misleading. Pinnock states that the reconciliation accomplished by Christ ordinarily must be ratified by the person, but in the case of persons who are incapable of such ratification, that requirement is waived or at least postponed. The problem of salvation of infants

22. Hazel W. Perkin, "God-fearer," in *Baker Dictionary of the Bible*, ed. Walter A. Elwell (Grand Rapids: Baker, 1988), 1:888.
    23. Pinnock, *Wideness in God's Mercy*, p. 162.

is of course notoriously difficult, but the solution Pinnock speculates about, namely, their growing up and then being given an opportunity, has no biblical basis, and he makes no claim for any. Suppose the other option is to be accepted then, namely, the idea that the requirement is waived. Apparently then all those who die in infancy are saved. To the extent, however, that these infants (who cannot meet the requirements because they cannot understand human language and concepts) are made an instance of the unevangelized (those who cannot meet the requirements because they do not hear), this has universalizing overtones, regardless of whether Pinnock may protest such an idea. The argument would be formulated as follows:

What is true of those who die in infancy is true of those who never hear.

The requirement of ratifying the reconciliation is waived for those who die in infancy.

Therefore, the requirement of ratifying the reconciliation is waived for those who never hear.

> This, however, seems to carry Pinnock further than he presumably would want to go. In light of that, he should perhaps restrict the alternatives to the requirement being postponed, rather than waived, in the case of those who die in infancy.

5. There is some definite slippage between a person not knowing the name of Jesus, as was true of persons like David, and not knowing any of the particulars of special revelation, as is true of at least some of the unevangelized. Pinnock does not really take into account and evaluate those differences.

An Alternative View

If the two answers we have examined must be deemed inadequate, what then will we offer as an alternative? We will seek to answer this by examining the biblical data, both Old and New Testament, to see what was involved in salvation, and what requirements had to be met to obtain it. The Old Testament is our first source of understanding.

Old Testament Teaching Regarding Faith

It is both difficult and important to identify and define correctly the nature of salvation in the Old Testament, which was broadly conceived. The Hebrew words for salvation derive from יָשַׁע (*yāšaʿ*), which means width, spaciousness, freedom from constraint, and deliverance. Consequently, these terms lent themselves to both general and specific applications. Broadly, salvation means deliverance from danger, enemies, or distress. This latter could be bondage in Egypt (Exod. 14:13), exile in Babylon (Isa. 46:13; 52:10–11), adversaries (Ps. 106:10), defeat (Deut. 20:4), or oppression (Judg. 3:31). Metaphorically, it means salvation from social decay (Hos. 1:7) and from want, the meaning approaching moral and spiritual welfare ("prosperity," Job 30:15). In Psalm 28:9 the reference is to religious blessing in general. "The Lord is my salvation" is the heart of the Old Testament, "always with an overtone of undeserved mercy." Later, Judaism anticipated a messianic period that would incorporate elements of political, national, and religious deliverance.[24]

Belief was always involved in this salvation. This, rather than fulfillment of the law, was the means of one being saved. The basic idea was that salvation was something accomplished by God. What, then, however, was the law and its purpose? The law was not the means of establishing God's favor and fellowship or of earning one's salvation, but rather, a means of maintaining fellowship with him. The same law that demanded a standard of holy living pleasing to God also provided for forgiveness and atonement for sin. Kaiser says, "One of the ways of 'doing' the law was to recognize the imperfection of one's life and thus to make a sacrifice for the atonement of one's sins. Thus Leviticus 18:5 was not a hypothetical offer of eternal life as a reward for perfect lawkeeping. The law itself assumed and provided for lawbreakers in the great sacrificial system which was a part of that covenant of law!"[25]

This idea of salvation also included a future dimension. The "day of the LORD" was the day on which the king would bring judgment upon the nations (Exod. 32:34; Deut. 31:17–18, 29; cf. Gen. 49:1; Num. 24:14; Deut. 4:30). It was even anticipated that an individual would do this. Zechariah particularly wrote about this one. God's work was to be accomplished through the king who would come, riding on a donkey, bringing salvation. He would even go forth and fight all the nations of the earth, which would one day gather to do battle against Jerusalem (Zech. 14). This was the suffering servant who would personally rule and suffer on behalf of all humankind. He would be rejected by men, whether it was his message (Isa. 53:1), his person (v. 2), or his mission (v. 3). He would personally effect an atonement between God and humans (vv. 4–6). Although he would submit to suffering (v. 7), death (v. 8), and burial (v. 9), he would subsequently be exalted and greatly rewarded (vv. 10–12).

---

24. R. E. O. White, "Salvation," in *Evangelical Dictionary of Theology,* ed. Walter A. Elwell (Grand Rapids: Baker, 1984), p. 967.

25. Walter C. Kaiser, *Toward an Old Testament Theology* (Grand Rapids: Zondervan, 1978), p. 113.

Yahweh was to return and gather Israel (54:5) and extend his "steadfast love" and "covenant of peace" (54:5, 9–10) to all nations through David's son (55:3–5; cf. 49:6; 55:1–2, 6–9; also Acts 13:45–49; 26:22–23).

This faith also looked ahead to an eschaton. This involved ending of "former things" (Isa. 41:22; 42:9; 43:9, 18; 44:8; 46:9; 48:3). Conversely, it meant the introduction of God's "new thing." There was to be new, sincere repentance (chaps. 58–59), a new Jerusalem (60), and new heavens and new earth (65:17–25; 66:10–24; cf. 2 Pet. 3:13; Rev. 21:1–4).[26]

What was to be the nature of this relationship? It certainly involved faith. This was the faith spoken of in Habakkuk 2:4, "the righteous shall live by his faith." When used of physical things, it meant "firmness" (Exod. 17:12); in the moral realm, it meant "moral firmness" or "trustworthiness" (Prov. 12:17). When used of God, it meant that his fidelity to his word could be trusted (Deut. 32:4). In usages like this in Habakkuk, it meant simply an unwavering trust in God's Word. It has been described by von Orelli as "a childlike, humble and sincere trust in the credibility of the divine message of salvation."[27]

This faith also has a negative side. It is a ceasing of all natural confidence in one's own strength and power, a renunciation of all trust in human support and assistance. So unbelief is described in Jeremiah 17:5: "Cursed is the one who trusts in man, who depends on flesh for his strength and whose heart turns away from the Lord." Faith renounces self-chosen human ways. It is a resting in, a quiet waiting for, God, as in Isaiah 30:15, "in quietness and trust is your strength." The result of this was a fearlessness of all human threats. Thus the psalmist said, "He alone is my rock and my salvation; he is my fortress, I will not be shaken" (62:6). This same concept is also found in Isaiah 8:12 ("do not fear what they fear, and do not dread it") and especially in Isaiah 28:16 ("the one who trusts will never be dismayed").

Positively, this faith was a setting apart of the Lord, as in Isaiah 8:13: "The Lord Almighty is the one you are to regard as holy, he is the one you are to fear, he is the one you are to dread." In Habakkuk 2:4, the faith of the righteous is contrasted with the pride and arrogance of the ungodly: "See, he is puffed up; his desires are not upright—but the righteous will live by his faith." The contrast here is with the Chaldeans, who, according to 1:11, are "guilty men, whose own strength is their god."

To summarize, then, this faith was an utter abandonment of reliance on one's own strength, righteousness, effort, or that of anyone other than

26. Ibid., p. 217.
27. Conrad von Orelli, *The Old Testament Prophecy of the Consummation of God's Kingdom, Traced in Its Historical Development*, trans. J. S. Banks (Edinburgh: T and T. Clark, 1885), pp. 325–26.

God himself. It was also a belief in the gracious, merciful provision of that holy, loving God. There was a belief in a day when God's cause would be vindicated and righteousness established. This belief was also related, in later Israel, to an individual who would suffer on behalf of the entire nation. There was even a belief that this salvation would be universal.

New Testament Teaching Regarding Faith

What, then, of the New Testament teachings regarding the requirements for salvation? We note throughout the New Testament writings a strong emphasis on repentance. It is found in the preaching of John the Baptist, being virtually his major emphasis (Matt. 3:2, 8, 11; Mark 1:4, 15; Luke 3:3, 8). It also played a very prominent part in Jesus' teaching (Matt. 4:17; 11:20; 21:32; Mark 6:12; Luke 5:32; 13:3, 5; 15:7; 24:47). It involves the idea of one's own personal insufficiency. It was significant in the apostles' preaching. Peter said, in the climax of his Pentecost sermon, "Repent, and be baptized every one of you in the name of Jesus Christ for the forgiveness of your sins" (Acts 2:38). In Acts 3:11–26, this same emphasis is repeated, in somewhat different words: "Repent therefore, and turn again, that your sins may be blotted out, that times of refreshing may come from the presence of the Lord, and that he may send the Christ appointed for you, Jesus" (vv. 19–20).

In addition to the need of repenting, there also was a strong emphasis on the need of understanding, belief, acceptance, and commitment on the basis of the facts of Christ's life. The life, death, and resurrection of Christ were highlighted at Pentecost (Acts 2:22–24). The death and resurrection are also central in Peter's message in Acts 3:11–16. And, in Paul's letter to the Romans, he emphasizes believing and confessing the lordship of Christ and the resurrection (10:9–10). Commitment was essential, rather than mere emotion and belief. Peter urged his hearers to "turn to God" (Acts 3:19). They are urged to "call upon the name of the Lord" (Acts 2:21; Rom. 10:13). Action was essential.

These are the factors specified in the New Testament for those who would find salvation. The enumeration of these elements does not necessarily exclude those who do not meet these conditions, but the preachers and writers do not pass up any opportunity to delineate such conditions.

Common Factors in the Two Testaments

We must now, however, seek to identify the factors involved in receiving salvation identified in both Testaments. There is certainly a need of awareness of and repentance for one's sin. This also means an awareness of the consequences of such sin for the person's relationship to God. Further, it involves the idea of inability to do anything about this predicament, to do anything to please God or to cover one's sins.

There also has to be, beyond the intellectual conviction of the wrongness of the situation, a turning from that way of life and from any sort of self-reliance.

There also is a trust in God's merciful provision for that sin. In the Old Testament, this was mediated through the sacrificial system that Jehovah had revealed to his people. In the New Testament, on the other hand, it was understood to have come through Christ's sacrificial death and victorious resurrection. To an increasing extent, in the Old Testament, this hope of the provision was identified with an individual who would come and bring about righteousness and salvation. It also came to be identified with the day of the Lord.

We must now ask ourselves, however, about the situation since that time. Could one be saved by the general response, rather than the specific? It appears from Acts 17:29–30 that Paul was saying that the situation has changed. He speaks of their past practice—of worshiping images made by man's design and skill, made of gold or silver or stone. He says that in the past God overlooked this (v. 30). Now, however, he commands all people everywhere to repent. Does this mean that the opportunity of that type is now closed? Was there previously a tolerance with respect to their lack of faith that now is no longer being exercised by God? Paul seems to be saying more than merely the fact that they now have heard of Christ removes any excuse. It is apparently urgent that these persons hear about and believe in Christ. That is why Paul is presenting the message to them. Similarly, although the Jews had the revelation in what we now know as the Old Testament, that did not prevent Paul from insisting that they must believe in Jesus Christ. Are we prepared to say that no Old Testament believer was saved or that such a person alive at or during the time of Christ's earthly ministry who had not heard of Christ could not possibly be saved? Paul's preaching to the Jews need not mean that salvation without hearing this was impossible, but only that it was improbable. Certainly God commands all persons everywhere to repent and believe in Jesus Christ, but what is the status of those who have not heard of this command?

There is a sense in which the salvation achieved by Christ's death is the permanent element within the varying forms of expression. In the Old Testament period, it was the sacrificial system that was the object of their belief and practice; in the New Testament, it was Christ's death. Yet those who believed in the former were actually saved by the latter. Is this not, then, a case of progressive revelation, so that the later supplants the earlier? The death of Christ is not simply another form; it is the reality, the only basis. If so, only belief in this would suffice. One could not continue to place one's faith in the former, even though it was understood that this was the means and expression of God's grace. For those before the latter event, the earlier was sufficient, but not for those after Christ's incarnation and sacrifice had occurred.

Chronologically Displaced Persons

What are we to say about those who live chronologically after the event of Christ, but who are epistemologically before it? In other words, we are referring to those who have never had any contact with special revelation at all, and thus cannot know the details of what God has done. They are caught in a sort of soteriological time warp, as it were. May they still be treated in the same way as those who lived before the completion of the plan of salvation and the revelation? Some may appeal to God's eternality, whereby he sees the past, present, and future equally clearly, and thus his knowledge is timeless. Although I once favored such an approach, I now believe that this is too artificial and speculative a solution.

A more helpful approach is to note that the responsibility was in relationship to the available understanding. Those who lived in the Old Testament were not held responsible for not knowing, believing, or responding to the fuller knowledge of God as found in Christ. That Old Testament revelation was, however, considerably more specific in content than we have sometimes thought.

What renders problematic the position that persons cannot possibly be saved through implicit faith is Paul's statement about those who have general revelation being without excuse (Rom. 1:20). In other words, if they are condemnable because they have not trusted God through what they have, it must have been possible somehow to meet his requirements through this means. If not, responsibility and condemnation are meaningless. What therefore must be the case is not that, on the basis of the internal law persons actually fulfill that law. Paul seems to be saying more than that no one fulfills the laws given to Moses, but that no one *can* be thus saved (Gal. 2:16, 21). If this is the case, then we must ask how one is saved, and the answer is that the law serves to make people guilty, to make them realize their need of grace, thus, to bring them to Christ (Gal. 3:24–25). Similarly, if individuals, on the basis of the inner law, come to realize their own sinfulness, guilt, and inability to please God, then that law would also have the effect of bringing them to grace.

But is this God, about which relatively little is known and understood by those who cast themselves upon him, really the true God, Jehovah, the God of Jesus Christ? If Paul is correct that these persons actually knew God but suppressed the truth, then it must be correct to say that on some level persons responding to the God of general revelation are genuinely responding to the true God. It also must be deemed to be the case, however, that while the knowledge of this God may not include all the details about him (which, to some extent, is true even of those who know him from special revelation), the conception of God should not be contradictory to the nature of the true God. Thus, one could not have been an "implicit Jehovist" while worshiping Baal, for instance. This would be true of the worship of many of those in other world religions. And it must be borne in mind that this implicit faith will always involve the idea of salvation by grace, which in its genuine form is so rare among devotees of the world religions. It must always be an abandonment of reliance on anything other than the grace of God himself.

What we are talking about in this latter part of the discussion is really how much information about the fuller revelation and the gospel may one be ignorant of and still be saved. That is a rather different question than how much of the fuller revelation and the gospel one may knowingly reject or disbelieve and still be saved. For as we have seen, there was for the Jews and Gentiles alike, a responsibility to accept and respond to the full message when presented, which removed any excuse of ignorance. We must make certain that our practice of evangelism is consistent with the answer we give. If one insists that to be saved in this era it is necessary to know and believe in Jesus, how much must one know, understand, and believe? Must one understand the incarnation, the fact that Jesus was both God and man? How orthodox must this understanding be? Is it necessary to believe that Jesus was deity just as was the Father, in the same sense and to the same degree? What if one believes that Jesus was the Son of God, but not actually God, or has not thought through what he or she believes by that expression? Must one hold the substitutionary-penal theory of the atonement, for that atoning death to be efficacious? What of the factual-historical-geographical questions? Could one be saved who mistakenly thought that Jesus lived in South America, or in the third century, or did not know when or where his life and ministry took place? Perhaps there is room for acknowledging that God alone may know in every case exactly whose faith is sufficient for salvation.

11

How Many Will Be Saved?

The issues of the immediately preceding chapters have in a sense been preliminary to the topic of this chapter. They have been oriented to the question of how persons are saved. That, then, leads logically to the question of how effective these several means or channels will turn out, in the final analysis, to be. How many will actually be saved, or more correctly, what will be the proportion between those saved and those lost? These two issues are related, but clearly distinguishable, for it would be quite possible to be an inclusivist and yet believe that very few if any will actually be saved through these alternate channels, and thus, that relatively few, overall, will be saved. Conversely, it is possible to be an exclusivist and to believe in most persons who will ever have lived being saved, if one holds that the exclusive gospel will be preached efficaciously, so that large numbers will respond and be saved.

We have examined the various positions taken and the reasons given in support of those positions. Some of those discussing these issues take the Bible more seriously than others. While recognizing that this is not the only or even the major authority for all, we must now necessarily ask first what the Bible says about how many will be saved. If there is a clear statement regarding this, then we will need to fit our theories to these data, or at least justify them on some other grounds.

When we look at the types of biblical data, we observe that they are basically of three types. The first are specific biblical statements addressing this issue. The second type consists of inferences from the practical instructions. Do these presuppose something about the people to be saved, about their number or some other significant characteristic of them? The third group of considerations are the inferences from other doctrinal considerations. The primary doctrine involved here is the doctrine of God. Does anything about his nature give us insight into the number who will be saved?

Didactic Scripture References

The relevant didactic Scripture references can be classified into four basic groups. The first are Scriptures that seem to indicate that all will be saved, thus favoring universalism. A second classification consists of passages that appear to refer to some being saved and some lost, but without specification regarding the number or proportion of each. The third are texts that speak of the saved as being many. Finally, there are biblical references to the fewness of the saved. It will be our task to examine carefully and to interpret precisely each of these, and then endeavor to find some way of combining them coherently.

Passages Favoring Universalism

The first group is sometimes given relatively little attention. These passages speak of the ultimate completeness and totality of the Lord's reign. Among those most frequently cited are John 12:32 (cf. 10:16); Acts 3:19–21; Rom. 5:12–19; 1 Cor. 15:22–28; Phil. 2:9–11; Col. 1:16, 20. Some of these are general enough regarding the outcome that they do not necessarily entail salvation as such. This would be especially true of Colossians 1:20. If the aim is simply bringing all things into subjection to Christ, then God's complete and final victory would be sufficient.

Somewhat more difficult is Philippians 2:10–11, which says that "every knee should bow, in heaven and on earth and under the earth, and every tongue confess that Jesus Christ is Lord, to the glory of God the Father." Does this not sound like saving faith, we must ask? It certainly is reminiscent of the wording of Romans 10:9–10. We must take note, however, of other passages that use similar language, but of persons who do not experience salvation. For example, in Mark 3:11, the demons are compelled to declare, "You are the Son of God!" This, however, does not constitute saving faith, but a forced acknowledgment of Christ's person. Similarly in Matthew 8:29, the demons ask, "What have you to do with us, O Son of God?" Hence, subjection to the Lord and acknowledgment of his rightful status do not necessarily indicate saving faith.

We come next to a pair of passages that draw parallels between Adam and the consequences of his sin, on the one hand, and Christ and the effects of his atonement, on the other. Romans 5:18 gives a rather striking instance. The language is the same in both parts of the verse.

Clearly, in the first part, the language is universal in its impact. What, then, about the apodosis? Must not this be assumed to be similarly universal? Certainly, this is the simplest and most obvious interpretation. Indeed, John Murray, a conservative and a Calvinist, says,

> There is no possibility of escaping the conclusion that, if the apostle meant the apodosis to be as embracive in its scope as the protasis, then the whole human race must eventually attain to eternal life. There is no escape from this conclusion in distinguishing between the objective provision and subjective appropriation. Nor is it possible to evade this inference by placing upon the justification of life an attenuated interpretation such as would be compatible with everlasting perdition. The justification with which the apostle deals in this verse is that with which he is dealing in this particular passage and in the epistle as a whole. . . . The righteousness and justification with which verse 18 deals can be nothing less than those which issue in eternal life, and the expression "justification of life" is itself capable of no other interpretation.[1]

If this were the only text that bore on the subject, Murray and we would probably come to this as our final conclusion.

In 1 Corinthians 15:22 we find a similar parallelism, which, if anything, is clearer than that in Romans 5. Paul seems to be comparing the two, Adam and Christ. If so, then the extent of Christ's work (namely, being made alive) would be expected to be as great as that of the effect of Adam's sin (namely, that all die).

Commentators have made significant efforts to avoid drawing such a conclusion. These have fallen into two major types or two major interpretations. On the one hand, some have said that we must understand a self-evident faith, namely, "so in Christ shall all (believers) be made alive." Augustine, Bengel, Rückert, Hofmann, Holsten, Beet, and Edwards have taken this approach. The other major alternative interpretation takes this to be a rising, whether to life or to condemnation. Chrysostom, Calvin, and Meyer, among others, maintain that this should be understood as a general rising, a resurrection either to life or to condemnation. Meyer says, "certainly no one shall be made alive except in Christ, but this will happen to *all*."[2]

There does seem to be yet a third possibility, however. Perhaps this is not a comparison but a contrast. Perhaps these are not mutually coterminous, but rather, mutually exclusive, groups. One must ask, "Does everyone die in Adam, and if so, in what sense?" That will, of course,

---

1. John Murray, *The Epistle to the Romans* (Grand Rapids: Eerdmans, 1959), 1:202–3.
2. Heinrich Meyer, *Critical and Exegetical Handbook to the Epistles to the Corinthians* (Edinburgh: T. and T. Clark, 1884), 2:57.

depend on the meaning one attaches to death, in the case of Adam. Was it merely physical, or did it go beyond that? It apparently was not simply, or perhaps even primarily, physical. If so, then based on God's statement, "In the day in which you eat thereof, you will surely die," if day is taken literally, Adam should have died immediately. It would appear rather that the primary reference of this death was spiritual, namely, separation from God, which eventually becomes eternal death or final and permanent separation. Seen in this sense, all who are in Christ die physically and receive spiritual death, but not eternal death. In other words, in Adam all die eternally *except* those who are in Christ. The problem with this interpretation, of course, is that it involves a shift in meaning that is not evident from the passage itself.

Texts Affirming Both Saved and Unsaved

If, however, we had only these texts, we would probably interpret them as teaching the eventual salvation of all persons. Yet these are not the only texts. While a certain type of biblical theologian might take the position that Paul teaches universalism here but not elsewhere, to the extent that we function as systematic theologians we must find some way to harmonize the interpretation of these texts with one another. This must be done with a number of texts that seem to teach that there will be both saved and unsaved, without indicating their relative proportions. Among these are 2 Thessalonians 1:8–9; Philippians 3:19; and Matthew 25:46. Other texts that assume an alternative to salvation without saying so explicitly are Matthew 12:42 and Mark 9:48.

One of the clearest of these is Matthew 25:46. This passage is, to be sure, put in the form of a parable. Nonetheless it purports to picture the future determination of humanity's destination. This determination is based on specific actions or failures to act. And it seems inescapably to be a part of this passage that there are two groups, permanently mutually exclusive of one another. Another such passage is 2 Thessalonians 1:8–9. The setting here also is the second coming, which presumably is the point at which judgment is administered. The text states, quite conclusively, that some persons will definitely be sent into a permanent exclusion from God's presence.

What is to be done with these passages? Some, to be sure, can be explained as hypothetical. On such an interpretation, they do not necessarily state that this *will* happen. Rather, these texts should be understood as descriptions of what things will be like if these persons do reject the Lord. In this case, these would be warnings similar to the hypothetical interpretation of the apostasy passages in the Book of Hebrews.

Yet this approach does not do full justice to the collection of texts. For underlying all of them is a clear distinction between two groups, those that are saved and those that are not. In Matthew 7:21–23, there is the statement, "I never knew you; depart from me, you evildoers." This is then followed by the parable of the *two* builders and the *two* houses. In Luke 6:43–48, Jesus describes those who address him as, "Lord, Lord," but do not do the things that he says. This passage also includes the parable of the two builders and the two houses. The conclusion that in Jesus' mind there were two contrasting groups seems inescapable.

We must, then, ask whether these two sets of texts can be harmonized in a coherent way. In general, the more dominant or clear-cut statements are those that assert a division. While it might be argued that these are primarily in parable form and therefore less emphatically doctrinal, the fact of the separation or division seems essential or fundamental to the point being made. Further, it seems easier to interpret the universal statements in a fashion that can be harmonized with the division texts than vice versa.

In particular, the Romans 5 and 1 Corinthians 15 passages are in contexts that affirm the work of Christ. They can therefore be understood as saying in effect *"but* in Christ persons are made alive." It should be noted that the expression "in Christ" is an exceedingly common and important one for Paul. It seems to be the key or inclusive concept designating the relationship that constitutes salvation. Thus, the contrast is in order to show what should have been the case or the predicament of those saved if they were not in Christ.

What seems then to be the most pertinent point of difference is between those who argue that many or a majority of those who have lived will be saved, and those who contend that relatively few will be saved.

Texts Teaching That Relatively Few Will Be Saved

Several biblical texts, all of them in the Gospels, seem to indicate that only a few, relatively, will come to receive eternal life. There are basically three of these (the reading of a fourth, Matt. 20:16, which appeared to support this concept being textually spurious and also a repetition of Matt. 24:14). For purposes of reference, we may quote them here.

> Enter by the narrow gate; for the gate is wide and the way is easy, that leads to destruction, and those who enter by it are many. For the gate is narrow and the way is hard, that leads to life, and those who find it are few. (Matt. 7:13–14)

> And some one said to him [Jesus], "Lord, will those who are saved be few?" And he said to them, "Strive to enter by the narrow door; for many, I tell you, will seek to enter and will not be able." (Luke 13:23–24)

> For many are called, but few are chosen. (Matt. 22:14)

On the surface, these texts appear clear: that few are actually saved, and many are not. According to their traditional interpretation, these texts indicate that relatively few will be saved out of the large number of those potentially saved. Yet a strong alternative position has been raised from a number of perspectives, maintaining that actually a large percentage of the world's total population over time will in the end turn out to have been saved.

Responses to the Fewness Texts

B. B. Warfield

The strategy of arguing for this alternative position comes from two directions. One is the negative approach, of contending that these texts, which seemingly teach the relative fewness of those saved, actually do not teach any such thing, when properly interpreted. One who has led in this endeavor is Benjamin B. Warfield, in a well-known essay, "Are They Few That Be Saved?" His thesis is stated clearly and directly: "A scrutiny of these passages will make it sufficiently apparent that they do not form an adequate basis for the tremendous conclusion which has been founded upon them."[3]

Warfield's general approach to these passages is to say that in all of them the Lord's purpose is ethical impression rather than prophetic disclosure. These statements were made under circumstances of the time to address the immediate needs of those about him. They can supply valid motivation to those with similar needs and in similar circumstances, but they cannot be generalized. There is no assurance that the circumstances implied by the original statements are necessarily constant and unchanging. Jesus' concern was to motivate his hearers to strenuous effort to make their calling and election sure, rather than to reveal to them the final outcome of his saving work in the world. In other words, the warning is about how difficult it is to enter in, not how few do. It is a description of the entering-in process, not an assessment of the number of those who actually enter in. He says, "When we read His words in the latter sense, we, therefore, do a certain violence to them; in deflecting them from their purpose we distort also their meaning and confuse their implications. We can always learn from these passages that salvation is difficult and that it is our duty to address ourselves to obtaining it with diligence and earnest effort. We can never learn from them how many are saved."[4]

3. Benjamin Breckenridge Warfield, "Are They Few That Be Saved?" *Biblical and Theological Studies* (Philadelphia: Presbyterian and Reformed, 1952), p. 338.
4. Ibid.

Warfield then proceeds to examine each of these texts specifically. He feels that what he has said in general is obvious on the face of Luke 13:23–24. We must understand this saying by seeing it in context. Coming right after the parables of the mustard seed and the leaven in the meal, it is sufficiently evident that Luke saw no intimation in our Lord's declaration that the number of the saved would be few, and Warfield observes that Theodor Zahn even supposed that Luke placed this question here, a question raised by the small and insignificant beginnings.[5] Whether this is true or not, Warfield feels that it simply would have been impossible for Luke to bring into immediate conjunction words that announce the complete conquest of the world by Christ's kingdom, and a declaration that those who are saved would be only a minority.[6] Warfield feels that the questioner asked this question because of his sense of the pitiful weakness of the kingdom, as he observed it. Jesus had gathered only a "little flock" to himself, and he had distinctly promised the kingdom to them (12:32). Yet he had been intimating increasingly clearly of late that the majority of people would be excluded from that kingdom. Warfield feels it is not difficult to imagine that the question stemmed either from distress over this confusing situation or from pride at being included in such an exclusive group. In either event, it was a natural question to ask.[7]

Jesus, however, gives no direct response to the question posed to him. Rather he uses this as an occasion for an exhortation and warning to "strive to enter by the narrow door" because "many will seek to enter and will not be able" (v. 24). There really is, in Warfield's judgment, no revelation that only a few will be saved, but a warning based upon the fact that many of those who seek to be saved fail. This is because the important thing for them is not curiosity about the number saved, but the necessity of applying themselves strenuously to their own salvation. The point of his remark is a warning against presumption. It is to be sought with earnest and persistent effort.[8]

Warfield considers Matthew 7:13–14 somewhat more complicated but no less clear. The major difference between this passage and the Luke passage is that the contrast between the two ways and the two doors is made more explicit. Here the difficulty of the task of entering into the narrow door is not as openly asserted. The mark of the correct way is not the fewness of those who enter in, but the narrow and constricted character of the way and the difficulty of traveling on it. The

5. Theodor von Zahn, *Das Evangelium des Lucas* (Leipzig: Deichert, 1913), p. 533.
6. Warfield, "Are They Few?" pp. 338–39.
7. Ibid., pp. 339–40.
8. Ibid., p. 340.

number of those entering by the one road and the fewness of those entering by the other road is presented as merely the result of the fact that the one is inviting and easy, the other repellent and difficult. "The lesson that is taught, therefore, is not that there are few that are saved but that the way of life is hard. It is, therefore, that the fundamental exhortation was not 'Go with the few!' but 'Go in by the narrow gate!'"[9]

Warfield acknowledges that it would not be unnatural to read the teaching as intended to convey the idea that the number entering the narrow gate is few, compared to those following the broad, easy way. He says, however, that "it would be wrong thus to transmute this vivid transcript of a phase of life into a didactic assertion of the ultimate proportions of the saved and lost."[10] He finds a warning to us not to engage in such calculation in the parallel instances in our Lord's parables. There is no more reason to draw from this parable the idea that the saved will be fewer than the lost than there would be to conclude on the basis of the parable of the ten virgins (Matt. 25:1–13) that the two groups will be exactly equal in number. There is even less reason to draw such a conclusion than there would be to conclude from the parable of the tares in the wheat (Matt. 13:24–29) that the number of the lost will be few compared with the number of the saved, since that is an important part of the teaching in that parable. Rather, what we have in this parable is a vivid picture of life, true to the life that lay before the eyes of his hearers and as it lies before us today as well, thus emphasizing the fundamental teaching of the parable—that the way of life is hard and that we must be diligent to walk firmly in it.[11]

On what grounds, however, asks Warfield, would we assert that this is how it must be true, equally, always, and everywhere? Has there never been a community, or is there no community today, in which a majority of the inhabitants are traveling the narrow way to the narrow gate? And, further, can it never be, or is it not to be, that the proportions of persons following "the two ways" shall be reversed? Nothing in this picture of life as observed by Jesus' hearers and by us would forbid the hope or the expectation of such a reversal. That could only be asserted if Jesus here didactically asserted that this was to be the case in the ultimate distribution of persons. But, Warfield says,

> That is so far from the case here, however, that the proportions of travellers on the two ways are introduced only incidentally and for the purpose of giving point to another lesson,—the difficulty of salvation and the con-

9. Ibid., p. 342.
10. Ibid.
11. Ibid., pp. 342–43.

sequent duty of effort in seeking it. If there be any intimation elsewhere in the Scriptures that the proportions of the travellers on the two roads may be altered as time goes on, there is no reason why we should insist, on the basis of this passage, that there must always be few following the narrow way and many the wide—with the result that the sum in the one case shall to the end remain small and in the other shall by the end become enormous.[12]

Somewhat different in nature is Matthew 22:14. Warfield believes that the parable of which these words form the concluding clause is no doubt historical in its teaching, picturing the offering of the kingdom of God to the Jews by the prophets and apostles and their rejection of the offer, followed by the turning to the Gentiles with the offer. Our Lord's summary of the results of this history in the statement, "For many are called but few chosen," has reference to the rejection of this invitation by the Jews and the sifting out of the unworthy among the Gentiles, symbolized by the lone figure in verses 12 and 13 who was not wearing a wedding garment. Our understanding of the teaching, says Warfield, will depend in part on whether these words of comment are understood as being a part of the parable, that is, the king's closing words, or whether they are Jesus' comment on the parable. If it is the latter, the terms in the saying need not, and probably are not, technical terms analogous to, though not identical in meaning with the terms, "called," "elect," and the like, in didactic portions of the New Testament. If it is the former, then these words most assuredly cannot and are not to be understood in that fashion, but must find their meaning in the preceding narrative. If these are the Lord's comments, he confines himself to the bit of history that he had recited, speaking from the standpoint of the moment rather than that of the judgment day, in the distant future. This bit of history, however, relates only to the rejection of the kingdom by the Jews and the consequent turning to the Gentiles. Warfield summarizes his interpretation of this saying: "It would in any event be incredibly harsh to take the word 'called' here with any other reference than that in which 'call,' 'called' are repeatedly used in the earlier portion of the parable. Whether, then, we assign the words to the king or to Jesus Himself, speaking outside the limits of the parable, their reference seems confined to the historical experience related in the parable, and that is as much as to say to the days of the founding of the Church."[13] Here again, Warfield feels that we must recognize our Lord's ethical intention, which was always a foremost concern in his teaching.

12. Ibid., pp. 343–44.
13. Ibid., pp. 345–46.

That ethical intention is to incite his hearers to see to it that they both respond to the invitation and live according to it.[14]

Warfield concludes, therefore, that these verses he has examined are too weak to provide a foundation for a doctrine of the scarcity of the saved. Nor can they be buttressed with other passages of a similar nature, which are somewhat difficult to find and present similar difficulties. Perhaps the most notable of these is 1 Peter 3:20, which points out that a few (only eight persons) escaped in the ark from the flood. The express mention of these few is certainly noticeable and prominent, and suggests that it was strongly in Peter's mind. We are not, however, justified in seeing in this an inclusive statement summarizing the overall response to the gospel as measured at the end of time. Rather, this should be seen as reflecting Peter's own experience of the rather meager response to the gospel as he had seen it.[15]

An interesting feature of Warfield's theology appears in his discussion of the actual historical results, even up to the time of his writing. He acknowledges that there are relatively few responding to the gospel, and states that unquestionably the kingdom of God began in very small beginnings, or more correctly has begun in small beginnings, for he feels that the church of the twentieth century is still the primitive church. To the Lord, his apostles, and his followers up to the present time, the kingdom must seem like the mustard seed, which is the smallest of all seeds, or like the mere speck of leaven, lost in the meal in which it is buried. What saves the picture from being as dark as it is painted is that in addition to the contrast between the few and the many another contrast runs throughout our Lord's teaching and that of his apostles, namely, that between the present and the future.[16] Here Warfield's postmillennial eschatology, combined with a belief that many more years and centuries lay ahead for the church, leads him to an optimistic prediction regarding the future. He says,

> These small beginnings are to give way to great expansions. The grain of mustard seed when sowed in the field (which is the world) is not to remain less than all seeds: it is to become a tree in the branches of which the birds of heaven lodge. The speck of leaven is not to remain hidden in the mass of meal: it is to work through the meal until the *whole* of it is leavened. The presence of this class of representations side by side with those which speak of few being saved necessarily confines the reference of the latter to the initial stages of the kingdom, and opens out the widest prospect for the reach of the saving process as time flows on; so wide a

14. Ibid., p. 346.
15. Ibid., p. 347.
16. Ibid., pp. 347–48.

prospect as quite to reverse the implications with respect to the ultimate proportions of the saved and the lost.[17]

Warfield rests his case at this point. He does not intend, within this treatment, to examine the positive evidence that the number of the saved will be large when compared with the number lost, in other words, that it will include the vast majority of the human race. It is sufficient to have shown that the evidence for the contrary position is not sustainable. He simply suggests that the constant teaching of Scripture includes a number of ideas that bear on this issue. One of these is that Christ must reign until he has put all enemies under his feet, which certainly must mean spiritual, not physical, conquest. Another is that the very idea of the salvation accomplished by Christ, who came as the savior of the world, contains inherently the idea that nothing less than the world will be saved by him. Finally, redemption as a remedy for sin cannot be considered to reach its final issue until the damage that sin has inflicted on the creation of God is repaired, and mankind as such is brought to the destiny originally designed for it by its creator.[18] He quotes with approval a statement by W. G. T. Shedd, that when the whole course of the gospel from beginning to end is surveyed, it will be found that, as Scripture says in Revelation 7:9 and 19:6, the elect or the church will be a great, innumerable multitude, out of *all* nations, kindred, peoples, and tongues. Their voice will be as the voice of many waters and mighty thunderings, saying, "Hallelujah, for the Lord God omnipotent reigneth."[19]

Clark Pinnock

There is not, in the literature of the present discussions, this thorough a treatment of the difficult passages. Insofar as this is done, much the same type of hermeneutic is employed. Thus, Clark Pinnock says that to make sense of Jesus' statement in Matthew 7:14, one must understand that he was here warning his hearers away from speculation and urging them to choose the hard and unpopular path. At the time of this teaching, the number of disciples was indeed few and conditions were arduous. In other contexts, however, Jesus encourages his disciples in the direction of the larger hope, perhaps to encourage them. Pinnock thinks this text teaching fewness cannot "be used to cancel out the optimism of salvation that so many other verses articulate."[20] With this

17. Ibid., pp. 348–49.
18. Ibid., p. 349.
19. Ibid., p. 350.
20. Clark H. Pinnock, *A Wideness in God's Mercy: The Finality of Jesus Christ in a World of Religions* (Grand Rapids: Zondervan, 1992), p. 154.

one exception, however, Pinnock does not in this treatise discuss any of the other texts adduced in support of the fewness doctrine, nor does John Sanders in *No Other Name.*

These two men give their attention to the other side of the evidence, the positive textual basis. We therefore will here examine their treatment of those texts. The tactic in general is to call attention to the places where Scripture speaks of the many who will be saved. Clark Pinnock writes of "optimism of salvation" and "a hermeneutic of hopefulness." He feels that it is possible either to concentrate on the passages that speak of the few who are saved, or the fact that many are lost, on the one hand; or to concentrate primarily on the passages that teach that many will be saved. He says, "To put it out in the open, I want evangelicals to move away from the attitude of pessimism based upon bad news to the attitude of hopefulness based upon Good News, from restrictivism to openness, from exclusivism to generosity."[21]

A number of biblical texts speak of the large numbers of the redeemed. One set of these involves the texts, such as Genesis 13:16 and 22:1, which speak of the vast, numberless descendants that Abraham will have, and evidently referring this to his spiritual descendants, or God's covenant people. This is then understood in light of Galatians 3:7 and 3:29, so that the prediction and promise to Abraham mean that there will be large numbers of believers. The other major place where these large numbers are mentioned is in Revelation, where in 7:9 John refers to "a great multitude that no one could count, from every nation, tribe, people and language." Appeals also are sometimes made to the descriptions of heaven as a broad and spacious place, whereas hell is narrow or small. This is especially found in the references to the city, the New Jerusalem. These texts must be seen as counters to the narrow road and gate idea.

For Pinnock, the argument proceeds along a path that is a combination of strictly biblical and more theological arguments. He notes the indications of God's universal salvific will and in particular argues at some length for the inclusiveness of the call and covenant with Abraham and the Jewish people.[22] This call is not in opposition to the universality of God's love and grace, and indeed is one of its very bases. God is in dialogue with the nations of the earth. Persons from the surrounding "pagan" nations are incorporated into Israel and even into the genealogy of Jesus Christ, the redeemer. This universality is even expressed in the psalms. In Psalm 47:1, the psalmist writes, "Clap your hands, all you nations; shout to God with cries of joy," and then goes on

21. Ibid., p. 20.
22. Ibid., p. 24.

to say, "God reigns over the nations; God is seated on his holy throne. The nobles of the nations assemble as the people of the God of Abraham. For the kings of the earth belong to God: he is highly exalted" (vv. 8–9). The prophets declare Jehovah's intention to make himself known to those outside the nation of Israel. So Isaiah writes, "The LORD Almighty will bless them, saying, 'Blessed be Egypt my people, Assyria my handiwork, and Israel my inheritance'" (Isa. 19:25). Pinnock's comment is, "The protolog of early Genesis agrees with the eschatology of the prophets and psalmists in stimulating hope in us for the substantial redemption of the world."[23]

Pinnock believes the major point on which the church has gone astray in its understanding of the gospel and the number of people included in the kingdom is the misunderstanding of the biblical teaching about election, an error he attributes to Augustine. The biblical doctrine is the corporate election of the nation of Israel to service. This was tragically and disastrously reinterpreted by Augustine to mean the selection of individuals to salvation.[24] Pinnock can understand why Augustine went in the direction he did, given the historical situation. One factor was the political situation, in which the church became a political power with the conversion of Constantine. Thus, the enemies of the state also became the enemies of the church, and such a situation is not conducive to the sort of open, loving attitude proper to Christian missions. Pinnock says, "In part this new attitude was due to a historical and not primarily a theological factor."[25] In addition, there were theological factors. The bitter Pelagian controversy led Augustine to overreact, so that the human contributed nothing to salvation.[26]

Another major factor in Pinnock's arguments is his contention that the fate of the world must be seen and understood in the light of the Noachic covenant. This was a covenant God made with all peoples, not just his chosen people of Israel. It involves the extent of salvation. While some interpret this covenant in a "minimalist way," seeing it as a covenant only of physical preservation and not of redemption, he believes otherwise.

> But surely this is a divine commitment and promise that transcends merely preserving the race from another flood. The promise to Noah prepares the way for the blessing of all nations through Abram a few chapters later. The call of Abram implements the promise to Noah. Both covenants are universal in scope. For a reader not to see this suggests a

23. Ibid., p. 30.
24. Ibid., pp. 24–25.
25. Ibid., p. 37.
26. Ibid., p. 38.

hermeneutical presupposition blocking truth out. Others do not miss the obvious point.[27]

Pinnock also argues from the texts, especially in Paul, which picture Jesus as the savior of the (whole) world and make redemption truly universal. Here, on the one hand, are cited the texts that speak of this salvation as pertaining to the world: John 3:16; 1 John 4:9, 14; 2 Corinthians 5:19. On the other hand, he appeals to the verses that seem to speak of this salvation as being to all humans. These include Colossians 1:16–17; Romans 5:18; 1 Corinthians 15:20–28; and Philippians 2:6–11. He says of the texts:

> Second, from the point of view of Christ's redemptive work, the dimension of universality is plain. Jesus is presented as the last Adam, representing the race as the first Adam had, except that in identifying with us Jesus Christ destroyed sin, defeated death, and won salvation through his obedience unto death and his glorious resurrection (Ro 5:18; 1 Co 15:20–28; Php 2:6–11). Truly, Jesus is the Savior of the world (1 Ti 4:10), the one Mediator between God and humanity (1 Ti 2:4–6), and the one through whom God has reconciled the whole world (2 Co 5:18–21). This is a most universal vision.[28]

There is also the refrain of God's universal salvific will. Repeatedly Pinnock returns to a discussion of God's love for all persons, and his expressed desire that all might come to saving knowledge of him. Surely, says Pinnock, this cannot be reconciled with the idea that God chooses to send to endless hell the majority of humans who have ever lived. Most prominent among these are 2 Peter 3:9, where Peter says that God "is patient with you, not wanting anyone to perish, but everyone to come to repentance"; 1 Timothy 2:4, "who wants all men to be saved and to come to a knowledge of the truth"; and Romans 11:32, "For God has bound all men over to disobedience so that he may have mercy on them all." This issue of the number saved comes down, he observes, to the question of God, of who or what he is and what he wants or intends. "Is he the kind of God who would be capable of sitting by while large numbers perish, or the kind to seek them out patiently and tirelessly? Does God take pleasure and actually get glory from the damnation of sinners as some traditions maintain, or is God appalled and saddened by this prospect? My reading of the gospel of Jesus Christ and my control belief causes me to celebrate a wideness in God's mercy and a boundlessness in his generosity toward humanity as a whole."[29]

27. Ibid., p. 21.
28. Ibid., pp. 33–34.
29. Ibid., p. 18.

Finally, Pinnock appeals to the pictures of the consummation, the end of history, as found in the Book of Revelation in particular. He likens John to Moses, who was permitted to glimpse the promised land, which in John's case is the renewed and transformed world. Here he sees the new Jerusalem coming down from heaven and the kings of all the nations of the entire earth coming to bring the glory and honor of their nations into it (Rev. 21:24–26). Nothing of the cultures and civilizations will be lost, but all will be incorporated into the new Jerusalem. The nations themselves, although smitten of God for their sins, can receive healing and restoration (Rev. 22:2). This is an all-inclusive picture of the all-embracing scope of Christ's redemptive work. Pinnock summarizes:

> According to John's vision, God is not even going to give up on the nations that fought and resisted him and persecuted his people so cruelly. God will finally win a victory over them, not through naked power, but through boundless love. It will not be a victory which will see them destroyed, but a victory in which they are healed. Though we are always tempted to doubt it, how could it be otherwise? How could the One who is "king of the ages," who created the whole world, and whose throne is surrounded by Noah's rainbow, not have a purpose for the whole creation or be content to rescue a pathetic remnant (Rev. 15:3; 10:6; 4:3)? Victory was on his mind: "The kingdom of the world has become the kingdom of our Lord and of his Christ, and he shall reign for ever and ever" (Rev. 11:15). Or again: "All nations will come and worship before you, for your righteous acts have been revealed" (Rev. 15:4).[30]

Analysis of the Arguments

Some analytical observations are now in order about the arguments that there will be large numbers.

1. We note in Warfield, and to a lesser extent in Pinnock, the tendency to assume that because an author presumably had a definite purpose for writing what he did, and made one central point, that only this conclusion can be drawn from that passage. Thus, if the primary purpose of a passage was to exhort the readers to faithfulness, one cannot draw from it any conclusions about eschatology, in the sense of the future facts. This, however, seems to me to commit the rather common "fallacy of a single teaching." Is Warfield's contention really true? By raising this question, I do not mean to suggest that perhaps there are multiple

---

30. Ibid., pp. 34–35.

parallel meanings of a given passage. Rather, it should be noted that an argument consists of a number of components or steps, or premises. The truth of the conclusion is based on the truth of the premises, or assumes their truth. While the major purpose is to teach the conclusion, the truth of the premises is also being asserted. So, with the eschatological teachings of Jesus, even those in parable form, we must ask, Why is he asserting this, or on what grounds is he contending for its truth? When we do this, we may well make some interesting discoveries, as that Jesus taught diligence in seeking to enter in, *because* few find that way. Only on the basis of a questionable assumption by Warfield can the claimed refutation take place.

2. The texts cited by Pinnock and others regarding the large number of persons, the great horde of believers around the throne in the final scene, are clear and correct. What is absent, however, both from these texts and others, especially where the number of the redeemed and those of the lost appears to be compared, is any indication that the lost are few. In other words, only an absolute many, not a relative many, is asserted.

3. Pinnock's arguments may establish more than he wishes to, or claims to, accomplish. The Scriptures appealed to are those often cited by universalists and in the fashion in which universalists frequently cite them, to establish that not merely many, but *all*, will be saved. Can Pinnock cite them this way, without distinguishing his interpretation from that of the universalists, and not draw their conclusions? It should be noted that his response is, in effect, we cannot be universalists, because that would deny human freedom. Is that the only thing that precludes universalism? If so, probably he should expound and defend his understanding of freedom somewhat more thoroughly, rather than operating from it as virtually a presupposition. As it stands, he seems vulnerable to conclusions that he does not want to be led to. As protective as John Sanders has been of him and others against what he feels are innuendoes of creeping universalism, is this not nonetheless a problem, or at least a potential problem?

4. Pinnock shows an awareness of the role of historical conditioning. Thus, as we have noted above, he attributes Augustine's coming to the conclusions that he reached to the historical situation of the church and the empire. He uses this to neutralize or relativize the disastrously mistaken Augustinian view, which may actually be a case of Pinnock committing the genetic fallacy. He also appeals to historical factors contributing to the view he espouses, such as the pluralism of our society. Yet, rather than

allowing these considerations to relativize his own view, he cites them as support for that view. This seems to be a blind spot on his part. Yet those who live by the sword of historical relativity will also perish by that sword.

5. It is notable that the statements of the large number of the saved refer to the absolute sense of those saved, rather than to some comparative number. To my knowledge, there are no instances where the number lost are indicated to be few, or where the number saved are described as many, compared to the number lost. Further, the analogy is used to say that some parables speak of the many lost and the few saved, but some, such as the virgins or the tares among the grain, or the kingdom as the leaven growing throughout the loaf, seem to indicate a relatively greater number of the saved. What is interesting, however, is that the numbers in the latter type of parable are either too specific or too vague, that is, the exact number of the virgins as five and five or the leaven spreading and growing, and no reference is explicitly made to a comparison. In addition, Jesus' statement in Luke 13 came in direct response to a question about whether the saved would be many or few. All of this suggests that we must take seriously the texts that propose relative fewness of the saved.

6. A further question must be raised regarding the issue of whether Jesus' statements about the few being saved addressed the proximate or the ultimate situation. In some ways, it could be argued that the response Jesus gives reflects merely the immediate situation, in which there was relatively slight response to the gospel. Note, however, that in the phrasing of the question in Luke 13, there is no real intimation of such a limitation. Indeed, if the question pertained to only the immediate situation, the answer would seem to have been fairly evident. One could see that there was not a large response. It was placed in the future tense, "Are only a few people going to be saved?"

7. If we seek to answer the question from an empirical-historical perspective, it appears that the more conservative estimate of the response is more in keeping with the facts. For certainly, overall, since the beginning of the church, the number of those who have responded favorably to the gospel percentage has been a relative minority. Even within the Book of Acts, this was the case. While we are impressed with the response of the three thousand at Pentecost, even this may have been a minority of those present. At any given time within the history of the church, the true Christians have ordinarily also constituted a minority. Does this not lead us to the conclusion on historical grounds, that the saved

will turn out to be actually only few? In the twentieth century the percentage of all kinds of Christians in the world has declined from 34.4 percent in 1900 to 33.7 percent in mid–1995. This suggests that Christianity has been failing to keep pace with the rate of growth of worldwide population.[31] Some opportunities for evangelization appear to be declining. This is true especially where national religions, especially Islam, are becoming more aggressive and restrictive. While some have eagerly hailed the opened doors of the former Iron Curtain countries, this enthusiasm may have been premature, in light of the influx of cult activity and resurgent nationalism. While the rapid growth of Christianity in Africa offers encouragement, no signs of worldwide revival can be clearly discerned.

We may, however, note that although postmillennialism has, because of considerations such as those just noted, fallen into considerable disfavor of late, there are some grounds on which one might expect a reversal of the situation. Because there are periodic revivals, and because an almighty God could bring about massive conversions, may it not be that in the future and endtimes, a large majority of people will turn to Christ? And if a large amount of time is left until the end of the world, and if thus, the preponderance of people who will have lived during the entire span of world history are either alive now or yet to be born, would this not argue that a majority will yet enter the kingdom of God? And, if there is actually the possibility of implicit faith for those who have not heard, might this so supplement the number of those who hear and respond overtly, as to constitute a clear enough majority?

In a sense, of course, we have no way of knowing just what the future will hold. This is what is distinctive about the future, that we have not yet experienced it. Yet there may be one hint in Jesus' eschatological teaching that would give us some assistance in this matter. His description of the last times suggests that it will be a time not of faith, but of infidelity (Matt. 24:9–14). Thus, a decline, rather than an increase, seems to be what we might expect. To be sure, it might be argued that what is described there is the very end, and that between now and then there will be large numbers of believers, and great success of the preaching. We simply do not have adequate basis to decide that. What indications we do have are not encouraging.

31. David B. Barrett, "Annual Statistical Table on Global Mission: 1995," *International Bulletin of Missionary Research* 19.1 (January 1995): 24–25.

Conclusions

Let us now draw some brief conclusions.

1. There will be persons present in the final kingdom from every tribe and nation. The gospel will be preached successfully, in the sense that it will be taken to every group and there will be converts from all nations.
2. There will be a large number of believers. On any way of calculating, the redeemed will be a great horde, beyond any crowd that we have ever encountered.
3. Nonetheless, they will be, when compared to the great number of unbelievers, a minority. It is not with any satisfaction that we arrive at this conclusion. On the contrary, it is with a great sense of sorrow that we conclude this. We could wish that it were otherwise. Yet, in the final analysis, it is not our wishes or desires that determine what is true. There is a sufficient number of reasonably clear biblical texts teaching this that we have no choice but to reach this conclusion.

12

Annihilationism

For those who believe both that there is some sort of future existence and that not all will be saved, a major problem remains. What happens to those who are not saved? The traditional view is that these persons experience endless suffering in separation from God. This is the doctrine of hell. Throughout the history of the church there have always been those who consider this doctrine unacceptably harsh. The view known as annihilationism is the conception that at some point human beings cease to exist at all. This may be found in several variations. Ordinarily it is the idea that only certain persons, usually those who have not believed or those who have not been saved, come to a state of nonbeing. Either they simply pass out of existence, or they are put out of existence. This may be believed to happen at the point of death, or at some subsequent point. Basically, there have been three major groups of theories.[1]

Theories of Annihilationism

Pure Mortalism

This is the idea that human life is inseparably bound up with the organism. Thus, with the death and dissolution of that organism, the person also passes out of existence. This is usually based on either a materialistic or pantheistic, at least pantheizing, philosophy. In the former, the soul is conceived of as simply a function of organized matter, so that there would not really be anything existing independently of that mat-

---

1. These descriptions are largely drawn from the overview given by Benjamin B. Warfield, "Annihilationism," in his *Studies in Theology* (New York: Oxford University Press, 1932), pp. 447–57.

ter. There is, in other words, really no spiritual entity, only a spiritual aspect of the person. In the latter case, however, the soul of the person is thought of as merely an individualized manifestation or, in effect, as a portion of the whole spiritual entity, and it is reabsorbed by that larger entity upon the dissolution of the individual organism. In rare instances the idea of the soul as a spiritual entity distinct from the material body but incapable of maintaining its existence separate from the body, is found. This understanding of annihilation in the broad sense, applying to all persons, is not commonly found in Christian theologies, because the emphasis on persistence after death is so strong within Christianity.

Conditional Immortality

This view is considerably more common within Christian circles. This conception agrees with the preceding view that the human is naturally mortal, but disagrees with it by saying that the human person can, under certain circumstances, become immortal, or as Paul put it, "put on immortality." The essential point, however, is that the human is not naturally immortal but must have such immortality conferred by God. For some, this stems from the understanding of the person as completely unitary, so that with the physical death of the person, there is no potential for continued survival. The soul dies with the body, and life beyond death is a matter of resurrection, which is essentially a re-creation of the entire person. Some would say that only the righteous are resurrected; others simply pass out of existence at death. Others, by contrast, maintain that all will be resurrected for the judgment, when the unrighteous will then be annihilated. Some of these hold that there will be a prolonged period of punishment, with annihilation taking place gradually. This may be a matter of persons simply losing their powers of existence, "wearing out," as it were. Yet others hold that there is a lack of any conscious existence until resurrection. The resurrection of unbelievers, on this view, occurs later than that of believers, and involves the unjust coming to life at the voice of God, becoming extinct in that very occurrence.

Annihilationism Proper

This view is based on the understanding of the human person as not naturally mortal, but immortal. Thus, the soul, or more correctly, the person, does not pass out of existence simply with the death of the person but ceases to be because of God's action. There is variation regarding when this will happen. It may be at death, at the general judgment, or at the end of a period of punishment that varies with each individual, according to the respective guilt of each. The means by which this is accomplished may be any of several possibilities: by a direct act of God, who cuts off the person; through the effect of the punishment administered; or through the effect of the sin itself. What all of these varieties have in common is that they regard the termination of the person not as the natural result of the end of life in the usual embodied form, but as a consequence of a definite act by God. It therefore relates to the other understandings of the end of the person's existence in a fashion similar or parallel to the relationship of active to passive euthanasia.

It should be noted, as Warfield has pointed out, that these types do not always or perhaps even often appear in pure or unmixed form. Because their advocates are not always careful to keep strictly within the logical limits of one of the classes of theories, we frequently find mixed versions of them. This is obvious in the versions currently being most energetically presented.

This overall conception has recently received renewed interest, exposition, and defense, and from somewhat surprising sources. A number of rather prominent evangelical theologians and leaders have in the past decade declared themselves to hold this view. Among these are John Wenham,[2] Stephen Travis,[3] Philip Edgecumbe Hughes,[4] Clark Pinnock,[5] and Michael Green.[6] At the Consultation on Evangelical Affirmations, held at Trinity Evangelical Divinity School in May 1989, debate broke out on this topic and it proved impossible to formulate an article that would represent the views of all those present.[7]

Arguments for Annihilationism

A number of arguments are advanced by those who currently represent this position. We shall examine several of these in turn.

The Issue of Mortality or Immortality

A first tactic, which is both theological and broadly biblical, is to examine and reject the idea that the human is somehow inherently immortal. The effect of this endeavor is to move the discussion increas-

2. John W. Wenham, *The Goodness of God* (Downers Grove, Ill.: InterVarsity, 1974), pp. 34–41.

3. Stephen H. Travis, *I Believe in the Second Coming of Jesus* (Grand Rapids: Eerdmans, 1982), p. 198.

4. Philip Edgecumbe Hughes, *The True Image: The Origin and Destiny of Man in Christ* (Grand Rapids: Eerdmans, 1989), pp. 398–407.

5. Clark H. Pinnock, "The Destruction of the Finally Impenitent," *Criswell Theological Review* 4.2 (1990): 243–59.

6. Michael Green, *Evangelism through the Local Church* (Nashville: Oliver Nelson, 1992), pp. 72–73.

7. *Christianity Today* 33.9 (June 16, 1989): 62–63.

ingly toward the position of conditional immortality. The reason for concern about this, argues Fudge, is that if the natural immortality of the soul is accepted, then the options are reduced to an unacceptable few.[8] He quotes Pusey, who says, "If man is admitted to be immortal, and punishment is not endless, there is no other conclusion but that he should be restored."[9] For those who accept this conclusion, and who, like the annihilationists, find either alternative unacceptable, rejection of natural immortality takes on special significance.

Part of the argument is the contention that the idea of the immortality of the soul is of Greek philosophical, rather than biblical, origin. It has found its way into Christian theology at a number of points. Some, especially the Reformed, maintain that this is part of the image of God and God's life-giving breathing into man the breath of life.[10] Critics, however, have claimed increasingly that this doctrine, which has had a rather long and in some periods unchallenged reign in the churches, is not really a biblical doctrine, in the fullest sense of the term. Rather, it is of pagan origin and crept into Christian thinking through Platonic philosophy. The Bible attributes immortality to the future glorified body, rather than to the present soul. Thus, the basis of confidence in life after death is bodily resurrection, not immortality of the soul.[11] While conceding that the early Fathers such as Origen and Augustine held to a type of view of the immortality of the soul, Fudge insists that their view was different from that of the Greek philosophers. Their view was not that the soul was inherently immortal, but came into being at the creative hand of God. Although it survives death, its future existence also depends on God's will. Others, however, such as Justin Martyr and Tatian, openly fought against the pagan doctrine of immortality.[12]

Coupled with this is a positive biblical doctrine of humanity and of the nature, if any, of immortality. Fudge maintains that the traditional arguments that the biblical view of the human includes immortality must be rejected. It does not follow, for example, from the human having been created in the divine image. Immortality is no more an essential quality of God, so that possession of the image would entail it, than is omnipotence or omniscience, which no one claims humans must have by virtue of possessing the image. Even if this were the case, it

8. Edward William Fudge, *The Fire That Consumes: A Biblical and Historical Study of Final Punishment* (Houston: Providential, 1982), p. 51.

9. Edward Bouverie Pusey, *What Is of Faith as to Everlasting Punishment? In Reply to Dr. Farrar's Challenge in His "Eternal Hope," 1879* (Oxford: James Parker, 1880), p. 27.

10. Harry Buis, *The Doctrine of Eternal Punishment* (Philadelphia: Presbyterian and Reformed, 1957), p. 8.

11. Fudge, *Fire That Consumes*, p. 54.

12. Ibid., p. 67.

might have been lost in the fall, since Genesis 5:3 states that Adam "be-
gat a son in his own likeness, after his image." Another argument is
from Jesus' statement in Matthew 22:32, that "I am the God of Abraham, the God of Isaac, and the God of Jacob." Surely, say some, this
must argue for the immortality of at least these three patriarchs. Seen
in context, however, it will be noted that Jesus is using this quotation
and thus his argument to prove the resurrection, not immortality. The
parallel passage in Luke makes clear that Jesus is speaking of the resurrection of those who belong to God, not the immortality of every person. Further, the presence of such expressions as "salvation of the soul"
in the Bible (e.g., Mark 8:35–38; 1 Pet. 1:9) does not argue for a separate
immortal soul. These are merely quotations of passages such as Psalm
16:9–11; 49:15; and 73:24, which speak of the psalmist's hope for abid-
ing fellowship with God, who will not let his own perish. The word
"soul," for both Old and New Testament writers, is here simply referring to the life of the person, not to some entity within him.[13]

This point is then developed at some length, through an examination of the biblical data from both testaments. The Hebrew word is
so rich and varied in its meaning that the translators rendered it in
forty-five different ways. The same terms are applied to both humans and animals. The conclusion to be drawn from such data is
that the human is an indivisible whole. When death occurs, it is the
death of the soul, the whole person, not simply the death of the body,
with the soul somehow surviving.[14] The New Testament gives a similar conception of the soul. The word ψυξή usually denotes the life
of the person, not some part of the person. Sometimes the adjectival
form of the word refers to the unspiritual or carnal person as contrasted to the spiritual person (1 Cor. 2:14–15), or the natural body
of this life contrasted with the spiritual body of the life to come
(1 Cor. 15:44).[15]

The Concept of Destruction

A second concept and argument centers around the idea of destruction, together with the concept of its means, namely, the consuming
fire. John Stott speaks of this as the argument relating to language. He
notes that the vocabulary of "destruction" is often used in relation to
the final state of perdition. The most common Greek words are the
verb ἀπόλλυμι (to destroy) and the noun ἀπώλεια (destruction). When
the verb is active and transitive it means to kill, as in the case of

13. Ibid., pp. 59–60.
14. Ibid., pp. 60–62.
15. Ibid., p. 64.

Herod's attempt to murder the baby Jesus and the Jewish leaders' plot to have him executed (Matt. 2:13; 12:14; 27:4). Jesus told his hearers not to be afraid of those who kill the body but cannot kill the soul (Matt. 10:28; cf. James 4:12). If, then, to kill is to deprive the body of life, it would seem that hell is a deprivation of both physical and spiritual life, in other words, an extinction of being. In the middle voice and intransitive, the verb means to be destroyed and so to perish, whether physically, as by hunger or snakebite (Luke 15:17; 1 Cor. 10:9), or eternally in hell (John 3:16; 10:28; 17:12; Rom. 2:12; 1 Cor. 15:18; 2 Pet. 3:9). Just as the believers are those being saved, so the unbelievers are τοῖς ἀπολλυμένοις (those who are perishing; 1 Cor. 1:18; 2 Cor. 2:15; 4:3; 2 Thess. 2:10). In his much quoted and debated statement about the broad and narrow roads, Jesus said that the broad road leads to destruction (Matt. 7:13; see also Rom. 9:22; Phil. 1:28; 3:19; Heb. 10:39; 2 Pet. 3:7; Rev. 17:8, 11). It would seem strange, then, says Stott, if those who are said to suffer destruction are not actually destroyed. He agrees with Edwards that it is "difficult to imagine a perpetually inconclusive process of perishing."[16]

There is, further, the biblical imagery of hell. The most prominent element in this imagery is, of course, the image of fire. This is commonly understood as teaching that those who are lost will eternally be submitted to this punishing flame, and will never be consumed by it. Jesus uses the expression "the fire of hell" in Matthew 5:22 and 18:9 and speaks of "eternal fire" in Matthew 18:8 and 25:41. The Book of Revelation refers to "the lake of fire" (20:14–15). Stott suggests that it is undoubtedly because we have all had the experience of the acute pain of being burned that fire is associated in our minds with "conscious torment." He maintains, however, that the main function of fire is not to cause pain, but to secure destruction, as all the world's incinerators bear witness. This also fits very well with the biblical expression "a consuming fire" and with John the Baptist's warning of the Judge "burning up the chaff with unquenchable fire" (Matt. 3:12; cf. Luke 3:17). Stott summarizes his conclusions from this data: "The fire itself is termed 'eternal' and 'unquenchable,' but it would be very odd if what is thrown into it proves indestructible. Our expectation would be the opposite: it would be consumed for ever, not tormented for ever. Hence it is the smoke (evidence that the fire has done its work) that 'rises for ever and ever'" (Rev. 14:11; cf. 19:3).[17]

16. John Stott, in David L. Edwards, *Evangelical Essentials: A Liberal-Evangelical Dialogue* (Downers Grove, Ill.: InterVarsity, 1988), pp. 315–16.

17. Ibid., p. 316.

Stott, however, notes and responds to four objections to his understanding of the lake of fire. The first is the vivid picture of hell as a place where "their worm does not die, and the fire is not quenched" (Mark 9:48). He points out that Jesus is quoting here from the last verse of Isaiah (66:24), which refers to the dead bodies of God's enemies being consigned to the city's rubbish dump, to be eaten by maggots and burned. While Judith (16:17) applied this to the everlasting pain for the nations hostile to God, Jesus in his use of Isaiah does not mention everlasting pain. Rather, in his words it is the worm that will not die and the fire that will not be quenched. They will not, at least not until their work of destruction is done. The worm and the fire are everlasting, not the persons who are experiencing their effects.

The second objection is Jesus' reference to "eternal punishment" in contrast to "eternal life" at the end of the parable of the sheep and the goats in Matthew 25:46. It is customarily assumed and even argued by some that if eternal life means that the righteous will live forever in conscious bliss in God's presence, the parallel requires that wicked unbelievers will forever experience conscious punishment in hell. Stott replies that this interpretation reads into the text what is not necessarily there. Rather, although Jesus said that both the life and the punishment would be eternal, he did not, at least in this passage, define the nature of either of these. Elsewhere (John 17:3) he spoke of eternal life as conscious enjoyment of God, but it does not follow that eternal punishment must be a conscious experience of pain at God's hand. "On the contrary," says Stott, "although declaring both to be eternal, Jesus is *contrasting* the two destinies: the more unlike they are, the better."[18] Clark Pinnock gives this response a slightly different shading. He also states that Jesus does not define the nature of either eternal life or eternal punishment in this passage. He simply states that there will be two destinies and leaves it there. In light of the interpretation of other teachings on the subject, one is free to interpret this text as meaning either everlasting conscious torment or irreversible destruction. The text allows both possibilities. All it teaches explicitly is the finality of the judgment itself, not its nature.[19]

A third objection is based on the parable, if that is what it was, of the rich man and Lazarus, as found in Luke 16. Did not the rich man (called Dives, after the Latin word for rich man) declare that he was "in agony in this fire" (vv. 23–24, 28)? That is true, yet Stott has several reservations about using this as an argument. We must be cautious in interpreting a parable (if it was that) that speaks of "Abraham's bosom" as

---

18. Ibid., p. 317.

19. Clark H. Pinnock, "The Destruction of the Finally Impenitent," *Criswell Theological Review* 4.2 (Spring 1990): 256.

well as hell fire. Further, since these experiences took place apparently immediately after the death of the two men, the most natural interpretation of the passage would be that it is referring to the intermediate state between death and resurrection. Stott, in fact, believes that this is when the lost come to the horrible realization of their fate. And such an interpretation is surely not incompatible with annihilation. In a similar fashion, because the "torment" of Revelation 14:10 will be experienced "in the presence of the holy angels and of the Lamb," that seems to refer to the moment of judgment, not to the eternal state. Not the torment itself, but the smoke, is the symbol of the completed burning that will be for ever and ever.

The Biblical Concept of Justice

Stott says that basic to this concept is the belief that God will judge people "according to what they have done," as described in such passages as Revelation 20:12. This implies that the penalty will be commensurate with the evil that has been done. This principle was of course followed in the Jewish law courts. Thus, if life had been taken, life could be taken in retribution, but if an eye, tooth, hand, or foot had been taken, then the penalty was limited to an eye, tooth, hand, or foot, respectively. This was spelled out, for example, in Exodus 21:23–25. There the lex talionis, or law of retribution, was followed, which limited the punishment to an exact retribution. If, however, there is eternal conscious torment as punishment for sins done in time, is there not a serious disproportion between the wrong and the penalty? Is not God guilty of the same sort of inequity that his law prohibited? This would certainly seem to follow. While not minimizing the seriousness of sin as rebellion against the Creator, he wonders if "eternal conscious torment" is compatible with divine justice as that has been revealed in the Bible. The only possible exception to this that he can see is if somehow the impenitence also continues throughout eternity.[20]

Pinnock also argues this point. In his case, the matter of utility enters in rather strongly. He contends that this is infinite punishment for finite sin, because a finite being cannot commit an infinite sin, even if against an infinite being. The major point, however, as he sees it, is that such unending torture of the wicked would serve no conceivable divine purpose except sheer vengeance and vindictiveness. It would spell endless and total unredemptive suffering, punishment for its own sake. There is no question here of reformation or reeducation of the wicked. There could never be any resulting good beyond the suffering itself. He cites with approval Hans Küng's observation that quite apart from the issue of the con-

20. Stott, *Evangelical Essentials*, pp. 318–19.

tradiction of a merciless God to all that we find in Jesus' teaching about the Father, such punishment is strangely out of harmony with our times. Currently in education and in criminology retributive punishments without an opportunity for probation are being abandoned. It is thus most inappropriate, and to most persons monstrous, that a God should administer not only lifelong but eternal punishment of body and soul.[21]

Biblical Texts Suggesting Universalism

Finally, Stott argues on the basis of the texts that have traditionally been used as the basis of universalism, including John 12:32; Ephesians 1:10; Colossians 1:20; Philippians 2:10–11; and 1 Corinthians 15:28. He is not led to universalism because of them, but raises the question of how eternal existence of the impenitent in hell can be reconciled with the biblical teaching of the apparent reconciling of all things to God by Jesus' final victory over evil. How can God in any meaningful sense be said to be all things to all people if a certain number of people continue in rebellion against him and under his judgment? He feels that "it would be easier to hold together the awful reality of hell and universal reign of God if hell means destruction and the impenitent are no more."[22]

The Doctrine of God

Pinnock has at least two more reasons for his belief in annihilationism. One is the doctrine of God per se. A God who would torment even the rebellious eternally is cruel and merciless. How is one to worship and imitate such a being? Everlasting suffering, especially if linked to soteriological predestination, according to which persons are lost because God predestined them to that fate, raises the apologetic task connected with the problem of evil to an impossible and hopeless level.[23]

Metaphysical Dualism

Finally, a metaphysical problem is involved in such a scheme. There is, under the arrangement of an unending hell, a similarly unending cosmological dualism. Heaven and hell just go on existing together forever. Pinnock feels that it would make better sense metaphysically, as well as biblically, morally, and justice-wise, if hell meant destruction and the wicked simply were no more. If this were not the case, the "disloyal opposition would eternally exist alongside God in a corner of unredeemed reality in the new creation."[24]

21. Pinnock, "Destruction," pp. 254–55.
22. Stott, *Evangelical Essentials*, p. 319.
23. Pinnock, "Destruction" pp. 253–54.
24. Ibid., p. 255.

Evaluation

We now need to offer an evaluation of annihilationism. Its opposite or contradictory is the traditional view that those who are not "saved" will suffer endless punishment in hell. The response will proceed in two parts: a criticism of certain of the arguments advanced by these persons, and a positive argumentation for the opposite view.

Philosophical Conceptions

It is necessary first to examine the philosophical conceptions present within the usual form of annihilationism. The major philosophical argument is that the eternal punishment view depends on the idea that the human soul is immortal, and hence cannot cease to be, or cannot be destroyed, even by God himself. The contention is that this idea does not derive from biblical sources, but from Greek philosophy, especially that of Plato. There are two assumptions or even two steps in the argument. The first is that similarity of two ideas demonstrates a common origin or cause, or that one of these originates from or is caused by the other. The second is the claim that a causal explanation of something adequately accounts for it, or settles the question of its truth.

These two ideas or assumptions must now be scrutinized. The overall difficulty with this argument is the lack of specificity and precision in the description of the Greek view. On many issues Greek thought was varied rather than monolithic. In Platonism (the view most frequently cited in these discussions) the idea of immortality is tied to a conception of preexistence of the soul. Thus, the soul is eternal or immortal in both directions, past and future, having neither beginning nor end. This is not true, however, of the Christian view. What is usually described as the doctrine of immortality in Christian theology is that the soul is immortal into the future but not into the past. It will never cease to exist at any point in the future, but has come into being at some finite point in the past. This is true, whether in the creationist view that God directly and specially creates each soul at the time of conception, or the traducianist theory that God created in seminal form all the souls of the human race at the beginning of the race, which then came into individual existence in the multiplication process of human reproduction.

There is a further significant difference. The Greek view was of natural or inherent immortality. The soul as soul is immortal. The biblical Christian view, on the other hand, is of a derived or dependent, and contingent or conditional, immortality. The soul does not have its immortality naturally. The ability to survive forever derives from God. In terms of physical immortality, the soul was potentially immortal when created, but would only become truly and everlastingly that if the requisite conditions were fulfilled, in other words, if the first parents of the human race obeyed God's command completely. We must therefore conclude that the causal connection has not been established. There simply must be more specific resemblance to establish any sort of derivation or common origin of the Christian from the "Greek" view.

Even if there were some sort of derivation or causation, however, it would not account for the Christian view of immortality. It might give a causal explanation of how this belief came into being, but not the reason for it. It would not have settled the question of its truth. One who holds that this does suffice would seem to be guilty of the genetic fallacy, of assuming that when one has explained the existence of an idea he has accounted for it. Rather, this may have been a factor that God utilized in the process of revelation.

General Theological Issues

A second point of evaluative concern relates to the general theological issues. The major concept here is the understanding of God. This difficulty appears at two specific points. One is the love of God, made clear many places in Scripture, but perhaps nowhere more so than in 1 John 4:8. We must, however, ask about the nature of this love. Pinnock, Stott, and others depict a sentimentalized version, in which God would not do anything that would cause anyone pain, displeasure, or discomfort. Thus, endless suffering would be incompatible with divine love.

We must ask, however, whether this really is the biblical picture of God's love. May it not be that God chooses some actions that cause some pain to some persons, for the sake of a higher good, namely, the greater joy or welfare of the whole of humanity, or more significantly, the good of the whole of reality, especially, the glory of the supreme being, God? (The issue of justice reflects another aspect of this same problem, and will be discussed below.)

There also seems to be a truncated understanding of God's will. This appears, for example, in Pinnock's complaint that if God does not want anyone to perish, then the idea of eternal conscious suffering for anyone is incredible. We must ask, however, whether there may not be more than one sense of God's will. Are there not situations in Scripture in which God willed to permit persons to do that which he really did not wish, or did not like? A clearly enunciated case of this would be Jesus' statement in Matthew 19:8 about divorce in the Old Testament era. God, because of the people's hardness of heart, permitted a situation that in the ultimate sense was apparently very displeasing to him. I have elsewhere distinguished between what I term God's "wish" and God's "will."[25] Certainly all of us as moral beings periodically make decisions contrary to our wishes. We choose to do things that we do not really like, and choose not to do things that we would very much like to do. This distinction, however, does not seem to enter into Pinnock's thinking. If God wants something to happen, and has the power to bring it about, then it must surely occur.

That brings us to the other general theological issue of justice. These theologians reject eternal conscious suffering on the basis that it is a punishment grossly disproportionate to the offense. How can a just God punish eternally or for an infinite period of time someone who has committed only a finite sin? How can a finite person be guilty of an infinite wrong?

This discussion, however, seems to assume that we are dealing with two basically equal partners, who therefore can negotiate a mutually acceptable agreement between them. In such a situation, the human might protest what is to him a disagreeable outcome. This is not the case here, however. One person is infinite, the other finite. The finite owes to the infinite person everything he has, including life itself. To fail, then, to honor God, obey him, accept what he says, and so forth, is indeed an infinite act of ingratitude and of rejection.

It is sometimes contended that there is no way that any sin or any combination of sins could be infinite. What must be measured, however, is the effect, which may seem to be out of all proportion to the act. Thus one person might make just a tiny pinprick in the body of another, so slight as to be scarcely noticeable. Yet if it is made in a crucial spot, or with a contaminated instrument, the effects may actually prove fatal. The act is, then, an absolute one, slight though it seems to be. The effect may also be specifically dependent upon the nature and condition of the person against whom the act is committed. The introduction of a particular substance into the body of another may not have appreciable effect. If, however, that substance is introduced into the body of a person who is allergic to it, the results may be fatal. It is important to remember that God's perfectly holy nature is totally opposed to sin. The point we are making is this. In protesting what they see as the injustice of everlasting suffering as punishment, the annihilationists assume that sin does not have that great an effect on God, and consequently should not be punished infinitely. But how do we know the full extent of sin's effect on a perfectly holy God, for whom sin must be exceedingly offensive, because it is a contradiction of his very nature?

The annihilationists also assume that the punishment that constitutes hell is something God administers by a deliberate, voluntary, and

25. Millard J. Erickson, *Christian Theology* (Grand Rapids: Baker, 1986), p. 361.

vindictive action by himself. The picture given seems to be of a God who chooses to send persons to such a punishment, when he need not. May it not be, however, that it is primarily the human person who chooses the eternal punishment, or at least chooses the action that leads to that punishment? Indeed, this is the very thing theologians such as C. S. Lewis have proposed as a possibility. On such a scheme, the fundamental characteristic of hell is not physical flame and attendant suffering. Rather, what is most characteristic of hell, what really makes it hell, is the absence of God, with the consequent loneliness, anguish, and longing, just as what makes heaven heaven is primarily God's presence. Thus, sin is a human being saying, "God, go away and leave me alone," and hell is God finally saying, in effect, "All right, you shall have what you wish." It is not, in the final analysis, God who sends persons to hell, but rather those persons themselves.[26]

May it not be that for persons to be what they are, so that salvation may be what it is, they must be so constituted as to have the potential of living forever? Perhaps this is one of those necessary matters, such as God's inability to make triangles without three sides, or circles in which all points on the circumference are not equidistant from the center of the circle.

Pinnock objects to this and similar attempts to minimize in some fashion the severity of hell. He refers to these as "taking the hell out of hell." He insists that the view of hell to be evaluated is that which has been most prominently held throughout most of the history of the church.[27] We must ask, however, why hell must be understood in the most offensive way possible. It almost seems as if the eternal punishment option is being stated as unfavorably as possible, to give rhetorical appeal to the alternative. This seems, however, to be a less than ideal way of handling a difference. One of Socrates' opponents or dialogue partners once complained that Socrates stated his view in the worst possible way. If true, that is a serious charge, since it suggests that one is attempting to gain an unfair rhetorical advantage.

The type of suggestion we have been developing is not, of course, well received in American society. In our society, the idea of individual responsibility is not popular, and even is not frequently mentioned. People do things that are unwise, and they are not regarded as really having contributed to the outcome of those actions. To suggest that the agent of the action is responsible may be thought cold- or hard-hearted. Persons who may have acted carelessly or irresponsibly (e.g., engaging in sexual intercourse under certain conditions), with

26. C. S. Lewis, *The Problem of Pain* (New York: Macmillan, 1962), pp. 127–28.
27. Pinnock, "Destruction," pp. 245, 254.

results which for them are undesirable or inconvenient (e.g., pregnancy) feel that they should have the right to reverse or, in effect remake, that decision (e.g., having an abortion) irrespective of the consequences for others (e.g., destruction of what may be a human life).

Reality, as defined by God, is not that way, however. Acts have consequences, and justice means that these must be experienced. That God provides removal of the eternal consequences for those who repent and accept his provision as grace. Justice, however, does not require that he cancel the inevitable results for those who continue to live independently of him.

Some other specific points in the arguments we have examined merit additional evaluation. We have noted that both Stott and Pinnock have appealed to the texts generally utilized by universalists. They feel, for example, that these texts speak of God's victory over all things, the way in which he reconciles all things to himself. Yet the universalists contend that this is not really accomplished without the actual restoration of everything, which would mean, not the disposal of anyone, as in annihilation. Annihilation would seem, according to these universalists, to be a matter of giving up on some of one's children as incorrigible. This would certainly not be the triumph of love. Rather, it would seem to be the surrender of love to the fact of failure.

The same problem applies to the question of God's love and justice. Pinnock has argued that they preclude endless punishment. For a universalist such as Nels Ferré, however, the problem is not solved quite so easily. In his thinking, the same principles preclude annihilationism. He argues for universal salvation and against annihilation, using terminology and arguments strikingly similar to those of Pinnock. (Actually, to avoid anachronism, we should say instead that Pinnock's arguments resemble Ferré's.) He contends that it is unjust if God gives eternal life to some or most, to allow or cause some persons to pass out of existence.[28] That would be a failure of sovereign love. Ferré would probably suggest that an expedient such as annihilation is a case of "taking the hell out of hell." Thus, on both these points, the annihilationists may be dealing with a two-edged sword.

Biblical Data

We must also examine the biblical evidence. Here, of course, the most significant text is Matthew 25:41–46. The usual argument is that just as Jesus is promising the believing everlasting life, unending bliss with him, he is also threatening the unbelieving with everlasting pun-

---

28. Nels F. S. Ferré, *The Christian Understanding of God* (New York: Harper and Brothers, 1951), pp. 242–43.

ishment. Fudge engages in an extensive argument attempting to show that when applied to nouns that speak of a resulting condition (such as punish*ment*), αἰώνιος does not denote eternity, as it does when modifying nouns that refer to activities (such as punish*ing*). Yet he does not really discuss the issue of parallelism in verse 46. A number of exegetes have insisted that the parallelism requires that if life here is of everlasting duration, punishment must also be eternal.[29] Perhaps the most impressive, because of its source, is this statement by John A. T. Robinson, a universalist:

> The genuine universalist will base nothing on the fact (which is a fact) that the New Testament word for eternal (*aionios*) does not necessarily mean everlasting, but enduring only for an indefinitely long period. For he can apply this signification to "eternal punishment" in Matt. 25:46 only if he is willing to give exactly the same sense to "eternal life" in the same verse. As F. D. Maurice said many years ago now, writing to F. J. A. Hort: "I did not see how *aionios* could mean one thing when it was joined with *kolasis* and another when it was joined with *zoe*" (quoted, J. O. F. Murray, *The Goodness and Severity of God*, p. 195). To admit that the two phrases are not parallel is at once to treat them with unequal seriousness. And that a true universalism must refuse to do.[30]

Another issue in this passage may provide us some guidance. The place to which these goats are consigned is referred to as "the eternal fire prepared for the devil and his angels" (v. 41). In Revelation, we gain more understanding of this future condition of the devil. In 19:20, the beast and the false prophet are thrown alive into the lake of burning sulfur. Then in 20:10, the devil is cast into the lake. It is said that they "will be tormented day and night for ever and ever" (v. 10). Verse 15 says that "if anyone's name was not found written in the book of life, he was thrown into the lake of fire." While the texts only say explicitly that the devil, the beast, and the false prophet will be tormented for ever and ever, there is no statement that the persons whose names are not written in the book of life have any different fate in the lake of fire. This lends the presumption that the punishment spoken of in Matthew 25:41, 46 is also everlasting in nature.

Is this fire everlasting, however? We can note, from Revelation 14:11, that the smoke curls up from this fire of torment forever. Fudge and

29. Among these are John A. Broadus, *Commentary on the Gospel of Matthew* (Philadelphia: American Baptist Publication Society, 1886), p. 512; Henry Alford, *The Greek New Testament*, rev. Everett Harrison (Chicago: Moody, 1958), 1:257.

30. John A. T. Robinson, *In the End, God* (New York: Harper and Row, 1968), p. 131, n. 8.

others like him contend that the smoke is everlasting, not the punishment. We must ask, however, how there can be smoke without something being burned? If these bodies are burned up, consumed, destroyed, how can there still be smoke? What would produce smoke, unless there was something to burn? For that matter, why would the lake of fire continue in existence, without something left to burn?

Contrast between Life and Punishment

Another point that needs evaluation is Stott's contention that the contrast between life and punishment requires maximum difference. That means that if the former is eternal, the latter is not. We must ask, however, whether this is really so. Upon what evidence is that contention based? And if it is valid, what does it really require? It would seem that the contrast is achieved by "life" and "punishment," and would necessarily preclude the latter. Indeed, eternality of each would seem to be the greater contrast. Overall, this argument is not impressive.

Metaphysical Dualism

Nor, it seems to me, is Pinnock's argument from metaphysical dualism. The dualism as such is not ultimate; it is a derived dualism in which the evil force has been created by and draws its life from God. Continuation depends on him. Yet its continuation is not even a dualism in the sense of being an active opposition. It presents no challenge or threat to God. It has been brought into complete and permanent subjugation. Thus, equilibrium has been attained or achieved in the universe. This would seem, therefore, not to be a genuine tension for this theology.

The Rich Man and Lazarus

The "parable" of the rich man and Lazarus has come in for a considerable amount of discussion of late. It has been examined in an earlier chapter, in connection with another topic. It also is significantly relevant here. It is frequently presented as an objection to the idea of annihilation. Actually, its application is somewhat narrower. Only the idea that unbelieving humans cease to exist at death is refuted by this story. While there is no assurance that these will not be annihilated at some later point, there is no explicit basis for believing in such, on the basis of these texts, and indeed the opposite would seem to be the case.

In view of these several considerations, we conclude that the theory of annihilationism in its various forms, as appealing as it may seem as a solution to some theological problems, cannot be sustained, philosophically, biblically, or theologically.

Part **4**

Practical Applications

13

The Salvation of Those Incapable of Faith

The topic of this chapter, the question of the destiny of those who die without ever reaching the capability of faith, has a special quality. Those incapable of faith are primarily infants and very young children, but also severely mentally retarded persons.[1] What becomes of them? Are all of them saved, some of them, or none of them? If some or all are saved, how are they saved? This issue carries a somewhat different emotional tone because of the emotion most persons feel regarding children and especially infants. It is a question with immense pastoral significance, which every pastor has to face sooner or later with grieving loved ones. It is an issue that many of us will have to face personally as well. Significantly, the author of perhaps the most thorough treatment of the subject of infant salvation, R. A. Webb, indicates in the dedication of the volume that he himself lost a child to death.

The topic is regarded by some as giving us a point of entrance or a possibility of unlocking the puzzle of the destiny of the unevangelized. As we noted earlier, the widespread belief that such infants go to be with the Lord was cited by Clark Pinnock as one example of persons who are saved without explicit faith in Christ. It is a real test of how we do our theology, for it is one of those areas where we have very little explicit statement in Scripture, and yet is an area where important doctrines intersect. It may well be one of the topics that will receive special

---

1. While the discussion will refer primarily to infants, it should also be understood as applying to those who may attain physical maturity, but never mentally pass beyond the capability of rather young children.

attention in the future, since in my judgment most theologians have never fully and adequately treated it.

The subject could and should be approached in a number of ways. One is to note the various Scriptures that seem to bear upon the subject. These should then be studied carefully, inferences drawn and compiled into some sort of synthetic doctrine. Another is to examine some of the varying solutions to the problem. We will attempt to do the former first, followed by a study of the latter type, with an aim toward arriving at some sort of acceptable conclusion. In so doing, we entertain no illusions regarding the difficulty of such an endeavor or the conclusiveness of our results.

Relevant Biblical Passages

Ideally, we would find definitive statements in Scripture either way regarding this matter of the salvation of the incompetent. There are, as Webb points out, fully one thousand occurrences in the Bible of the words that are translated *child*, together with their cognates and combinations. Yet, as he says, "when he has looked at them every one he will be surprised and disappointed to find that not a single text explicitly and dogmatically tells us what is the fate of infants dying in infancy."[2] While we would wish for even a single passage addressing this matter explicitly and directly, the best we may be able to hope for is the possibility of passages implying something of significance for our purposes. A large number of passages alluded to, both in terms of examples of children and teachings about children, really do not seem to bear sufficiently upon the issue to be of help. We will note two that have traditionally been used, which in my judgment carry some weight, but even these carry fairly significant problems. We will, however, need to reach whatever conclusion we can on the basis of these passages, as well as more general theological considerations.

Probably the most directly relevant Old Testament passage is found in 2 Samuel 12, in the story of the illness and death of David's illegitimate child, born to him and Bathsheba, and his reaction to those developments. David is unconsolable while the child lies ill. When, however, the child dies, he arises, apparently taking heart, and declares, "I will go to him, but he will not come to me" (v. 23). This particular statement has been quoted at numerous funerals of infants. Webb feels that what is especially significant is the change that takes place in David at the

---

2. R. A. Webb, *The Theology of Infant Salvation* (Harrisonburg, Va.: Sprinkle, 1981), p. 11.

point of the child's death. The deep sorrow and remorse changes to a mood of comparative optimism. The only thing different, the only piece of information David had that he did not have until this point was that the child was now dead. From this Webb infers that during the child's illness, David had no knowledge of the child's destiny. Now that the child is dead, David recognizes that the child will be in heaven in the future state, and therefore knows that he will see him.[3]

Even if we are inclined to follow this line of logic, certain objections arise. One is the question of the extent of the understanding of the future life that David and other believers of his time possessed. Although clearly a supporter of the "wider hope" regarding the salvation of persons in general, John Sanders is quite reserved about the number of children who will be saved. He says of this passage, "The text may mean no more than David would eventually join the boy in the realm of the dead."[4] This particular objection does not deal with Webb's point about the change of heart on David's part when the child dies. More evidence also is emerging regarding the Old Testament belief in the afterlife than was previously credited.[5] A more serious objection, in my judgment, which is perhaps shared by persons of a wider assortment of theological views, is the issue of the status of David's statement. Was he speaking by divine inspiration? If not, what authority do we attach to what was essentially merely David's opinion? Yet, we should note that David was frequently the channel of divine revelation, authoring many of the psalms, and that Luke twice refers to the Spirit as "speaking through David" (Acts 1:16; 4:26). This most assuredly does not guarantee divine origin of all that he says, and it should be noted that David erred on occasion in ordinary matters of opinion. It does, however, lend considerable credibility to this statement, which is certainly of a theological character. Webb mentions two other objections. The first is that as a monument to David's sin and guilt, the child's death relieved David. The second is that this was a special case, in which the double crime associated with the child's conception and birth, and of which it was innocent, really called for compassion for the child and retribution on the father, under divine justice. Neither of these seems an adequate explanation of the particular hope David expresses, however.

The other major significant biblical text is found in connection with the little children coming or being brought to Jesus, found in the parallel passages Matthew 19:14–15; Mark 10:13–16; and Luke 18:16–17. The

---

3. Ibid.

4. John Sanders, *No Other Name* (Grand Rapids: Eerdmans, 1992), p. 289.

5. See, for example, Robert A. Peterson, *The Doctrine of Eternal Punishment* (Philadelphia: Presbyterian and Reformed, 1995), chap. 4.

disciples try to prevent these children from coming to Jesus, but he responds by saying, "Permit the little children to come to me, and do not forbid them, for of such is the kingdom of God" [or of heaven, in Matthew]. Both Matthew and Mark add that he put his hands on the children, and Mark specifies that he blessed them. Mark and Luke add Jesus' statement that whoever does not receive the kingdom of God as a little child simply will not enter in.

Some interpret this as merely an object lesson by Jesus, in which he tells his hearers that unless they display this same childlike simplicity and trustfulness, they will not participate in the kingdom. Certainly Jesus was teaching this, as indicated by the words in Mark and Luke. The issue, however, is whether this is all that can be derived from the passage. Sanders apparently follows the single teaching approach to this, as well as to other passages of Scripture, since he says, "Did he mean that heaven is filled with little children, or did he mean that all must become like little children to enter the kingdom? The context favors the latter."[6] Apart from whether heaven "is *filled*" with children, which would suggest children remaining in that state of development, and not many of any other type of person, the question is, must it be either/or? Obviously, something about children made them suitable illustrations of the quality Jesus was looking for. What was that? Could it be that Jesus was using as the object lesson in his plea for a certain quality, individuals who did not actually embody that quality? That would seem strange indeed. Thus, if Jesus was affirming that those who would enter into the kingdom must be like these children, he seems to be asserting, as a premise in his argument, that these children were in the kingdom.

Part of the difficulty here is that we do not know the exact age of these children. The word παιδίον frequently is used of young children, even virtual newborns, as in Luke 2:17, 27, and Matthew 2: 8–9, 11. It can also be used of youths, however. Just what are we to make of this? It would seem that they had to be young enough so that their attitudes and behavior constituted that trust and humility found in young and "innocent" children.

Are we to attach a great deal of significance to the fact that these children were brought to Jesus? In other words, can we maintain that only those brought to Jesus are of the kingdom? This would lend support to the idea that children of elect parents are themselves elect. On this basis some pastors will baptize infants whose parents are themselves practicing believers, but not those whose parents request baptism of their children but display no grace of salvation in their own lives. This seems, however, to attach too much significance to their presence. Jesus com-

6. Sanders, *No Other Name*, p. 290.

mended the qualities of such as these children, thus suggesting that all such children were of the kingdom. Does this argue that all children are "saved," which lends some credence to universalism? We must ask later in our discussion whether a change takes place at some point in life that introduces a separation within the human race, as persons grow older.

The Variety of Approaches

A large number of approaches have been attempted. Some take their primary inspiration from a particular understanding of sin and the human predicament, some from an understanding of the means of grace, some from the doctrine of God. While some rely almost exclusively on biblical references, others are primarily dependent on more emotional considerations.

Pelagianism

The original presentation of this approach occasioned the first real discussion of the problem of the salvation of infants. Augustine, the greatest theologian of the church's first millennium, found himself theologically at odds with Pelagius. Out of that controversy and the literature it engendered came a rather complete doctrine of humanity and of sin.

To a large extent, the problem of the salvation of infants arises out of belief in original sin, that is, the belief that all persons begin life, not in a state of innocence, but involved in sin, because of Adam's sin. There is great disagreement regarding the extent and severity of this sin, and the means by which it is transmitted, but the effects of the sin are usually thought of as involving two factors: depravity or corruption of nature, and guilt. The problem centers especially on the matter of guilt. If all infants are by nature guilty and thus incapable of believing and receiving God's provision for cancellation of sin through the atoning death of Jesus Christ, how is it that such infants are not condemned? Must not their sinful condition and their guilt separate them from God?

To the Pelagian, in a sense there really is no problem of the salvation of infants, because they do not need to be saved. They have no guilt, for they are innocent of any wrongdoing. For Pelagius, the only sin of which human beings are guilty and for which they can be held guilty is sin they have personally committed. There is no such thing as original sin. In his commentary on Romans, Pelagius argued against the idea that Adam's sin somehow brought condemnation on his descendants. Dealing with Romans 5:12–21, Pelagius contends that the parallelism between Adam and Christ means that if the sin of Adam brings death to all persons without their having personally sinned, then the death of Christ also automatically brings life to all. Further, if original sin is removed by baptism, then there is nothing for a child to receive from two baptized parents.[7] Pelagius emphasized strongly the effect of example on others. The sin of Adam affects his followers, then, through the bad example he gave them.[8] The upshot of this, for our purposes, is that unbaptized infants who die are not condemned.[9]

What Pelagius had seemed only to imply was made quite explicit in a summary by another Pelagian, Celestius:

> Adam was created mortal and would have died whether he had sinned or not sinned; the sin of Adam injured only him, not the human race; the law leads to the kingdom [of heaven], just as the gospel does; even before the coming of Christ there were men without sin; newborn infants are in the same state in which Adam was before his transgression; the whole human race does not die through the death and transgression of Adam, nor does it rise again through the resurrection of Christ.[10]

Thus, the unbaptized infant constitutes no problem, for until a person commits his or her own first sin, there is no guilt. Thus, a person at the point of awareness of moral issues becomes guilty only of any sins he or she might personally perform from that point onward, not acquiring any responsibility for Adam's sin. Adam's sin had no direct effect on his immediate descendants, or any other later descendants. Its only effect was in his giving us a bad example to follow, not in any more direct actual influence.

Sentimentalism

Another approach is what Webb calls the sentimental approach, because it really does not discuss the question of guilt and of transmission of the effects of Adam's sin, but rather, derives the solution by inference from the nature of God. Although perhaps oversimplifying a bit, he correctly observes that the basic difference among religions and theologies is in their understanding of God.[11] That observation seems to be correct, which is partly why theology in the broad sense is called that, even though it deals with many more issues than simply the nature of God. It is because the understanding of God colors the understanding of each of these other areas.

---

7. Pelagius, *Expositions on Thirteen Epistles of Paul*, on Rom. 5:15.
8. Ibid., on Rom. 5:12.
9. Pelagius, *On Nature* (in Augustine, *On Nature and Grace* 10).
10. Augustine, *On the Proceedings of Pelagius* 11:23; *On Original Sin* 11:12.
11. Webb, *Theology of Infant Salvation*, p. 103.

The specific form of the argument from the nature of God relates to the divine love. Certainly God, as a loving Father, would not want anyone to be lost, especially helpless infants. In this model, God's love is seen as benevolent, so that he wills only the best for his children. The concept of God's holiness or justice is not prominent in this theology, to say the very least. While not speculating about the mechanism by which salvation is applied to infants, this view's proponents are convinced, merely on the understanding of God, that infants must be saved, or more correctly, that there is no damnation of infants, but only eternal life, however that may be defined.

One who has expressed this position quite clearly is George A. Gordon, for many years minister of the Old South Church in Boston. He criticizes the Augustinian conception of predestination as being inconsistent, for it considers God partial in his treatment of members of the human race. Gordon says,

> But the Absolute will is absolute in goodness; therefore the deduction that God is on the side of some men and against others is an illogical deduction. . . . The reference to the Infinite will of an eternal passion to save a given number of souls, and of complete indifference to the remainder, is the same logical error over again. . . . [Predestination] must express the will that is never at war with itself, that is always and only on the side of every soul that it has made.[12]

Gordon even makes this the key to understanding the incarnation: "The fundamental idea of the gospel may be stated in a sentence. The glad tidings consist in an ideal incarnation of God in the interest of a universal incarnation."[13]

A variation on this approach rests the salvation of infants in the very creative act of God, as that relates to the human race. In other words, because of the fatherhood of God, all persons are children of God. Fatherhood and creation are really inseparable. This is virtually irrespective of the moral condition of the persons involved. It is not so much a statement about the condition of the persons, as is the case for purer or more doctrinaire Pelagianism, as it is about the nature of God and his relationship to those persons. Consequently, the picture of God is more nearly drawn from the parable of the prodigal son (or the forgiving father) than from the imagery of the righteous judge. Atonement, as the necessary appeasement of a God who has been sinned against, rebelled

12. George A. Gordon, *Ultimate Conceptions of Faith* (Boston: Houghton, Mifflin, 1903), pp. 126–27.

13. George A. Gordon, *The New Epoch for Faith* (Boston: Houghton, Mifflin, 1901), p. 128.

against, and offended, becomes redefined as more a restoration of a lost or broken fellowship. Robert Smith Candlish says, "Rightly understood, as it seems to me, the paternal relation, in the first place, implies the enjoyment by those towards whom it is sustained of a permanent footing in the family, as opposed to one that is contingent and precarious (John viii. 35). And secondly, in consequence of its implying this, it excludes the idea of punishment properly so called; admitting only that of chastisement (Heb. xii.)."[14]

This particular orientation of theology strongly emphasizes God's concern for his children's welfare and happiness. In that sense, it is very much in keeping with the ethos of late twentieth-century American culture, with its anthropocentrism, and, for that matter, the mood of much American popular religion. The idea of God doing anything that does not accord with the wishes and comfort of a human child is unthinkable. All persons are by nature children of God, unless and until they declare themselves otherwise. Incapable of having done such, the infant is still safe in the Father's gracious care and keeping. It would be unfatherly for him to allow any one of them to perish. Webb describes this approach as follows:

> And were he, in the exercise of his judicial or sovereign prerogative, to actively consign one of these little ones to hell, at the same time holding within himself the power to save it (for infants have no free will to oppose him), he would be a virtual Moloch, causing his children to pass through the fire. It is therefore a moral impossibility—according to this type of theological opinion—for any infant dying in infancy to be other than saved because God is the Almighty, Regnant Father, always yearning for his child, absolutely able to save it, and is in no sense a cruel monster.[15]

The force of this argument is seen to lie in the conception of God and of human beings' relationship to him. The question, as Webb correctly observes, rests on whether the major premise is correct, or whether God is naturally the father of humans, and humans are naturally the children of God. That all human beings were originally the children of God is not to be disputed. The real issue is whether all still are, in their natural condition, to be considered children of God.

---

14. Robert Smith Candlish, *The Fatherhood of God* (Edinburgh: A. and C. Black, 1866), p. 120.
15. Webb, *Theology of Infant Salvation*, p. 142.

Arminianism

The Arminian theory approaches the issue from a rather different starting point. In this scheme, all persons, infants and adults alike, are seen as fallen, sinful, depraved, and guilty in the sight of God. This view, in other words, takes seriously the idea of the fall. In this respect, it resembles, to this point, the Calvinistic understanding. Similarly, both views hold it necessary that change in the human, be that infant or responsible and capable adult, take place. They agree that somehow the grace of God must intervene to nullify the effects of sin in these two respects, namely, by negating the guilt of original sin, and removing the guilt that is present. This view finds its solution to the problem of human guilt, however, in the understanding of the nature, extent, and means of application, of the atonement.

This application is somewhat differently conceived of by different Arminian theologians. Some, such as the Remonstrants, deny that the sin of Adam, in the sense of guilt, was imputed to his posterity.[16] Charles Carter interprets Arminius's doctrine of original sin as being deprivation, an absence of original righteousness, rather than the imputation of guilt for Adam's sin.[17] In the Arminian thought of John Wesley, because of prevenient grace, original sin does not lead to damnation. Prevenient grace is the doctrine that God restored to all persons the ability to believe. Wesley wrote to the Calvinists: "But that any will be damned for this alone [original sin], I allow not, till you show me where it is written. Bring me plain proof from Scripture, and I submit; but till then I utterly deny it."[18]

Probation of the Infant

On this view, the infant is born guilty and corrupted, and leaves this life in this condition. Then, however, regeneration, and with it, justification, take place. Some, such as Augustus Hopkins Strong, speculate that the regeneration takes place in connection with the first glimpse of Christ, in heaven.[19] This is, in some ways, a Calvinistic solution to the problem. A more Arminian solution requires the possibility of a responsible decision by each person, a responsible belief in and acceptance of

16. H. Orton Wiley, *Christian Theology* (Kansas City: Beacon Hill, 1952), 2:108.

17. Charles W. Carter, "Hamartiology: Evil, the Marrer of God's Creative Purpose and Work," in *A Contemporary Wesleyan Theology: Biblical, Systematic, and Practical*, ed. Charles W. Carter (Grand Rapids: Francis Asbury, 1983), 1:238.

18. John Wesley, "Predestination Calmly Considered," 34, in *The Works of John Wesley* (Grand Rapids: Zondervan, 1958), 10:223.

19. Augustus Hopkins Strong, *Systematic Theology: A Compendium Designed for the Use of Theological Students* (Philadelphia: Judson, 1907), p. 663.

Christ. Thus, in the view of some, the infant must grow to adulthood, or at least to an age of moral responsibility, and then be given an opportunity to make such a decision. This view assumes the true and full sinfulness of the infant, in terms of both guilt and depravity. It further sees the infant, prior to death, as morally and spiritually incapable. It maintains that it is not possible for any other person to make a decision for this infant, or, for that matter, for any other person. It sees the options as only three: that the dead infant must be taken into heaven, unjustified and unregenerated; that the infant is regenerated and justified by the sovereign heavenly Father, without any agency and consent of its own; that the infant must be brought to a state of maturity within the intermediate state, and then be allowed to settle its own destiny by its own free choice and upon its own responsibility. Taking original sin seriously but also laying a heavy weight on the importance of individual responsibility, this view, which is in many ways Arminian, is left with the third option as the only really feasible choice.[20]

Baptismal Regeneration

This approach, rather popular in terms of the number of persons affiliated with denominations teaching it, takes seriously the effects of Adam's sin on his descendants, including infants. All persons, on this view, are born in a state of both guilt and depravity. It is necessary for these to be removed for the person to enter into eternal life. This predicament of the person is then related to the church's sacramental system. This sacramentalism includes the idea that God has entrusted the means and dispensing of grace to the church, and made certain rites called sacraments the means by which this grace is transmitted to those in need of it.

For purposes of our present discussion, the sacrament of baptism is the means by which regeneration is effected. When a person receives baptism in water, with the due intent of the person administering it to baptize, then the waters of baptism remove the guilt and taint of sin. Scriptural support for this doctrine is found in biblical texts that refer to water and its cleansing power. A primary text is Jesus' statement to Nicodemus in John 3:5, "unless one is born of water and the Spirit, he cannot enter the kingdom of God." It is also seen in the Great Commission, where Jesus instructed his disciples to go and make disciples, baptizing them (Matt. 28:20). A final text frequently appealed to in support of this teaching is in Titus 3:5, "he saved us . . . by the washing of regeneration and renewal in the Holy Spirit."

20. Clark H. Pinnock, *A Wideness in God's Mercy: The Finality of Jesus Christ in a World of Religions* (Grand Rapids: Zondervan, 1992), pp. 167–68.

The major group holding and practicing this view is, of course, the Roman Catholic Church. The last major official conciliar pronouncement of the Catholic Church on this matter was in the sessions of the Council of Trent. The following articles were directed to this subject:

> Or if he denies that that merit of Jesus Christ is applied both to adults and to infants by the sacrament of baptism rightly administered in the form of the Church, let him be anathema.[21]

> If any one says that baptism is optional, that is, not necessary for salvation, let him be anathema.[22]

Not only the Catholic Church holds this view, however. Of the groups involved in the initial round of the Reformation, the Lutheran Church made the least change in the church's sacramentalism. Also holding to original guilt and corruption, Lutheranism insists that baptism is necessary for the salvation of infants. Much of their doctrinal declaration was enunciated in protest against the Anabaptist views. So, for example, the Augsburg Confession says, "Of Baptism they [Lutherans] teach that it is necessary to salvation, and that by Baptism the grace of God is offered, and that children are to be baptized, who by Baptism, being offered to God, are received into God's favour. They condemn the Anabaptists who allow not the Baptism of children, and affirm that children are saved without Baptism."[23]

Calvinism

Finally, Calvinists have approached this question, as indeed they do each such issue, from the perspective of the doctrine of predestination. A beginning point for all Calvinistic doctrine is the fact of universal sinfulness and guilt, known as total depravity. Webb refers to this as the decree of nature, that all, apart from the grace of God, are lost and condemned. Unless something intervenes to counteract the effects of this fact, damnability must inevitably result in actual damnation. This, then, is the decree of grace, unto salvation. This predestination is not based upon any foreseen merit, or even any foreseen faith, on the part of the one elected. This means that infants, as well as adults, may be objects of God's electing grace. The Calvinist sees the infant as helpless and incapable of believing, but the adult is as well, although in a some-

---

21. *Canons and Decrees of the Council of Trent*, trans. H. J. Schroeder, fifth session, "Decree Concerning Original Sin," 3 (St. Louis: B. Herder, 1941), p. 22.

22. Ibid., seventh session, "Canons on Baptism," canon V, p. 53.

23. Trans. Charles P. Krauth, in *The Creeds of Christendom* by Philip Schaff (New York: Harper and Brothers, 1877), 3:13.

what different sense of incapability. Thus, there is no more inconsistency in the infant being saved by Christ's atoning death than in the adult being saved.

The child may therefore be regenerated and thus have the depravity and guilt of sin removed, by the working of the Spirit, in applying the grace of Christ's atonement. What, however, about repentance and faith, which are generally understood to be the preconditions of all saving benefits? Here Webb states that these are not meritorious grounds of salvation. Like many if not most Calvinists, he maintains that they are the manifestation and the result of the regenerating work of the Holy Spirit. They are actually the bringing to consciousness of the benefits of Christ's atonement. In other words, their effect is not to save, but to reveal salvation in human experience. Thus, they are not necessary in the case of the infant. Webb says, "Consequently, since an infant dies in the preconscious period of its life, these instrumentalities of faith and repentance have no office to perform, for the reason that there is no self-consciousness to be enlightened."[24] He likens the child to an heir to the throne who has the title to that throne as a birthright, but whose coronation serves to make him conscious of the fact of the prerogatives.

All infants, although guilty because of the Adamic sin, are nonetheless salvable because they are electable; and they are electable because in election God is agent, and the person elected is patient. We must ask, however, whether all infants who die in infancy are elect, or whether some of them may not be elect. Webb insists that Calvinists hold that if there were such nonelect, nonredeemed, nonregenerated children who died in that condition, they would be justly damnable because of their guilt. Yet, he says, Calvinists "assiduously teach that the hypothecation is a sheer impossibility, for as a matter of fact no reprobate infant does, or can die, in its infancy."[25] Some elect infants die in infancy, and some grow to maturity. In each case, they are saved because they were elected by the Father, redeemed by the Son, and regenerated by the Spirit. Those who die in infancy would have believed, been repentant, and been obedient to the gospel had they lived to moral maturity. Those who grow to maturity in the fullness of time evidence their salvation by actually believing, repenting, and obeying the gospel. Of reprobate infants, on the other hand, none of them die in infancy, but all come to maturity, and then "express the evil that is in them by sundry voluntary and conscious acts of transgression, of varying degrees of heinousness; which overt acts call up into consciousness the sinfulness which is subjective to the natures with which they are born, and so give to them a

24. Webb, *Theology of Infant Salvation*, p. 281.
25. Ibid., p. 284.

ground, in conscious experience, for recognizing and appreciating their condemnation."[26]

Webb argues for this view through an exposition of the nature and purpose of suffering as penal. He distinguishes between two kinds of suffering, penal suffering and disciplinary suffering. Penal suffering, which is inflicted because of guilt, is inflicted by justice, whereas disciplinary suffering is inflicted by love. The purpose of disciplinary suffering is chastisement, intended to improve the person upon whom it is inflicted. Penal suffering or penalty, on the other hand, is intended to bring the person on whom it is inflicted into conscious connection with the suffering that justice judges to be proportionate to, and merited by, the offense committed against law. Webb says this distinction must be carefully preserved and understood if one is to avoid great confusion in this matter of salvation of infants. He distinguishes between the role of the official beating his son, as a convicted citizen, at the public whipping-post in fulfillment of the orders of the court, which would be punishment, and administering the same punishment to his son in the back yard with the same rods, which would be chastisement.

It is essential, for punishment truly to be that and accomplish its rightful purpose, that the person being punished be aware of the punishment and the reason for it. Therefore, an infant, being a sentient creature, is capable of suffering, but being an unconscious creature, is too immature to understand and appreciate the reason for suffering; therefore, the infant is incapable of being punished, strictly and truly speaking. Its only guilt being Adamic and federal, it is guilt of which it is not aware and of which it can only become aware by growing to maturity and expressing its sinfulness in its own voluntary and conscious acts of transgression. If such an infant were sent to hell, it would be aware that it was suffering, but would not know or understand why it was suffering. If someone else were to tell the child why it was suffering thus, the child might believe on the testimony of this other, but would be experientially blank and nonunderstanding. Webb says that for suffering to be truly penal two conditions must necessarily be satisfied: There must be a reason satisfying the conscience of the one inflicting it, and there must be a reason certifying guilt to the conscience of the one who experiences the suffering. Thus, children could not really be punished with penal suffering. Webb says, *"Providence must delay the death of the reprobate infant until he comes to maturity, and translates his original sin into conscious actual sin, so there may be a basis, not simply in law and truth, but in consciousness and conscience and experience for penalty."*[27] Conse-

---

26. Ibid., p. 285.
27. Ibid., p. 291.

quently, a reprobate infant cannot die in infancy, for that would defeat the very purpose of justice. And, by deduction, all infants dying in infancy are elect. The death of an infant is, therefore, the absolute proof of its salvation.[28]

Critical Evaluation and Construction

We must now offer some evaluation of the several theories that we have examined. Each has certain points of difficulty that makes it less than fully satisfactory. The Pelagian view simply seems to require ignoring too many data, both scriptural and experiential. The teaching regarding the universal coming of sin on the entire human race, and statements such as that of David regarding his very iniquity from his mother's womb (Ps. 51:5) seem to contradict this as well. The universal human propensity to sin also argues for this. Pelagianism, the belief in the inherent goodness of human beings, is a very widespread and persistent belief. It is, however, a view that appears to be contradicted by human behavior, including that within the history of the twentieth century. It is an unrealistic view.

Arminianism is more biblically based, holding to the doctrine of universal sin. By its doctrine of prevenient grace, however, it involves itself in many of the same empirical difficulties as does Pelagianism. Further, it is based on a theological concept regarding which there appears to be real biblical silence. Although it has a strong appeal in many ways, it also must be deemed inadequate.

The idea of baptismal regeneration is widely held. It enables one to maintain belief in original sin and also provides a definite means by which salvation is effected. It suffers, however, from the difficulties that beset the whole sacramental system, which cannot be gone into in detail here. Specifically, it attaches more significance to the practice of baptism than the biblical texts cited would seem to justify. It is not really a viable option for anyone holding the view of the nature and means of salvation adopted in this volume.

The concept of postmortem probation and decision is a truly creative one. Whereas it does not solve the problem of the destiny of those dying in infancy by guaranteeing that all are saved, it at least removes something of the apparent injustice by allowing everyone a chance to make a responsible decision, thus giving these infants the same opportunity as adults, and apparently guaranteeing a more direct and explicit hearing of the gospel than some obtain. It also draws on what is probably a

---

28. Ibid.

correct insight in concluding that children will not remain children throughout eternity. There are two difficulties with it, however. First, there is no real biblical basis for such a postmortem opportunity. Second, this is really not a view of the salvation of infants, as such. It says that infants must become adults, for only then can they be saved. While this is not, in itself, necessarily a significant problem, it does in a sense place this view outside the class of those we are examining here.

I would suggest an explanation that basically is Calvinistic and in many ways follows Webb's interpretation. There are some nuances of this view, however, and they are related to the imputation of sin. I would agree that all persons participated in the fall, in the sense that the fall was not simply the sin of one isolated individual, but that the person who sinned was the entire human race. This is the "realistic" theory propounded by Augustine, or the theory of the natural headship of the human race by Adam. This is tied to what used to be termed the traducianist view of the origin of the human soul. On this view, the soul is not created by a special act of God at the point of conception and united with the physical nature. Rather, all human souls were present in Adam in seminal form. We have received our entire nature, physical as well as psychological and spiritual, by generation through descent from Adam. There are numerous scriptural and natural evidences for this view. The reference in Hebrews 7:10 to Levi paying tithes to Melchizedek, because Levi was at the time in the "loins" of Abraham, is an example of the former. The essential unity of human nature, as well as the inheritance of psychological traits from one's ancestors, are examples of the latter type. Thus, each person participates in the first sin, and justly receives, as a result, a corrupted or depraved nature, as well as the guilt for that sin.

We must ask further, however, about the basis and time of reckoning or imputation of the guilt. Here we must turn to the locus classicus for the reckoning of guilt, Romans 5:12–19. The most pertinent verse for our purposes is verse 18: "Consequently, just as the result of one trespass was condemnation for all men, so also the result of one act of righteousness was justification that brings life for all men."

The same thought is expressed in more concise fashion in 1 Corinthians 15:22: "For as in Adam all die, so in Christ shall all be made alive." The problem comes in the strong parallelism between the two parts of each of these statements. If all die in Adam and all come to life in Christ, does this not result in universal salvation? The usual argument given is that Christ's atoning death that gives life is only of benefit when accepted, or ratified, by the free choice of each individual person. There is no such thing as an automatic effect of the atonement-redemption in anyone's life. But what of the parallelism? Is it possible that the imputation of Adam's guilt is like the imputation of Christ's death? May it be that there must be some type of conscious ratification of that sin by the person, since none of Adam's descendants was conscious of the act or personally willed it in an intentional fashion? We are at best attempting to form some sort of interpretive or integrative construct to deal with this problem. Consequently, it is not always possible to verify or validate directly each factor in the scheme. Its verification must be relative and issue from the ability of the entire integrative scheme to fit the whole complex of factors that such a theory must account for. My current explanation is as follows.

Until the first conscious or responsible moral action or decision by a person, there is no imputation of the Adamic sin, just as there is no imputation of Christ's righteousness until there is a conscious acceptance of that work. In the case of the sin, there is a period at the beginning of life when one is not really capable of distinguishing between good and evil. This is because there is, in effect, actually no awareness of the concept of rightness and wrongness or of responsibility. This is prior to what we term the "age of accountability." That there is such a time of nonculpable behavior can be seen illustrated in principle in Deuteronomy 1:39. God has pronounced, through Moses, his word of judgment on the people who had rebelled against him, and who consequently were not to be allowed to enter into the promised land. Only Caleb and Joshua, the two spies who had brought back a favorable report from the promised land and had maintained that the people of Israel would be able, with Jehovah's help, to enter into it and capture it, would be allowed to enter. There was one other group that would be excepted from the penalty: "And the little ones that you said would be taken captive, your children who do not yet know good from bad—they will enter the land. I will give it to them and they will take possession of it." Israel was to turn around and go back into the desert, where they were to wander for forty years as punishment for the disobedience, disbelief, and rebelliousness of the remainder of the group until they had all died. It appears that these little ones, despite the principle of corporate solidarity that was so genuine in Israel, were not deemed responsible for the sin of the nation. While one cannot make a direct transference from this situation of sin and punishment to the matter of guilt for original sin, there appears to be a principle here that is applicable in the latter situation. There is a time of moral responsibility, or an "age of accountability," and sin is not reckoned prior to that.

Two other Old Testament passages allude to this concept. In the messianic prophecy in Isaiah 7, there are two references to the time when the boy "knows enough to reject the wrong and choose the right" (vv. 15–16). It could, of course, be argued that the boy knows the difference between the two, but has not matured to the point where he is wise enough to choose what he knows to be right, rather than what he knows to be wrong, but that is a rather forced interpretation. At the end of the Book of Jonah, God responds to Jonah's complaint over his not destroying Nineveh. He replies, "But Nineveh has more than a hundred and twenty thousand persons who cannot tell their right hand from their left, and many cattle as well. Should I not be concerned about that great city?" (4:11). The association of these undiscriminating persons with the cattle seems to be that they are similarly innocent of any culpable wrong.

This moral accountability with accompanying acceptance of the Adamic sin does not require any actual sinful act as such. It is not that one is innocent and free of any guilt until he or she commits a first act of personal sin, for which he or she then becomes responsible and hence guilty. It is rather that in the moment one becomes conscious of the reality of right and wrong, that person becomes aware that past actions he or she has performed are indeed sinful. In other words, one in effect becomes aware of the inclination toward sin, or the sinful nature, or depravity. The appropriate moral and spiritual response to this awareness should be an abhorrence of it, a rejection of it. This would, in other words, be a rejection and repentance of the sinful nature one possesses. The person typically does not do this, however. By failing to reject that sinful inclination, one acquiesces in it or accepts it. This constitutes a ratification of the first sin of the human race, an accepting it as one's own, and therefore guilt comes on the person as well. This enables us to preserve the parallelism between Adam's sin and the resulting death spreading to the entire human race, and between Christ's death and the resulting life made available to all persons. While the results are universal, in each case the results only become effective when ratified by the person involved.

What is the bearing of this question of accountability on the salvation of the morally incompetent? It means that because there is no capability of making one's own moral choice, the infant who dies in infancy never comes to the age of accountability and thus never ratifies the Adamic sin, or accepts the effects of that sin for his or her own life. The same would be true for those who attain physical maturity, but never come to this point of moral responsibility. Consequently, there is no imputation of guilt. There need not be, in a sense, justification.

What, however, is to be done regarding the sinful nature, the depravity, of the child? Is this not a continuing problem? It most certainly is. For if depravity is transmitted, then it is present, whether moral accountability or responsible action regarding sin has occurred or not. This is a subject regarding which Scripture does not really inform us.

Somehow, in connection with the transition from this life and its experience to the presence of God, there must be a purification of that depraved nature. Note, however, that this problem is not qualitatively, but only quantitatively, different from the problem of the change of all believers. For unless one is totally sanctified prior to the occurrence of death, there must be the completion of that process in what we usually refer to as glorification, since, as the Bible contends, "we shall be like him, for we shall see him as he is" (1 John 3:2). We are not told that we must take any special action at that point. It appears, rather, that the very appearance of Christ has this effect. But if sanctification and glorification are but the continuation and the completion of the renewing work begun in regeneration, may it not be that much the same thing, albeit on a more complete scale, is done for infants dying in infancy?

How, we must ask, does this question bear on the larger question we have been discussing in this volume? Does it give us a clue about the possible salvation of those who have never heard? Because these infants are persons who receive eternal life without any explicit faith, may it not be that those who do not have explicit faith because they have never heard may also be saved? It seems to me, however, that this consideration does not bear directly on the issue. Both classes are constituted of persons who in some sense do not believe explicitly because they are unable to do so. The inability is of two different types, however. In the case of the capable, morally responsible unevangelized, their difficulty is lack of information. Yet we have contended that, on the basis of biblical testimony or the testimony of special revelation, we must conclude that they do have an opportunity of sorts, because they have a degree of knowledge or information, namely, through general revelation. Hence, there is a responsibility for what is done or not done regarding that revelation. In the case of the infant, however, there is inability to respond to the gospel as found in the special revelation, even if directly presented with it. Thus, the child cannot respond to either special revelation or general revelation. There is not responsibility with respect to either of these, for there is no ability to respond. The inability of the first class of persons is accidental with respect to special revelation and personal and responsible with respect to general revelation. The inability of the second class of persons is essential or necessary, but not personal and responsible.

One other issue needs some probing. If it is indeed the case that all who die in infancy enter into the presence of God, are we not faced with an unusual dilemma? For by allowing children to mature to the age of accountability, we doom some of them to eternal damnation, on the assumption that not all will accept Christ and receive eternal life. On such grounds, would it not be the most efficient means of evangelism and the most compassionate treatment of such children, to practice mass infanticide? In fact, instead of opposing abortion and stigmatizing those who practice it, should we not commend and praise the practice, since those fetuses, if they indeed are persons, are guaranteed eternal life, which we cannot say for adults?

The response that must be made is that this is indeed a logical conclusion from the premises. The difficulty, however, is that this attempts to promote a good end by the use of very evil means, means which are severely condemned in Scripture (e.g., Gen. 9:6), if the child is indeed a person. Thus, we must continue to avoid and to oppose such practices.

14

The Implications for Missions and Evangelism

One issue that often overhangs the discussions we have examined, becoming explicit in many cases, is the question of the relationship of one's theory regarding the future destiny of the unevangelized to the effort in evangelism and missions: What impact does the adoption of this particular view have on the missionary enterprise? Presumably, from the perspective of the person raising the question, anything that reduces the urgency or motivation of missionary endeavor is a negative.

We should note, immediately, that this criterion in itself is not the sole or even the major consideration in evaluating one of these views. The reason for this is that the missionary endeavor is a means to an end, not an end in itself, although those personally involved in missions sometimes express themselves as if the latter were the case. If, for example, there is no eternal loss for those who do not hear, then, at least on the conventional grounds, failure to tell them about the future would not be a negative factor. As John Sanders has pointed out, utility does not establish truth. He uses the illustration of possibly trying to motivate his children to get ready on time for church and Sunday school by telling them that it is later than it actually is. In this case, the success of the technique would not prove that it really was 9:15 rather than 9:00[1]

---

1. John Sanders, *No Other Name: An Investigation into the Destiny of the Unevangelized* (Grand Rapids: Eerdmans, 1992), pp. 283–84. Sanders has apparently misspoken, for he says that if telling his children that it is 9:15 rather than 9:00 works (i.e., gets them to hurry and get ready), "I don't take that as evidence that it really is 9:00." Presumably, he meant to say, "that it really is 9:15."

nor of course would the end justify the means. So, unless we hold the pragmatist view of truth, we must really determine which view of the future is correct, and evaluate the evangelistic endeavors in light of this.

Yet having said this, it should be noted that virtually all schools of thought recognize that the church has been given a commission to proclaim the gospel. The question then becomes, in effect, what is that understanding of the future that would justify such a command being given to the church? To put it another way, why would Jesus have commanded his followers to evangelize, if it were not really necessary? What we will therefore do in this chapter is to examine the rationale for missions given by the adherents of each of these views, analyze the issues involved, and seek to draw some conclusions.

It should further be noted that in the long run, those views that give the greater urgency to evangelistic motivation will tend to be the more prevalent, because they will add more to their numbers. Conversely, the less evangelistic will decline, on a relative basis. This can be seen with respect to certain of the more extremely Calvinistic groups that opposed any sort of evangelistic endeavor.[2] It can also be seen emphatically in the sharp numerical decline of "mainline denominations" in our time.

The Variety of Views

Universalism

Many of its critics maintain that universalism cuts the nerve of evangelism, rendering it either unnecessary or illogical. Yet its advocates maintain this is not the case. Two major types of responses or reasons have been given.

The first is that although there is no eternal hell, no everlasting condemnation or separation from God, yet there is a hell, and it is a most unpleasant experience. Consequently, anything that can be done to spare people this experience, or to reduce its duration, should be done. Nels Ferré, for example, says that the message of universalism is not what should be preached to sinners. Such a message will not reach them where they are, fearing and hating God. One would have expected him to say the exact opposite, that such a person needs to have the animosity removed, and that knowing God's love and goodwill expressed in his not ultimately condemning anyone would serve to accomplish this. Rather,

---

2. See, e.g., Robert G. Torbet, *A History of the Baptists* (Philadelphia: Judson, 1950), pp. 278–80.

says Ferré, such preaching would only "secure them in their sin and self-sufficiency."[3] A very different type of message is needed:

> Therefore, headed as they are away from God, they must be told: Repent or perish! It is a terrible thing to fall into the hands of the living God. You are going to hell, which means you are going to face the consequences of your disobedience and faithfulness, not only in this life, but especially on the other side of death. But hell is real without being eternal. Only God's love never fails or never ends. God's final victory involves his total work of redemption which is in eternity and not limited to our earthly time.[4]

Ferré is apparently saying that hell, although not eternal, is real, and people need to be told that unless they repent, they will go there. Thus the preaching is necessary to prevent what is a real, if not infinite, loss.

A second universalistic approach is found in the thought of John A. T. Robinson. He approaches the issue under the general topic of the relationship of human freedom to the divine will to save everyone. He notes that there is a paradox, not only for universalists, but also for Calvinists, between their professed belief and their actions. If one is certain one is bound for heaven or for hell, then why be concerned, since nothing can be done about it? "Yet neither of these classes of men appears to be characterized by any less moral earnestness. They reveal a concern for converting and improving the world at least as serious as that of any other Christians."[5] How are we to account for such a strange phenomenon?

Robinson directs us to the distinction between objective and subjective truth, drawing on the thought of Søren Kierkegaard and Emil Brunner. If one merely looks at this question from the perspective of objective logic, then the divine omnipotence makes human action superfluous, if indeed it does not eliminate it completely. It is different, however, for the person who has experienced the love of God subjectively. Such a person, even when knowing that God will love him no matter what he does, would not think of presuming upon it. Only the person who does not really love would think of such things. So, Robinson says, "There is no real need to treat seriously the objection to universalism that it is morally or spiritually debilitating. The objection rests upon a misunderstanding into which no one who makes an existential profession of the belief is in any danger of falling."[6]

3. Nels Ferré, "Universalism: Pro and Con," *Christianity Today* 7.11 (March 1, 1963): 24.
4. Ibid.
5. John A. T. Robinson, *In the End, God* (New York: Harper and Row, 1968), p. 126.
6. Ibid., p. 127.

The other consideration with which Robinson grapples is the question of hell. He quotes with approval T. F. Torrance's statement that there is an infinite urgency in the fact that life and death hang in the balances and that there is a possibility of choosing either one, and that any doctrine that cuts the nerve of that urgency is a menace to the gospel and to mankind. His comment is, "To those words anyone who would be faithful to the New Testament must subscribe."[7] Here also, if one treats the issue from the perspective of objective speculation, that nerve will be cut. If, however, one approaches it from the existential viewpoint, that urgency need not be denied. Jesus, indeed, refused to give a precise objective answer to the question of whether all men will be saved.[8]

Salvation is a state of having chosen, and this requires the realization that there are two alternatives. Robinson says, "As long as a man presumes that the truth of universalism relieves him of reckoning with hell or making a decision, then he is not even on the road to the valley—or, rather, he has implicitly chosen hell." This is the reason for preaching the doctrine of hell: "If, therefore, the universalist insists on the seriousness of choice, and consequently on the reality of an alternative, it is because he sees in desperate earnestness the nature of truth as subjectivity: it is not because he regards hell as an indispensable piece of bluff required to keep men moral."[9]

It is not enough to say that hell is a possibility and only heaven is a reality. That would be to treat the two myths with unequal seriousness. There is a paradox here, because one myth teaches that hell is a reality, while the other teaches that it is impossible. These two conceptions cannot be resolved into a third conception. They must be held together. If they were treated as parallel objective statements about the ultimate outcome of the universe, one would have to be false and the other true. They are rather statements from two different perspectives. One statement is true from the standpoint of God and those who are already in the faith. The other is true from the perspective of those who are still wrestling with decision.[10]

What, then, are we to make of Robinson's rather puzzling presentation? The key would seem to be to interpret what he has said in light of the concepts to which he appeals and the analogies he draws. This is particularly the case with the concept of subjective truth, which he borrows from Kierkegaard. In that way of thinking, truth is not so much

7. Ibid., p. 128.
8. Ibid.
9. Ibid., p. 129.
10. Ibid., pp. 129–30.

the objective state of affairs, but rather the truth as personally assimilated and internalized. Thus, in this case, it may well be that God loves everyone and that in the end his love will prevail, so that all will be saved. Indeed, it is not completely inappropriate to say that all persons are already currently saved. Yet they are not experiencing the reality of that salvation. Such only becomes the case when they wrestle with the choice of relationship to God and love for him, versus indifference toward God. To presume upon the teaching of universalism is to fail to be subjectively in the truth, although objectively correct. Thus, one has salvation, but fails to live in its subjective reality and benefits.

One other clue to understanding this is the parallel Robinson draws between Calvinism and universalism, regarding the relationship between belief and practice. Calvinists frequently say that the outcome or the end is certain to God in each case, but he predestines the means to the end, faith, as well as the end in itself, salvation. For the elect to be saved requires their coming to faith. The means to that faith is the hearing of the gospel. Thus, there must be preaching. If this analogy applies here, then it would seem that although persons are objectively saved, the means by which that salvation is brought about is the subjective choice of Christ. For that to be realized requires that persons be made aware of the options and the decisions. Hell must be preached as a very real option, enabling genuine decision to take place.

It would appear that in Robinson's view, there is greater urgency to getting the Good News to persons during this lifetime than there is in Ferré's view, which allows for change of mind and heart after death. The force of the impulse to proclamation is weakened even further by views like Origen's that rest the ultimate reconciliation of all things to God on his nature, rather than emphasizing the need for the human response.

Exclusivism

It would seem that traditional exclusivism must provide a strong urgency to the missionary enterprise, for if there are two possible destinations for humans and the difference between them is on the basis of their faith and decision, then everything possible must be done to make it possible for them to fulfill these conditions. Consequently, the application of the view to the question we are considering in this chapter is direct and forceful. In fact, it is probably safe to say that this view gives the strongest and most conclusive argument for the urgency of the Great Commission of any of these views.

This strong sense of urgency grows out of several of this view's major doctrinal tenets. The first is the human race's universal sinfulness and lostness. Whether based on the church's teaching regarding grace and its role in dispensing it, or on a strong conception of biblical authority, this view sees everyone as a sinner, by nature and by choice. Whatever resources are available to everyone are apparently insufficient to prevent persons from being sinners, or to enable them to escape that condition.

Second, this view insists on the necessity for salvation of Jesus Christ's work. "Neither is there salvation in any other, for there is no other name under heaven given among men, whereby they must be saved" (Acts 4:12) is a powerful consideration, from the perspective of exclusivism.

Third, the benefit of this work of Christ's depends on personal faith, and that in turn requires knowledge of him and what he has done. It is not sufficient to have implicit faith. There must be knowledge of Christ's work. While the content of this saving faith may have changed over the years, it has changed in response to the progressive nature of special revelation. This is a permanent and irreversible change, however. So, for example, James Borland writes, "Since Calvary, the unchanging required content of one's faith is the gospel. Nothing else saves, while all else damns. No substitutions, additions or imitations are permitted. Any other gospel is not another that can save. It only brings with it an anathema (Gal. 1:6–9)."[11]

Fourth, this necessity of hearing the gospel in order to have faith and be saved gives urgency to the missionary endeavor. The apostles did not take it upon themselves to decide that those who did not hear the gospel were lost. Rather, they were simply following Jesus' marching orders. He said, after all, "It was necessary for the Christ to suffer and to rise from the dead the third day, and that repentance and remission of sins should be preached in his name to all nations, beginning at Jerusalem" (Luke 24:46–47).[12]

This command of Christ's to his disciples was obviously given because it was necessary, and it is still in effect today. As Borland puts it, "If it was necessary to go then, why not now?" He adds, "If taking the gospel to every creature was a concern of Christ's two thousand years ago, why should his *modus operandi* be abandoned now, especially without a word from him to that effect?" His concluding word sums up well both the position of a number of exclusivists and the reason for their concern about some other approaches: "To hold out the possibility of any other way of salvation does not add to God's greatness but depreciates his Word and the work of the Church through the ages. To

11. James A. Borland, "A Theologian Looks at the Gospel and World Religions," *Journal of the Evangelical Theological Society* 33.1 (March 1990): 9.
12. Ibid., p. 11.

teach any other way of salvation for the heathen diminishes missionary zeal and leaves the helpless hopeless."[13]

It should be noted that the exclusivist's motivation depends on the conviction that there really is no biblical justification for the idea of an alternative source of saving knowledge. Consequently, the necessity of people hearing is absolute, not merely relative. Further, exclusivists believe that the argument from fairness some urge against the exclusivist position has no validity. If one were to follow that argument, where could one logically stop? After all, there are those who have heard, but only from persons whose lack of personal credibility undercuts the effectiveness of their witness. And if some have the opportunity only to hear the general revelation, but others hear the message overtly, then there is still inequality. Finally, there is insufficient justification for the urgency with which Christ gave the Great Commission, if it is only in order that some might have the joy of salvation earlier than they would otherwise have it.[14]

One problem that sometimes arises for this approach attaches particularly to the Calvinistic view that God has chosen some for eternal life while bypassing or even rejecting others. What God has decided will certainly come to pass. Consequently, some might draw the conclusion that evangelism and missions are unnecessary, as did some of the Calvinistic Baptists in response to William Carey's professed call to world missions. Calvinism is sometimes charged with leading to such passivity.[15]

Does this follow, however? It is notable that more thoughtful Calvinists see no conflict between the end being decreed and activity, even intense evangelistic activity. This is because both the end and the means to the end have been foreordained by God. Loraine Boettner, for example, finds in the fact that those without the gospel are lost the strongest motivation for missions. While recognizing that God can work however and wherever he chooses, the ordinary method is to save persons from among the unevangelized.[16] Actually, of course, the Arminian, who believes it certain that whoever is going to believe will believe, is not in a radically different situation. The only way to avoid this predicament is to hold that it is uncertain who will believe, which involves abandoning the doctrine of God's omniscience. Pinnock, seeing the problem attaching to foreknowledge, has been willing to take this step.[17]

13. Ibid.

14. Robert H. Gundry, "Salvation according to the Scripture: No Middle Ground," *Christianity Today* 22.5 (December 9, 1977): 16.

15. Clark Pinnock, *A Wideness in God's Mercy: The Finality of Jesus Christ in a World of Religions* (Grand Rapids: Zondervan, 1992), p. 177.

16. Loraine Boettner, *The Reformed Doctrine of Predestination* (Grand Rapids: Eerdmans, 1954), p. 119.

17. Clark Pinnock, "God Limits His Knowledge," in *Predestination and Free Will*, ed. David Basinger and Randall Basinger (Downers Grove, Ill.: InterVarsity, 1986), pp. 141–62.

Pluralism

What of those who hold to the idea that salvation may be found through all religions, that salvation is not the exclusive possession or prerogative of any one religion, or that, in fact, at base the several religions really are the same? Here we may distinguish between the possible logical implications of the position and the actual stance taken on this issue.

In theory, pluralists should be expected to emphasize the importance of avoiding any sort of aggressive or exploitative missions, for that would disregard the legitimacy of the other religions and would be a form of degrading them. Yet, on this view, it should not really be thought wrong to go to those places and persons where there is no other major religion. Supposedly, these people need to be reached by some religion, which could as well be Christianity as any other. The question of folk religions is a question of the degree to which pluralism is carried out consistently and extensively. To the extent, however, that there is belief that apart from a relationship to the higher power, however understood and named, a person is "lost," effort should be made by some religion to reach them with the gospel. Consistent, however, with the pluralist view, it would be improper and an act of encroachment to engage in missionary activity in a geographical area where a missionary religion of another type is the dominant or even official one.

This should also lead to a sort of ministry on behalf of other religions. That is to say, those who are only nominally adherents of other religions should be encouraged to become more committed and devout followers of those religions. Typically, such persons have in the past been considered prime objects of evangelism by Christian missionaries. Since, however, there is really no basic major difference among these religions, the persons should rather be encouraged to deepened experience within their own religion, unless there has been some sort of strong negative reaction against that religion.

In practice there is a somewhat more passive approach than the foregoing might suggest. This, however, is also consistent with the basic theoretical tenets, when these are fully understood. The idea that those who are not already reached by or enlisted in Christianity or one of the other major religions are somehow in need of "salvation" is a basically Christian conception. At least this is true to the perceived urgency of the task. In this matter, however, as in all matters, the true pluralist cannot really consider the Christian revelation regarding the human predicament uniquely authoritative. Perhaps the effects of not evangelizing are not so great as we have thought from our rather ethnocentric position. Hinduism does not consider the outcome of life for non-Hindus to be as serious as that which orthodox Christians see for non-Christians. Failure to do missions and evangelism must be evaluated using some more common denominator.

It is this common denominator, however, which some pluralists insist must not be sought. We might at this point distinguish between more conservative and more liberal pluralists, or perhaps we could speak of objectivistic and subjectivistic pluralists. Indeed, perhaps the distinction should be between pluralists and relativists, or between modern and postmodern versions of pluralism. Knitter acknowledges the criticisms by some of "objectivism" and "foundationalism."[18] The persons making these criticisms maintain that even to speak of a soteriocentric approach is to assume some common ground.

Pluralists, however, are not just indifferent to missions. Ordinarily, attempting to evangelize or engage in missions with respect to those of other religious commitments is either an explicit or an implicit rejection of the legitimacy of the other person's position. It is believed to have accompanied, or been accompanied by, a political and economic imperialism, and appears to be this religiously. Consequently, pluralists, if true to their major conceptions, ordinarily do not encourage or even condone the usual type of mission endeavor.

In general, one does not find a strong urgency for proclamation among pluralists. This is probably in part because, given the type of pluralistic orientation described above, there is little basis for certainty regarding salvation as some sort of future life with God. Here pluralism differs from universalism. Usually, Christian universalism believes in at least some sort of reasonably traditional Christian conception of salvation, its nature and its need. Although everyone will sooner or later be saved, that will be by being reconciled to the Christian God, and giving them the Christian message is the means to this. Robinson therefore is right in this respect, in likening the universalist to the Calvinist. On the other hand, pluralism does not necessarily see a Christian type of salvation as the goal of life, nor belief in the Christian message as necessary to obtaining that goal.

The Implicit Faith Approach

As we noted earlier, inclusivists who base their view on the idea that one may come to an implicit faith without an explicit knowledge of Christ find examples of such persons in the Bible. This idea, that salva-

---

18. Paul F. Knitter, "Toward a Liberation Theology of Religions," in *The Myth of Christian Uniqueness: Toward a Pluralistic Theology of Religions*, ed. John Hick and Paul F. Knitter (Maryknoll, N.Y.: Orbis, 1987), p. 190.

tion is not only possible, but in a number of cases actual, without the knowledge of the gospel, of course has the implication that for such persons the missionary or evangelistic endeavor is not necessary, at least not for deliverance from eternal damnation. But does this not then reduce somewhat the urgency of the task?

These theologians continue to insist on the importance of the missionary mandate. In general, however, the strategy employed in their arguments is to reexamine just why the gospel is preached, or what is the good that the preaching of the gospel aims to achieve. This has a number of variations.

Pinnock poses the question of whether it is really urgent to take the gospel to persons if they have access to salvation, no matter where or when they may live. He notes that the response of conservative-evangelical theology has been that the adoption of such an understanding of inclusivism must inevitably lead to diminishing missionary effort. He believes, however, that this results from the belief that the main motivation for missions is rescuing persons from eschatological wrath. The objection is not an idle one. Given that understanding of the motivation for missions, the need for hearing the gospel would be nonabsolute. It would be for a clearer, more explicit message, but a message already available to everyone.[19]

In Pinnock's judgment, however, some persons use this argument who really have no right to, namely, the Augustinians. After all, if it is determined from all eternity who will be saved and who will not, why should it be necessary to preach the gospel? Such a determinist scheme undermines motivation for any kind of human action, not merely missions. In fact, this may be why the Reformers were relatively uninterested in missions, whereas Erasmus was.[20]

What we must do, says Pinnock, is to examine the understanding of the motivation for missions. He suspects that we have unduly narrowed the motivation for missions, making it just one thing: deliverance from wrath. He says, "I object to the notion that missions is individually oriented, hellfire insurance." The traditional view of God and the human situation relative to him as depicted by traditional missions is of a God who hates sinners and delights in sending them to hell. Jesus, however, did not come to condemn the world but to save it. Consequently, our mission is to proclaim to the world, not the bad news, but the good news. This is not the news that there is now grace where there was none before, but that something new has occurred, that God has reconciled the world to himself in Jesus Christ.[21] What is really involved here, although Pin-

19. Ibid., pp. 176–77.
20. Ibid., p. 177.
21. Ibid., pp. 177–78.

nock does not say so explicitly, is a correct understanding of the gospel and consequently, even of salvation. Salvation should not be thought of primarily in a negative fashion, as deliverance from hell. It is the good news of the coming of the kingdom. The task of missions is of course, quantitative, to evangelize and form congregations. It is also, however, qualitative, to change persons' outlook, to bring them hope, love, and responsibility for the world. Thus, the main motivation for missions is to see the kingdom come and God's rule established.[22]

How does this understanding bear, then, upon those who "have responded favorably to the light they have received"? The motivation for preaching to them is "that they might learn more about the source of that light, have a fuller experience of salvation in the dimension of Pentecost, and be caught up in the kingdom surge."[23] In other words, while they have salvation, they do not have its fullness. The purpose of preaching is to bring them these additional dimensions of it. "The fact that people can respond to cosmic revelation does not mean that the word about Jesus need not be proclaimed to them. They need to hear it by way of fulfillment and assurance."[24]

Sanders also is sensitive to the charge that "wider hope" theories remove the need for evangelism and missions. He responds with four reasons why those who hold such views are actually strongly motivated to share the gospel with the unevangelized. The first is simply because Jesus commanded us to go. We are to go for the glory of God. Jesus' explicit words should be enough motivation for anyone. If not, then perhaps they are not as committed to the authority of Jesus as they think. A second motivation is the desire to share what we have experienced, so that others "might share in the private and social blessings that come from a personal relationship with Jesus Christ." The third motivation is that God desires to provide fullness of eternal life to everyone now. Even if some already have eternal life and others will be presented with the opportunity to accept Christ after death, only by knowing Christ overtly can one live a truly human life and enjoy full peace and hope. Finally, there is an ongoing warfare with evil in this world. Many who have not overtly heard of Christ are living in and contributing to this evil. By proclaiming the Good News, we can help alleviate this evil in the world.[25]

Eschatological Evangelization

Those who hold this view present an argument similar in many ways to those who maintain that all may be saved through general revelation.

22. Ibid., p. 178.
23. Ibid.
24. Ibid., p. 179.
25. Sanders, *No Other Name*, pp. 284–85.

They contend that it is better to experience the benefits of salvation earlier rather than later. So, even those who would hear and believe during the life to come are better off if they know now rather than later. There is a quality to life that comes with knowing Christ, and failure to experience this is indeed a large loss. Therefore, we should take the gospel to everyone. Further, there is no assurance that all who hear in the life hereafter will respond favorably. Consequently, we should seek to evangelize when we can.

Pinnock recognizes the criticism that will be raised regarding this view. Would it not be better to leave someone like Job unevangelized until the postmortem encounter with Christ after death? Certainly that would be more compelling. He says, however, that this question would have greater force if we could identify the premessianic believers. Unfortunately, they are mixed in with others, so we must simply present the gospel to all, indiscriminately. Besides that, "even if we knew their identity, we would be obliged to tell them of the greater light and salvation that they long for."[26]

Analytical Observations

We must now examine these several views more closely. The one that deserves first additional interest is the eschatological evangelism view. What are this view's implications for missions?

We begin with a supposition that encountering Christ and his claims and the offer of salvation beyond this life would be more impressive and powerful than any such introduction within this life. It is difficult to know just what circumstances would accompany such a presentation because very little is said in Scripture about such a situation, which in itself should be a caution to us. In particular, how this relates to the biblical data regarding the intermediate state is quite unclear. If, however, the hints we are given regarding the intermediate state (e.g., Luke 16:19–31; 23:39–43; 2 Cor. 5:1–10) apply to this situation as well, then there will presumably be awareness of the ultimate consequences of one's decision for or against Christ. So, the rich man in Luke 16 saw the disadvantages of failure to believe, although in that story he has no further recourse. On the other hand, Abraham indicates that the rich man's brothers would not believe even if someone came back from the dead to tell them, although that of course is still different from going to the state of the dead and experiencing it personally.

26. Pinnock, *Wideness in God's Mercy*, p. 172.

If, however, a presentation of the gospel after death has greater vividness and consequently greater persuasiveness than does such a presentation before death, then those who hear only postmortem are likelier to believe than are those who hear only within this life. Consequently, if hearing within this life disqualifies one from any opportunity to hear after this life, we are not necessarily doing persons a favor by telling them the good news now. It would actually be better for them in the long run if they did not hear until later. While Pinnock recognizes the potential problem with respect to those who are already "messianic believers," the problem is much broader than that, extending to all who have not heard.

The answer to such a question depends in part upon who actually will have a postmortem opportunity. Is it all who have not been exposed to special revelation during life, or only those who, not having heard special revelation, have responded favorably to the light of general revelation? Part of the difficulty of untangling this question is the apparent confusion or contradiction, or at least combination, of both approaches in Pinnock's writing. At times, as we noted earlier, he seems to be saying the former and at other times the latter. The logic of the immediately preceding paragraph would apply more strongly to the former than to the latter.

Another consideration of this type applies even to the exclusivist approach. This view usually allows for some variation of destiny, depending on the nature of the opportunity. So, for example, Loraine Boettner and others argue that those who reject the gospel when it comes to them overtly will be punished more severely than will those who merely reject the natural light or general revelation.[27] The preaching of the gospel worsens the ultimate state of those in the latter group who reject it. On the other hand, those who hear and accept the Good News are given a better state of affairs than they would otherwise have had. The point is that the result of missions activity, according to exclusivists, is not to improve the ultimate condition of every person who hears. It really is not possible for humans, with their limited knowledge of the future and of an infinite number of factors, to decide whether on balance it is better to take the gospel to every creature. Fortunately we do not have to engage in that type of calculus. We are called simply to obey the Great Commission. And by giving us that commission, Christ has declared that in his judgment it was better that we should preach thus.

We should note, in all of this discussion, that we have been considering the logical implications of each view. In so doing, we are really speaking of the type of inferences that theologians would draw. Yet, as we are coming increasingly to recognize, not all persons, including Christians, are completely rational and logical. Consequently, the atti-

27. Boettner, *Reformed Doctrine of Predestination*, pp. 120–21.

tude, "if they're all going to be saved anyway, why get so excited about missions?" is more emotional, almost as a sense of relief, than the more logically nuanced argument that a fuller experience of salvation is important and therefore these who are already justified through implicit faith need to hear the full message nonetheless.

It is also worth noting that evangelism and missions are not the only activities in which our Lord has commanded the church to engage. Worship, fellowship, prayer, edification, discipleship, care for the needy, and other activities are also enjoined. One might well argue, "How can a Christian spend time in these activities when there are persons who have never heard of Jesus Christ and are consequently failing to experience any of these blessings?" Only if one makes evangelism and missions so supreme that they must override other plain responsibilities of Christians can such a question be asked. Looking at the model of our Lord himself, who did not spend all of his time in proclamation, is a helpful clue here.

We also need to realize that while evangelism is the responsibility of the entire church, it is not necessarily the exclusive or even the primary responsibility of every member. It is worth remembering the point C. S. Lewis made in his essay on "Learning in Wartime."[28] Some asked how anyone could waste time on the study of trivialities such as literature, art, mathematics, or biology, when persons were going to hell. Yet, as Lewis points out, the Bible considers all of life as sacred. Paul told his readers to get on with their jobs, and Jesus attended a wedding at which he turned water into wine. As important as is evangelism, it is not the Christian's exclusive concern.

We may now summarize briefly the findings of this chapter.

1. The strongest motivation for evangelism is attached logically to the exclusivist view, since without hearing the gospel explicitly, people are eternally lost. At the same time, it simply is not true that no other view supplies a motive for evangelism and missions.
2. Those views that hold that the opportunity for being saved does not change at death reduce the urgency of proclamation to persons while they are still alive.
3. The nature of the state of lostness directly affects the force of the evangelistic impulse. While annihilation is a serious outcome of one's life, it is not as serious as eternal suffering, and consequently annihilationism weakens somewhat the force of the evangelistic impulse.

28. C. S. Lewis, "Learning in War-Time," in *The Weight of Glory and Other Addresses* (New York: Macmillan, 1980), pp. 20–32.

4. The nature of the motivation, and to some degree, its strength, is related to the understanding of the nature of salvation. If salvation is positive, involving the quality of a person's relationship to God, then there is motivation even if the person is not going to eternal punishment without hearing explicitly.

5. The primary basis for concluding that the church is to engage in evangelism and missions comes from the fact that Christ has commanded it to do so, rather than from any calculation of its relative need.

6. The degree of strength given to the motivation to evangelism and missions, while an important consideration in evaluating a given approach to the question of the destiny of the unevangelized, is not the sole or even the primary one. To make it so involves the adoption of a pragmatic theory of truth.

7. Evangelism and missions, while important responsibilities of the Christian and of the church, are not the only ones. Making them so results in a truncation of the understanding of both the Christian life and the church.

Subject Index

Scripture Index